DICK VERMEIL

Whistle in His Mouth, Heart on His Sleeve

Gordon Forbes

TRIUMPH
BOOKS

Library of Congress Cataloging-in-Publication Data

Forbes, Gordon, 1930–
    Dick Vermeil : whistle in his mouth, heart on his sleeve / Gordon Forbes.
        p. cm.
    ISBN 978-1-60078-241-1
        1. Vermeil, Dick. 2. Football coaches—United States—Biography.
    3. Philadelphia Eagles (Football team) I. Title.
    GV939.V47F67 2009
    796.332092—dc22
    [B]

                                                              2009012158

This book is available in quantity at special discounts for your group or organization. For further information, contact:

Triumph Books
542 South Dearborn Street
Suite 750
Chicago, Illinois 60605
(312) 939–3330
Fax (312) 663–3557
www.triumphbooks.com

Printed in U.S.A.
ISBN: 978-1-60078-241-1
Design by Patricia Frey
Page production by Amy Flammang-Carter
Photos courtesy of AP Images unless otherwise indicated

To Marie, my partner of 10 years and a dedicated New York Jets fan, and to Skylar and Kaitlyn, my two young granddaughters who have the looks and pep of future cheerleaders

Contents

Foreword

I remember my first year with the Los Angeles Rams, where Dick Vermeil was an assistant coach. What was really obvious was the incredible enthusiasm and passion he had for the game. He was in excellent physical shape and he almost moved around like a player. He was just an exciting guy to be around.

During his years as head coach with the Philadelphia Eagles, he never lost that passion. He made me a better quarterback in so many ways, starting with emphasizing work ethic. He felt there was a price to be paid for success, and if you were willing to pay that price, you could become successful.

Coach Vermeil worked us incredibly hard. On Monday, Wednesday, and Friday in the off-season, the quarterbacks would be throwing the football, working on our drops, and working with the receivers. Then we would get in our conditioning work, running and weight lifting and all of those things. Mike Dougherty, our film director, would tape everything. And this was the *off-season*. But that's how we got better. And we accepted that. We accepted the team concept.

Coach taught us how important it was to continue to improve. Beyond the physical things, it was preparation. Studying your opponent. Looking for an edge. Understanding what defenses were trying to do. Reading your keys. Any way you could get that edge. Coach Vermeil just made me an incredible student of the game. In that regard, I think he taught me the things from the mental side of the game that led to a second career for me in broadcasting.

No question, Coach Vermeil was naive about point spreads, gambling, and things like that. He only cared about winning and ultimately respecting his opponent. He loved to compete against Tom Landry. But he never embraced the idea of piling on. He had too much respect for the profession. We would back off in the fourth quarter when we were ahead. Just run out the clock. I used to get negative mail when we won games but didn't cover the point spread.

They said he was too conservative, a coach who just liked to run the football. But there was a reason for that. He was building a physical football team, and the running game was that side of it. But as he grew, he worked to improve our ability to throw the football, too. Remember, he brought in Sid Gillman, the father of the modern-day passing game, to work with us. As time went on, Coach Vermeil became much more open, much more aggressive in his game plans.

I remember the Monday night game in 1979 when we finally beat Dallas. We had lost 13 straight times to the Cowboys in Dallas. Wilbert Montgomery was our guy, our star back. The Cowboys liked to load up to stop him. Coach Vermeil decided to open up that night. He sent in 39 pass plays, an unheard-of number for him. Eleven of the first 13 plays he called were passes. Most of them were off play-action, faking the run with Wilbert. We even scored on a daring fourth-and-1 pass from the Dallas 32-yard line. It was a beautifully designed game plan and we executed it almost flawlessly. After the game, there were tears of joy in Coach Vermeil's eyes.

In 1980, we went to the Super Bowl with a team that wasn't the most gifted in the league. Wilbert was a phenomenal football player, probably our best player. Other than that, we were just a bunch of scrappy guys, a team built on our work ethic. We had no speed among our receivers. We had to line up Wilbert outside just to give the illusion of having a deep threat. We weren't the altar boys most people believed we were. But we cared for each other and we covered each other's asses.

I can remember looking at tapes until 1:30 in the morning. And I had to be up at 6:00 AM to go to practice. Coach would call me, knowing I'd be watching tapes. He'd want me to see something about our red-zone offense on the tapes. He'd be briefing me on the next day's practice. We would bitch and we would moan about all the work. But we understood why he was working us that hard. That's how we got better. We all loved him because of his emotion. We knew he was working while we were sleeping. He was cultivating his talent.

I think the game wore Coach Vermeil down, especially during the players' strike of 1982. I thought that Eagles team was going to be the beginning of something special offensively. But when we came back from the strike, we were not the same football team. He was not the same coach. We were a team based on discipline, repetition, and preparation. When we came back from the strike, it was just a mess. The last few weeks of that season, Coach Vermeil was even more emotional than usual. To a certain degree, it seemed like he had lost control of his players.

I wasn't surprised that he came back after 14 years in television. Actually, I was disappointed that he didn't come back sooner. I had retired in 1990 and wasn't playing anymore, but I was around the league. I didn't see any Dick Vermeils out there. I didn't see any guys who cared about their players like he did, who cared for his coaches like he did, or cared about the game like he did. I saw a lot of guys coaching, and it was just their job. It was what they did. It wasn't their passion.

Coach Vermeil has always been my inspiration and, I believe, an inspiration to all his other players and coaches. Look at what he's done, from high school coach, to college coach, to pro coach. He paid his dues all the way along. I can't tell you how overjoyed I was when he came back and the Rams won the Super Bowl. If there was a guy who ever deserved to win a Super Bowl, it's Dick Vermeil. I always kind of felt that his legacy might be our loss in Super Bowl XV, but he certainly made up for that loss by winning it with the Rams. The guys I've spoken to from our '80 team were all so happy that Coach Vermeil was able to win a pro championship, even though it wasn't with us.

I know how many people he helped and how many people he touched along the way to make them better people. I'm not even talking about football, just about making them better people. With this book by Gordon Forbes, who covered the Eagles during the exciting Vermeil years, I think he can reach a lot more people and have a positive effect on their lives. Coach Vermeil has said he didn't think anyone would be interested in his life story, but that's the humility of Dick Vermeil.

—Ron Jaworski

Introduction

Coaches dating back to the old smashmouth days of George Halas and Curly Lambeau have always been fascinated by the game of pro football. Why the fascination with a job involving such wild and crazy hours and the uncertainties of a bouncing ball?

"The battle, that's probably the biggest attraction, or the biggest addiction," said Tom Flores, who won two Super Bowls with the Oakland/Los Angeles Raiders. "Winning is also an addiction."

It took Ted Marchibroda 31 years before he realized the reason for his love affair with the game. Marchibroda, who began his pro coaching career in 1961, had an epiphany during Mass soon after he was hired as head coach of the Indianapolis Colts.

"I never realized myself until the priest finished his sermon," said Marchibroda. "He said, 'Your life is lost when you know the outcome.' That's why I love football so much. You never know the outcome."

"I hate to say it's the limelight, or the glory, or the ecstasy of winning," said Wayne Fontes, who coached the Detroit Lions for eight-plus seasons and reached the playoffs four times. "I just think myself, personally, it's fun. I wouldn't know what else to do. This is more fun than being behind a desk or working for some IBM place or something."

Dan Reeves, the former Denver Broncos, New York Giants, and Atlanta Falcons head coach, grew up working a mule-driven plow on a 275-acre cotton and peanut farm outside Americus, Georgia. The work ethic he developed, all sweat and weary muscles, became the basis for his life in football.

"I started plowing with a tractor when I was nine years old," said Reeves. "Then one summer, Dad thought it would be great to plow with a mule. It didn't seem like much fun, two legs keeping up with four. But I guess that was his way of teaching me about hard work.

"That's the reason I like football. It's like life itself. Life has its ups and downs, just as football does. So I think you have to work hard. That's something that's instilled in me. We'd have to get up early and do a lot of the farm chores. We had hogs and cows, and we had to feed them and water them. I'd get up at 4:30 and catch a bus at 6:30 for a little ol' school."

Reeves became a player/coach with the Dallas Cowboys at age 26. He eventually won 201 games as a head coach. He lost three Super Bowls in Denver despite a high-scoring offense that featured John Elway's powerful arm at quarterback. The demanding Broncos fans remember the lopsided championship defeats (by a combined score of 136–40), and that's all many of them remember.

They blame Reeves, not the Broncos defense that gave up 136 points and 1,462 yards in those three humiliating losses.

Reeves tried to win with players who showed character, even if they were a half-step slower than some of the more problematic players in the league. "When you get people with character and great intensity, all the other things fall into place," Reeves said. "Things like competing, pride, and wanting to be the best. But you've got to have the physical tools, too. You can't just go out and find a lot of good ol' boys to play." In 12 seasons under Reeves, the Broncos sent only six defensive players to the Pro Bowl. The Oakland Raiders, known for their cast of rogues and renegades, sent 11. So much for character.

Don Shula, who won a league-record 347 games and coached for 33 NFL seasons, felt like Tom Flores about his job. Shula cited the excitement of the game as his reason for coaching until he was 65. "It's an exciting lifestyle," Shula said. "The competition on Sunday afternoons or Monday nights. The playoffs and the Super Bowl. You can't find something to replace those moments."

Jimmy Johnson, who won back-to-back Super Bowls in the 1990s with the Dallas Cowboys, still misses the weekly challenge. "I miss preparing the team for a big game, that's what I miss," said Johnson. Now he prepares for the Fox Sports pregame show, flying 2,330 miles each week to Los Angeles from Miami to join Howie, Terry, and the boys for a pregame analysis of the week's matchups.

The Fox show has a rollicking flavor to it, somewhat like having a bunch of retired players on the set, which some of them are, laughing about the good times. But Johnson concedes it's not the same as preparing a team and wondering if your game plan will be as good in Sunday's battle as it seemed during practice.

"Bill Parcells told me one time that he doesn't know how long anyone could go at our pace," said Johnson in his autobiography, *Turning This Thing Around*. "I do this job and put in these hours because I enjoy it. And when it gets to the point where I don't enjoy it, that's when I'll stop and head out to the beach for good. It could happen when we're winning, if I get to the point where I don't enjoy putting in these hours. I don't have any burning desire to be the winningest coach or to win so many titles, or accomplish so many things."

After winning those Super Bowls with the Cowboys, Johnson and maverick owner Jerry Jones engaged in a nasty power struggle. Owners, of course, always win these exhibitions of sporting muscle, and Jones won this one. Johnson was dismissed, a shocking development that proved Vince Lombardi was right when he called pro football "a game for madmen."

Two years later, Barry Switzer won another Super Bowl using Johnson's players. Jerry Jones beamed once again, and everything was right in Dallas again. Yet, Jones wouldn't have pulled his axe out if Lombardi had been his coach. Vince might have "flailed away with his fists" before leaving, as he admitted doing with a few uncooperative players in Green Bay.

But three years later, Jimmy Johnson was back. The Miami Dolphins, his new team, seemed like an ideal fit. He had won a national championship with the University of Miami, a team that included some rebels of the kind that often find a home in the NFL. Besides, Johnson was a lifelong beach bum who loved to fish and execute pirouettes on the surf with his trusty waverunner.

Yet, Johnson never came close to winning another Super Bowl. He retired after four seasons, humiliated in his last game, a 62–7 thrashing by the Jacksonville Jaguars, a fifth-year expansion team. Jimmy Johnson was still the same brilliant coach he was during those big years in Dallas. He was undermined by two factors: too many obligations under the new salary cap system that changed the face of pro football in 1993, and the age of his quarterback, Dan Marino, who was 35 when Johnson arrived.

In the years before Johnson took over the coaching whistle from the legendary Don Shula, the Dolphins had committed to 13 high-priced free agents. Their average length of service: 2.16 years. Only two of the free agents, tight end Keith Jackson and fullback Keith Byars, made significant contributions. Most of the others hung around for a year or two and then were cut loose. The Dolphins, however, had to include their prorated signing bonuses against their salary cap. These mistakes stymied Johnson, who didn't sign a single free agent that made a difference in his four years with the Dolphins. Working within the cap was just one more complicated aspect of the game that coaches in this new era had to learn.

The late Bill Walsh, who never had to deal with the cap, said he was fascinated by the anticipation of each new season. "We always have exciting things happen to us," said Walsh. "We conclude one experience and begin another one anew as a given season. So many men I know envy that kind of life. It gives life a lot of meaning because from year to year, there is anticipation. That's the exciting part of coaching. Now, there's a downside, too. That's very evident."

Walsh, of course, meant the insecurity of the job. There are impatient owners to please. There are stadiums packed with critical fans, some of whom have been known to toss more than vocal insults at head coaches. There are star players like receiver Terrell Owens, who have huge egos and, in their self-centered minds, game plans of their own that are better than the coach's. There are media types sitting in the press box, at least 50 yards from the action. Nonetheless, they can spot open receivers and wonder why the quarterback can't see the same player from 15 yards away. Of course, there aren't any 6'5" pass rushers obscuring the views of the press-box quarterbacks.

Brian Billick, who won an unexpected Super Bowl in 2001 with the Baltimore Ravens, still isn't sure what led him to the coaching profession. "I have wanted to be a coach for most of my adult life," Billick has said. "I can't really tell you exactly why I love this game and precisely why I enjoy coaching so much. But I do. When I first got into coaching, a veteran coach told me, 'If you can do without this profession, do so. You and your family will be much happier.' Obviously, I can't do without it because I can't imagine doing anything else professionally."

Yet, seven years after upsetting the New York Giants in Super Bowl XXXV, the Ravens fired Billick and hired John Harbaugh, a 10-year career special teams coach, save for one year coaching the secondary in Philadelphia. Billick's problems involved injured quarterbacks and an unexplained inability to defeat the Cincinnati Bengals, a division rival.

Of course, no discussion of the crazy world of NFL coaching would be complete without some input from Bill Parcells. In his time, Parcells has jumped from New York (Giants), to New England, back to New York (Jets), and on to Dallas, a team he once despised. He is currently employed by the Miami Dolphins as vice president of football operations. This job isn't nearly as crazy as coaching a team, and the lights aren't on in his office at midnight. But Parcells brings his own sense of the bizarre to the game, meaning anything can happen in Miami.

"The scrutiny you're under is so much different now from when I took over the Giants," Parcells said when he was coaching the Patriots. "If you can't absorb a little criticism, you can't do this job. Reconstructing a team isn't that much different than it was when I first started out, although free agency gives you another tool to implement. I'm a football coach. That's what I am. I like the people in football, generally speaking. Football still has that appeal to me. It's been the game all my life."

Parcells has undergone heart bypass surgery and other heart procedures partly because of the stress of the game and the long, lonely hours of the job.

His wife (they have since divorced) used to wonder about the appeal of this highly stressful sport.

"My wife has a question she's asked me every year for 10 years," Parcells said. "And she always words it the same: 'Explain to me why you must continue to do this, because the times you're happy are so few.' She has no concept."

Judy Parcells asked the question that surely has passed through the minds of every NFL coaching widow. Why do their husbands work until 2:30 AM, in some lonely stadium, drinking cold coffee and watching small figures run around on videotape? Why do they take the abuse from crazy fans who don't know a thing about game plans? And why do they risk their health for some job that can end at the whim of the owner, or the failed foot of a kicker?

And just because a coach produces a winning record doesn't mean he'll be back the next season. Marty Schottenheimer's San Diego Chargers, with its basic "Marty-Ball" offense and a swarming defense, posted a 14–2 record in 2006. Yet, the Chargers fired Schottenheimer because of a philosophical rift with general manager A.J. Smith. A game for madmen, indeed.

* * *

This is the kind of job that Dick Vermeil accepted in 1976 when he agreed to leave the California sunshine and coach the struggling Philadelphia Eagles. Vermeil had served his apprenticeship under some distinguished pro coaches: George Allen, Tommy Prothro, and Chuck Knox. He knew nothing about Philadelphia and little about the Eagles, except that they were an old, established franchise and had lost to the Los Angeles Rams 34–3 in 1972, the year that Vermeil coached the Rams' quarterbacks.

The Philadelphia coaches who preceded Vermeil, Mike McCormack and Eddie Khayat, were popular men. McCormack was a Hall of Fame offensive tackle with the once-powerful Cleveland Browns and blocked for legendary back Jim Brown. Khayat was a defensive tackle on the Eagles' 1960 championship team that handed Green Bay coach Vince Lombardi his only playoff defeat in a bruising title game. Neither could build a winner for one simple reason: the Eagles couldn't score. Under Khayat and McCormack (Jerry Williams was fired after three lopsided losses in 1971 and replaced by Khayat), the Eagles scored 14 or fewer points in 30 games. Their average point total in 67 games during the Khayat-McCormack years: 16.7. Understandably, they were hooted out of town by the league's most passionate fans.

Yet, McCormack still thinks highly of the city. "I think Philadelphia is an outstanding place to coach," he said years later. "I've said it many times that when you're coaching the Eagles, at the start of every game, they're your fans. They may not be at halftime. But no matter what happens the week before, they're your fans. Coaching there prepared me for a lot of other things. After three years there, you don't think anything can happen that will affect you. You know you've been hardened to everything."

So, did Dick Vermeil realize the crazy level of the pro game he was getting into, a sport that regularly chews up talented head coaches and spits them out every year? Probably not. If he had, he may have remained on the West Coast at UCLA. In some ways, at least on the field, Vermeil was a 1970s version of Vince Lombardi, who loved his Packers but treated them "all alike, like dogs," as tackle Henry Jordan had said.

Vermeil never fought with any of his players, as Lombardi used to do. But at training camp in 1980, Vermeil lost his head during an offensive drill. He watched in mounting anger as a free-agent guard named Mike Siegel kept missing his blocks. Finally, Vermeil ordered player personnel director Carl Peterson to cut Siegel, right on the spot. Siegel turned and began undressing as he headed for the locker room. The helmet hit the ground. Then his No. 64 jersey. Then his pads, cleats, and pants. Siegel left a bizarre trail of equipment, reaching the team dressing room wearing only his shorts and jock. Seeing Vermeil's snarling face, none of the Eagles laughed until they reached the privacy of their dorm rooms.

So, is there any doubt that this is a "game for madmen," as Lombardi had said?

"I am a religious man, whose religion, as all true religions, is based on love of fellow man," Lombardi said in a 1967 article in *Look* magazine. "And yet each week, as I talk about our opponents, I almost snarl against them. Why? It is as simple as this. When Bob Jeter, our right cornerback, has to play against

Baltimore's Raymond Berry, or Herb Adderley, at our other corner, is going against Detroit's Pat Studstill, the hate has to build, layer by layer."

That's right. Vince Lombardi, the St. Vincent of Green Bay, preached the value of hate. "You must have that fire in you, and there is nothing that stokes that fire like hate," Lombardi used to say. Former Los Angeles Rams and Washington Redskins coach George Allen didn't go that far. But he once admitted that when his team was losing and getting outhit, he would send in a rowdy second-stringer to throw a few punches in a pile to get the benches cleared, like they do in hockey. Thus aroused, Allen figured, his team would become angry. And the pent-up Redskins would respond by hitting anything across the line, starting with the other team's quarterback.

Before his death in 2007, Bill Walsh told me that he didn't totally disagree with Lombardi's characterization of pro football as a maddening game. "I'd agree with that," said Walsh. "I think you have to be a little bit crazy to be a coach. I really do. You have to be willing to go over the line. You have to be the kind of person who really isn't afraid to go over the line a little bit to make things happen."

Over the years, coaches have been guilty of spying, stashing players on injured reserve, and employing other forms of cheating to get an edge. Going over the line, as Bill Walsh said. The Baltimore Colts once hired a professor from Gallaudet University, a school for deaf students. "He'd sit in the press box and read a coach's lips," said Mike McCormack. "That's when you started to see coaches put a clipboard over their microphone."

Sam Wyche, who took the Cincinnati Bengals to a Super Bowl in 1988, says the NFL is filled with coaches who stretch the rules and rewrite the book of ethics. "I don't think anybody would stop short of anything that gives them a chance to win," said Wyche. "There's such a tight bond among coaches. They're like brothers. They call each other about players. For example, one might tell another coach that a certain nose tackle tips a stunt by backing off the ball. Or a certain wide receiver, when he splits 12 yards, is going inside; 10 yards and he's going outside. Sharing information isn't cheating; taping signals is."

So now, nearly 40 years after Lombardi's death from colon cancer, pro football is still regarded as a wild, unpredictable game, and most of its coaches as tyrants. Don Shula coached for 33 years, winning a record 347 games. He had a Hall of Fame quarterback named Johnny Unitas in Baltimore, where Shula won 73 games in his first seven seasons. He didn't need any tricks of the trade, not with Unitas and that pounding Colts defense.

Shula's early success gave him stature and confidence. Then he moved on to Miami, where he had two additional Hall of Fame quarterbacks named Bob Griese and Dan Marino, and kept on winning, including the NFL's only perfect season—17–0 in 1972.

At the 1992 winter meetings in Phoenix, Shula gathered on the freshly cut croquet lawn of the Arizona Biltmore for the annual photo of the 28 head coaches. Shula looked around. Missing were nine veteran coaches, including Sam Wyche, Chuck Noll, Dan Henning, Lindy Infante, Jerry Burns, John Robinson, and Chuck Knox, all respected head coaches. Noll had retired after 23 years and 209 victories. But all the others had been told to head past the office Christmas tree and out the door, and not to bother looking back at their secretaries. They would probably be leaving, too.

Shula was disturbed by the absence of so many former head coaches. Oakland Raiders owner Al Davis believed that coaches should retire after 10 years anyway because of job stress. Shula was disturbed by that idea, too.

"I didn't know that Al would be an authority on that," said Shula. "I think every situation is different. Chuck Knox coached for a long time. And Chuck Noll had a great career. So I don't know that what Davis says is gospel." Yet, league figures that year supported Davis. Only Shula (20 years), Knox (19 years), Joe Gibbs and Reeves (11 years), and Mike Ditka and Marv Levy (10 years) had coached at least 10 seasons.

Flores, who coached for Davis, said they had discussed the possibility of coaches taking time off, a one-year sabbatical. "That's not a bad idea," said Flores. "But it doesn't work that way. There were nine coaches this year told to take a year off. So it doesn't work that way."

When he coached the New England Patriots (1991–92), Dick MacPherson wanted to work until he was 70. "If I win, no doubt about it," MacPherson said. "If we don't, I won't be coaching. I'll be too old. They'll say, 'Cripes, he can't remember names anymore.' But if we win, they'll say, 'Boy, he's got a lot of energy. He's a young man at heart.'"

MacPherson's first Patriots team went 6–10, losing eight of its first 11 games. The quarterback was Hugh Millen, who threw 18 interceptions. The next year, the Patriots plunged to 2–14 and MacPherson, looking much older than his 62 years, was fired.

Prior to Dick Vermeil's arrival in 1976, the Eagles had one winning season during the past 14 years. During most of those frustrating losses, the Eagles were a collection of marginal players, scattershot quarterbacks, and big talkers. But Vermeil thought he knew how to stop the bad play and the casual country-club atmosphere that existed in the Eagles locker room. He had learned about the value of hard work a long time ago from his father in Calistoga, California, his birthplace. He had absorbed the lessons of coaching strategy from Bill Wood at the high school level, Bob Bronzan and John Ralston at the college level, and George Allen, Tommy Prothro, and Chuck Knox at the pro level.

He would work these Eagles, condition them, and teach them. Separate the workers from the jokers. He would acquire the fitting nickname "the Little Dictator." And he would win in Philadelphia, whatever the cost to his life.

Chapter 1

Calistoga Roots

The sleepy town of Calistoga sits at the north end of Route 29 in northern California's Napa Valley. Tourists pass dozens of vineyards along the way, some dating back to the 1880s. To most of them, Calistoga is just the northern tip of the vineyard industry, a town of about 5,100 residents that offers such attractions as $49 mud baths, views of the Old Faithful geyser, and nearby hot-air balloon rides over the lush green countryside for $200 per passenger.

But to the natives, like the family of Louie and Alice Vermeil, Calistoga has always meant far more than just another winery attraction. "My mother was an invalid," Alice Vermeil once told Stan Hochman, the Philadelphia sports columnist. "We moved to Calistoga for the mineral waters. My father was working class. When we first moved here, my grandmother said I couldn't play with the Italian boys. But who else was there? Then I started dating Louie, and he's French."

Louie and Alice married and raised four children, all of them smart, honest, and instilled with a strong work ethic by their demanding father. Louie worked at the Owl Garage, a converted barn where he—and later his sons, Dick, Al, and Stan—worked long, weary hours repairing cars. Louie's father, also a mechanic, worked until he was 86. "He died at 96," Louie said. "Retirement must not have agreed with him."

Louie himself died from cancer in 1987 at the age of 75. A car buff, Louie took his last vacation in 1946, when he went to see the Indianapolis 500. "I always worked long hours," he said. "I guess it rubbed off [on his sons]. I used to go out at 7:30 or 8:00 AM, come in at 5:00 or 6:00 PM and eat, then go back to work until midnight. Then I'd get up in the morning and do it all over again."

The Calistoga people involved in winemaking were hard workers, too. "If bad weather wiped out a grape crop, they could handle that, and look forward to the next year," said Hochman. "Hopefully, the harvest would be better and the wine would be better. It's what happens when you're in an industry that depends on Mother Nature. I guess you take on that attitude, you know, that you can't fight it. So you just absorb the beating one year and look forward to coming back the next year."

There was always love and discipline in the Vermeil household. And on those sun-drenched summer days, with a light fog drifting down at dawn from Mount St. Helena to the north, you could almost sense that time had stopped and you were back in another era: the simpler 1950s, when neighbors shared intimate stories, recipes, and morning coffee.

To the north of Calistoga, steep trails lead to the 4,343-foot summit of Mount St. Helena. In 1880, Robert Louis Stevenson and his wife spent their honeymoon on the mountainside. According to historians, they lived in an abandoned bunkhouse of the old Silverado mine. In the summer months, the reddish-orange California poppies bloomed, giving the mountainside a colorful blanket.

"It's a little more than a one-stoplight town," said Hochman, who spent a week in Calistoga before Dick Vermeil's first Super Bowl game. "It may be two or three stoplights at least in the whole town. Everybody I talked to mentioned that Dick's parents still lived in that historic house that Robert Louis Stevenson once lived in, and how the main floor was tilted. If you laid a Coke bottle flat at one end of the room, it would roll down to the other end."

Hochman found the Calistoga natives very knowledgeable about their most famous industry. "They were very careful about recommending, or touting, if you will, some new wine," he said. "For example, if you asked about Diamond Creek, which was just becoming famous at that time, they would say, 'That's a nice bottle.' A nice bottle? It now sells for $200. Even though they knew it was going to be great stuff, they didn't go overboard." Robert Louis Stevenson, after whom a scenic park was named, always believed that Napa Valley wine was bottled poetry.

One of the most famous Calistoga wines is the Jean Louis Vermeil cabernet sauvignon, developed by winemaker Paul Smith and partner Dick Vermeil in honor of the Vermeil family. It is offered by OnThEdge winery. One tester described the wine as "stunning for its inky/ruby/purple hue that is accompanied by beautiful pure aromas of *crème de cassis*, subtle wood, smoke, and licorice. [Vermeil's] initial dive into the wine world is impressive. It goes against the rule-of-thumb that celebrities rarely achieve anything special in the world of wine."

According to Calistoga lore, the town's name originated from a slip of the lip. Sam Brannan, a noted entrepreneur, constructed a hotel and spa in Calistoga in 1859. He compared the site to Saratoga Springs, the famous spa in New York. But Brannan mispronounced the name, making it sound closer to Calistoga, and the name stuck.

The Owl Garage, which opened in 1939, was located behind the Vermeil household on Washington Street. Over the years it became the most famous and respected repair shop in Napa Valley, if not all of northern California. Louie Vermeil guaranteed his work, and his prices were extremely reasonable. There were always two tow vehicles available, a 1952 GMC and a 1930 Model-A Ford that Louie had converted into a tow car. And, of course, Louie always had a sizable list of repair jobs to assign to his sons.

"Dick's always been the one to pretty much go ahead on his own. He's always been that type of person. He's always been aggressive."

Louie Vermeil

"I used to pull cows out of mud holes and wells, stuff like that," said Louie Vermeil. "Work's work. But I always tried to make time to see how Dick and later, Al, were doing in sports. I wasn't pushing them. I just wanted to watch them. It's normal, and, hell, they were growing up. I grew up once myself, if you can believe that."

Actually, Louie Vermeil once played as a two-way guard on the Calistoga Bears town team (1932–37). There was no pay, no insurance, and flimsy uniforms. Players played "just for the fun of it," said Louie. They stuck their necks into blocking wedges and hoped they'd come out alive, or at least make it back to the next huddle.

"In 1928, we had some turmoil about guys who had moved in from San Francisco," Louie said. "They kicked them off the team. Then we had go play at Redwood City. We played them to a 0–0 tie, but pushed them all over the field. And damn near beat them."

Louie played right end on defense. Redwood City ran two plays at him and Louie wrestled the ball carrier down each time. On third down, they swept the other way and Louie, pursuing from the backside, again dropped the runner, preserving the tie.

The sign hanging from Louie's Owl Garage seemed to say it all: "Anyone Who Enjoys Work Can Have a Helluva Time in This Place." Louie proudly thought of himself as a seven-day mechanic. But on Sundays, he made sure that the noise from the Owl Garage didn't disturb the services at Our Lady of Perpetual Help, a Catholic church located just 30 feet away from his garage.

The entire Vermeil family, excluding Louie's wife Alice, always pitched in with repairs, sometimes working into the night while other families sipped Napa Valley wine with their leisurely dinners.

"Take pride, that's all," Louie would say, then resume working on some clunker that needed a tune-up.

"Hell, I can remember putting an engine together, a whole damn engine," Dick Vermeil once said. "[My dad] asked me whether I had checked something. I'd say, 'Dad, I can't really remember.' Then I'd have to tear the whole engine out, take the whole damn thing apart, check it out, and put it back. Those things left an impression on me. I learned that you just flat-ass take pride in what you do."

* * *

The Vermeil children—daughter Laura and sons Dick, Stan, and Al—were raised in a white, gingerbread-style house that was built in 1873. The floors creaked, and the front room had that crazy tilt to it. The Vermeil home was a gathering place for athletes, parents, and fans after Friday night football games. Even Bill Wood, the Calistoga High School coach, would show up. The Vermeils welcomed them all with ice cream and sodas, although Louie would sometimes skip out to the Owl Garage to change a flat.

Alice Vermeil decorated the house with plants and colorful flowers. She would throw up her hands in frustration over Louie's habit of scattering car parts around the yard. But inside the house, she lined the windows with plants that she watered and fertilized on a regular schedule. "Gee," kidded Louie, "pretty soon you're going to need a machete just to move through the house."

"Dick was used to working and having responsibilities. It was second nature to him. He wanted things done and done right, and if it took long hours, he'd put them in."

ALICE VERMEIL

Dick was easily the leading athlete of the family. He was a four-sport star at little Calistoga High. "Dick was a leader," Alice Vermeil said. "He was always being chosen captain. Stan was only a year behind, and he was content to let his brother do it all."

Dick was a 5'5", 125-pound option quarterback. Coach Wood took over a listless 1–7 team and turned it into a 7–1 team using only 17 players. "I thought we had a remarkable group of kids," he said. "Good-sized tackles. Good guards. And we had Dick, which made a big difference offensively. Plus, we had a couple of kids who could run. Throwing off the run, Dick was agile, strong. He ran the quarter for me in track. We had little intention of doing a lot of passing. Why should we? You move it on the ground. You don't mess around."

Accordingly, Vermeil got his belief in a strong ground game from Wood. Also, Wood's routine of lengthy practices ("Till we got it done," according to Wood) would resonate with Dick Vermeil as he climbed the coaching ladder.

"Dick was a great competitor," said Wood. "You could see right off he didn't want anybody to get the best of him. I had no time for kids that didn't care. Let them go home. And if you would end up with only 12 who stuck, you'd still be better off."

Yet, no matter how many sports Dick played, he spent an equal amount of time in the Owl Garage alongside his father. Louie was a short, stocky man who always wore grease-stained chino pants, a black shirt, and heavy boots to work. Dick always talked about his father as the toughest man in Calistoga, though Louie never believed him. "I'm tough?" said Louie. "I'm a little surprised at that statement. I don't think [Dick] is that tough. He's a success-type person, yes. Whatever he does, he does it well. He always was a perfectionist. Whatever he did, he wanted to do the best he possibly could to his ability. Dick's always been pretty much the one to go about on his own. He's always been aggressive. He has always been a leader, whether it was getting a job done, going hunting with the boys, or playing sports."

The only thing that troubled Louie Vermeil in a life dedicated to his family and the American automobile was the occasional appearance of a foreign car. "He preferred to work on American cars," said Stan Hochman. "Since his repair shop was about 20 or 30 feet from the church, he had to be careful about the hours he worked. He didn't want to be banging and making noise during church services. But he was a good guy. And he and his wife had a good relationship."

"They ask me the difference between me and Dick," says Al Vermeil, the most engaging of the Vermeil clan. "I tell them, 'About a million bucks.' Then they ask me what it's like being Dick's brother. I tell them, 'Now I know how Lady Godiva's horse felt.'"

When the Vermeil boys weren't playing sports, they engaged in the usual yard games, but rarely got into trouble because of jealousy. "[Dick] was a leader in everything he did, from games of hide-and-seek to always getting chosen captain," said Stan Vermeil, who was born 11 months after Dick. "He had that uncanny ability, so that the other kids would listen whenever he talked. We looked so much alike, so close in age, that everyone thought we were twins. We shared a bedroom. His side was nice and clean; mine was a mess. He worked hard in school; I didn't."

Louie and Alice used to take their sons to see the San Francisco 49ers play during the years of Y.A. Tittle, Joe Perry, Leo Nomellini, and Hugh

McElhenny. The Vermeils were also ardent fans of auto racing. Louie Vermeil used to drive sprint cars and officiate at the Calistoga Raceway. But Stan was the real star competitor on the track. The cars were built for speed by tinkering with the engines and reducing air drag with some tricks of the trade. All very legitimate, of course; Louie's tricks were always done by the rule book.

Occasionally, the Vermeil boys would wander into trouble. Alice Vermeil used to dutifully dress them for church services, usually in freshly pressed sports jackets and open, light-colored shirts. While waiting for the family to assemble one Sunday, Dick spotted a paint can and got a devilish idea.

"When I came back, they were smeared with purple paint," said Alice. "Dick had gotten hold of some paint and splashed it all over Stan." Stan retaliated, smearing his brother with what was left in the can. The purple color was in marked contrast to their tousled blond hair. On another occasion, Alice returned from a shopping trip to find Dick and Al on the roof of their tank house. They were waving umbrellas, ready to jump off and execute perfect two-point landings 20 feet below.

Mostly, however, the Vermeil boys loved to compete. There was always a pool table, electric trains, and other games in the house. Among the boys, Dick was usually the first to offer a challenge, or to accept one.

"They played all of those sports," Louie Vermeil said of his three sons. "If they weren't in school, they were in sports. They were into football, baseball, track, and basketball. I never held them back from that. When they had sports, they had sports. The other times, they worked here."

Dick worked in the shop repairing cars while he was attending high school. "Dick's a pretty good mechanic," said Louie. "He could put on a pair of overalls at 8:00 in the morning and at 5:00 or 6:00 that night, they looked just the same. And he got a lot of work done."

> *"It's been that way since he was a kid. Playing the trumpet. Going on a hunting trip. Playing whatever sport. Nobody ever had to tell him it had to be done. It's his own instinct."*
>
> ALICE VERMEIL

Al Vermeil put it another way. "Dick, he was like a guy who could wear a pair of overalls and look like he was wearing a tuxedo," he said.

Working those crazy hours in the Owl Garage sometimes played tricks with a teenager's social life. Stan Vermeil once had a Saturday night date to go dancing. Stan didn't finish his job until midnight. By the time he arrived at his date's home, she was asleep. "I chatted for a few minutes with her dad and went on home," he said.

Under Bill Wood, Dick became a star option quarterback at Calistoga High, even though he weighed only 125 pounds. There were only 28 students in his senior class, so he was easily the best athlete in the school. Dick also began concentrating on his studies, which had slipped during his previous three years, perhaps from spending long hours with Carol, the school's bouncy cheerleader.

"He was far behind," said Alice Vermeil. "And when he went to take his college entrance exams, a counselor told him, 'Go on home, there's no way you can do it.'" Instead Dick enrolled at Napa Junior College, ignoring another counselor who told him, "After reviewing your grades, I think you should go to work in your father's garage."

Vermeil refused to believe him. He played two seasons at Napa in the same option quarterback role. His body had grown to about 140 pounds, and his knowledge of football had grown, too. In his second season, Napa finished 6–4, a triumphant season for such a small school.

Before a crucial game against Sacramento, Dick severely sprained his ankle. "They thought it might have been cracked," said Al Vermeil, who was a drive blocker on that team. "All week long, they told me he wouldn't be able to play on it. But all along, we knew he would play. And he did. They wrapped 40 rolls of tape around it and he played. You do that, it's got to have an effect on the people around you."

Stan Vermeil remembers a major upset of American River. Dick threw the winning touchdown pass as time ran out. "A kid named Dunstan caught it," said Stan Vermeil. "I was the place-kicker and I had already missed two kicks. The coach tossed the kicking tee onto the field, I tossed it back. I wasn't anxious to try again."

But Stan Vermeil found strength after talking to Dick, a conversation somewhere between encouragement and demand. Dick held as Stan swung his foot. "I kicked it and we won," said Stan.

"He wasn't a bad player at Napa Junior College and at San Jose State," said former Stanford coach John Ralston, who hired Dick in 1965 as the school's first freshman head coach. "I'd say he was a good little player. I don't think he had an overwhelming arm or anything. He was just like I was. I used to play football so I could learn to be a coach. I wanted to coach since I was 13 years old."

Ralston played for Pappy Waldorf at the University of California. "I wasn't worth a damn," he said. "I had five years of high school football, too. And then Pappy hired me back after my last year at Cal. Boy, I loved that guy, Pappy."

Meanwhile, Dick was totally in love with Carol Drake, the petite, green-eyed Calistoga High cheerleader. After he learned to drive, Dick bought a 1936 Ford coupe for $15 to use on dates.

"He is really a driven person," Carol Vermeil once said. "He told me it's an obsession with him. You either put up with it or you don't. As with any wife, you just have to make a decision as to whether it's worth it or not. For me, it certainly was. I think I'm really lucky. Dick is a fantastic person and I think there are a lot of ladies who would like to be in my shoes."

"I had some great coaches [at Stanford]. Bill Walsh, Mike White, Rod Rust, Jim Mora. But Dick Vermeil was head and shoulders above all of them."

JOHN RALSTON,
FORMER STANFORD HEAD COACH

Carol remembers those Calistoga days with special feeling. "We were in high school," she recalled. "I was hanging around his house all the time. We used to work on his car together, that '36 black Ford coupe he bought. I even learned to change the carburetor. I'll never forget it. He had it all jazzed up. It was really a neat little car. We would go all around in it. I wish we still had it, it was so nice."

Carol quickly learned that all of the Vermeil boys were expected to work during their free hours. "The garage was right there, about 150 feet behind the house," she said. "It was part of their life. I grew up in the '50s when we were taught to forsake our careers for our husbands and families."

* * *

Dick Vermeil and Carol married in 1956. By then, Vermeil had become serious about his future. He was no longer the little option quarterback thrilling the girls at Calistoga High with his hip-twisting heroics. Now, feeding off Bill Wood's advice, Vermeil's mind had swung over to the coaching side of football. He was a backup quarterback at San Jose State, overcoming the handicap of his size (155 pounds) with his fearless attitude, his insight into the game, and his growing self-confidence.

"I played against him in college," recalled Tom Flores, who attended the College of Pacific. "We were head-to-head quarterbacks. He was more of a running quarterback, an option quarterback. He wasn't very tall, so I didn't know what kind of thrower he was because we dominated it pretty good for two years."

Ironically, Vermeil and Flores would face each other 22 years later on a much higher level as opposing Super Bowl coaches.

Vermeil's hero, aside from his father, was John Ralston, the quiet, thoughtful head coach at Stanford. After graduating from San Jose with a master's degree in 1959, Vermeil began picking up obscure coaching jobs in the northern California area: head coach at Hillsdale High in San Mateo (17–9–1 in three seasons); backfield coach at San Mateo Junior College; and head coach at Napa JC, where he compiled a 7–2 record in 1964.

When he wasn't on the sideline, Vermeil was turning up at every football clinic within 200 miles. Whether the clinic was in Sacramento or San Francisco, Vermeil would be there with his tape recorder and his yellow note pad, which would become staples throughout his coaching career. He would always sit in the front row, as if the seat had been assigned to him. Vermeil would take notes feverishly and shoot questions at the speakers.

"You'd be speaking and he'd be taking notes," said Ralston. "He'd go home and he and his wife would put them in order. And the notes would be on your desk when you got there on Monday morning, neat and very readable. So finally, I hired Bill Walsh in my first year at Stanford and Dick the second year."

Ralston's offer to Vermeil was made at one of these clinics.

"How'd you like to be the freshman coach at Stanford?" he asked.

"How soon do you want me to report?" said Vermeil.

"He didn't ask how much money he was going to make or anything," said Ralston. "I was making $16,000. I don't think the assistant coaches were making more than $10,000 or $12,000. We had a summer camp program where they all could earn an extra $1,000."

To this day, Ralston can't quite believe Vermeil's work ethic. "No question, it was phenomenal," said Ralston. "No one worked harder than Dick Vermeil. And he and his wife, the two of them, are super people. When we had athletes coming to visit, he'd take them home to his house. He's just the best coach that I can think of. Everything he did was perfect. I've never seen a guy like him."

Over the next five years, Vermeil would follow the coaches he admired. He moved downstate to join the Los Angeles Rams as their first special teams coach. George Allen, the Rams' head coach, regarded kicking, punting, and covering kicks as a vital extension of the offensive and defensive units.

Vermeil kept moving. He was on Tommy Prothro's UCLA staff for one year, then returned to L.A. to coach the Rams' quarterbacks, including Roman Gabriel, Jerry Rhome, James Harris, and a fast-talking kid from Youngstown State named Ron Jaworski, who had the best pure passing arm of them all. And when Chuck Knox replaced Prothro after disappointing 8–5–1 and 6–7–1 seasons, Vermeil stayed on. The Rams lost to eight losing teams in Protho's two seasons, and missed the playoffs by one game in 1971 and two games in 1972.

> *"Dick always had an edict that he got from George Allen. You know, one thing I know is that I can outwork my opponent. I will spend more hours at it and therefore I will be successful."*
>
> CARL PETERSON, FORMER EAGLES PERSONNEL DIRECTOR AND CHIEFS PRESIDENT

"When he first came to the Rams [in 1969], Dick was the first special teams coach in football," recalled Roman Gabriel. "He had a tremendous amount of enthusiasm and it carried over when he started coaching quarterbacks. But Dick was smart enough to know that the system that Ted Marchibroda had put in worked. So basically, I did what Ted had told me, and Dick oversaw all that. Marchibroda was the best quarterback coach that has ever been in the league."

Later, when he began his NFL head coaching career, Vermeil sometimes frustrated his quarterbacks in practice by telling them when to deliver the ball. "Let it go, Ron, let it go," Vermeil would yell. And Ron Jaworski would fire the ball downfield on orders, not upon reading the defense. Gabriel, however, said this never happened to him with the Rams. "Dick knew I had been in the league for five or six years, so he figured I knew when to let the ball go," Gabriel said.

Tommy Prothro, the new Rams coach after George Allen bolted for the Washington Redskins, used a screwy blocking scheme, flip-flopping guards and tackles depending on whether the play was a pass or run. "The year before we did that, we had one of the best pass-blocking lines in the league," said Gabriel. "When we began flip-flopping, Joe Scibelli, our right guard, would block Bob Lilly on running plays. On the next play, Tom Mack, our other guard, would block Bob Lilly. Listen, it was tough enough for the guards and tackles to block the same guy."

As he did later on in his career, Vermeil ran on cold coffee and Carnation breakfast bars. He drilled his players until they were weary-legged. In those early years, when Vermeil was in his thirties, he worked long into the night. He would flick on a 16-millimeter projector and watch the movements of his players, back and forth, back and forth. His comments would be saved on a small tape recorder. He kept the recorder with him wherever he went—even to bed—in case a new wrinkle on a screen pass popped into his head at 3:00 AM.

Presumably, there were some of Vermeil's assistants who felt overworked and underappreciated, as they say at the office water cooler. Finally, one of them decided to speak out. The coach was Dick Tomey, a UCLA assistant under Vermeil in 1975 when the Bruins shocked Ohio State in the Rose Bowl.

"There are a lot of things you do in coaching, and when you think back, you ask yourself, would you do that again?" Tomey asked rhetorically. "That particular year I was gone so much from my family. Looking back, I don't think it was worth it. Besides, I think we could have won the damn thing [Rose Bowl] anyway."

Tomey said his respect for Vermeil hadn't changed because of his crazy, dawn-to-midnight schedule. "Now don't get me wrong," Tomey said. "I'm for Dick Vermeil. I have the greatest respect for Dickie. He's a very, very close friend. But to contrast myself to him, well, football is not the most important thing in my life. If you've got to work all day and all night every day to be a football coach, I don't want to be one."

Dick Vermeil, however, willed himself to be a football coach, a great coach. And if the Dick Tomeys of the coaching world objected to his hours, then let them find another job. Let them punch the clock at 9:00 AM and leave at 5:00 PM and be home in time for a hot dinner. Let them gather around the television set and watch NFL football. Let them miss the feel of the greatest game in the world. Smelling the action. Tasting victory. Fighting defeat.

As a coach, you never knew which plays would work and which would fail. But hopefully you would experience that moment in time when you embrace your quarterback, hugging him around his sweaty jersey, to celebrate after winning one of those chess battles. The celebration might only last a few hours under Vermeil. But it was joyful and true to the work ethic of the little head coach. A defeat? There will be another war the following weekend. But there will be lonely nights to keep beside that projector, and whips to crack during practice. And if the Dick Tomeys don't understand that sometimes you have to put football ahead of your family, they don't understand the game.

That's what Dick Vermeil did during most of his seven seasons as "the Little Dictator" of the Philadelphia Eagles. From July through December, football came first, followed by his family and his religion. Even Vince Lombardi, who sometimes used to actually scuffle with his players in training camp, always put his family ahead of the game.

In a 1967 article in *Look* magazine, Lombardi said, "Each year, I tell our team that, during the football season, there are only three things in which a man should be interested: (1) his family; (2) his religion; and (3) the Green Bay Packers."

When he became an NFL head coach, Vermeil thought he could win by outworking everybody. Give him a decent quarterback, some fast receivers, some linebackers who could "flash" (Vermeil's pet word to describe an outstanding individual play), and some fine drafts and he could beat anybody. Where else are the lights burning at 4:00 AM? What other team lives by the motto, "No One Ever Drowned in Sweat"? What other coach grew up working in the Owl Garage until midnight on Saturdays?

So Dick and Carol Vermeil would leave California for the big city to become, of all things, wide-eyed easterners. Vermeil, the coach, would carry the work ethic that father Louie had taught him to the extreme. He would work himself to exhaustion and nearly suffer a mental breakdown. Only then would he learn to believe what Dick Tomey had believed years ago.

Chapter 2

Turmoil in Philly

When he was a schoolboy growing up in rural Shenandoah, Pennsylvania (population 5,624), Jerry Wolman was a dreamer. Let the other kids dream of their sports stars and Hollywood heroes. Young Wolman wanted to own the Philadelphia Eagles. He often hitchhiked to the city and stood outside the gates at old Shibe Park, eyes riveted on the nearest security guard for any sign of a wave or a nod. He was usually inside by the start of the third quarter.

It was a time when the NFL was secondary to college football. The pros played in old baseball stadiums with wooden bleachers and chopped-up grass fields. As former two-way All-Pro Eagles guard Bucko Kilroy put it, "We didn't play for money. Seventy-five hundred dollars was the average salary. We played for fun."

Wolman was a high school dropout. He began driving trucks for his father, who was in the wholesale fruit and produce business. Several years later, after he married, Wolman and his wife Anne drove blindly away from Shenandoah, not really sure of where they were going, only that they wanted to leave the little country town that held no future. They had been living in a $6-a-week room, cooking meals on a hot plate. They were too adventurous, too restless, to keep scuffling for a bare living, and they kept thinking about the bright lights of some big city.

"Anne wanted to go to New York," said Wolman. "I liked Philadelphia. So we made a pact. We decided to pick up the first hitchhiker we saw and go where he was going." Near Mountain Top, Pennsylvania, they picked up a George Washington University student and headed south. That was the foundation for Jerry Wolman's boyhood dream.

The construction boom of the '60s was under way. Wolman jumped in with every dollar he could hustle and started his own construction firm. Eventually, he saved enough of his profits to make a winning bid of $5.5 million for the Eagles. On January 21, 1964, the kid from Shenandoah, who had followed a hitchhiker and a dream, was officially confirmed as the new owner of the Eagles.

Then came a terrible miscalculation. While Wolman was busy learning the book on pro football ownership, his company began work on its most ambitious project: a 103-story, $50 million office and apartment complex in Chicago known as the John Hancock Center. The project quickly became tangled in mistakes, most of them relating to the foundation.

"We had caisson failures," said Wolman. "They were big, round tubes that were put into the ground, and then cement was poured into them. That's where it all went wrong. It was the way the caissons were pulled. When it was all said and done, we probably lost $20 million." Wolman also lost his boyhood dream, the Eagles, despite a lengthy court fight with future owner Leonard Tose over a controversial buyback arrangement.

Wolman, playing bad odds, couldn't pull it off. His reorganization plan stalled in the courts, like the Eagles offense did on most Sundays. He eventually sold the team to Tose, a trucking executive, for $16.1 million. Six years later, a federal judge ruled that Wolman's buyback arrangement with Tose was nullified by an August 1, 1969, deadline.

"First of all, it was a bit of an ego trip, which is the case with most owners," said a glum Wolman. "I thought of the team becoming a winner. The Eagles were my team. I still feel a great deal of loyalty to the Eagles. I love Philadelphia. I love the people of Philadelphia. And I love the fans. We had crab fests there. We invited the players' wives. We were all very close, more like a family."

But now the owner was Leonard Tose, a 54-year-old playboy who wore $2,000 form-cut suits and sported a winter tan from regular trips to Miami Beach and Las Vegas and Acapulco. Tose, however, didn't fly to these paradises just to hang around the pool and watch the action. He was a very serious gambler. Indeed, gambling at the blackjack tables became a disease that left the Eagles in a very rocky financial state. Even as dismal as the team was in the early part of the Tose era, the Eagles packed Veterans Stadium, their new 65,000-seat home.

Tose was the son of a Russian immigrant who founded a highly profitable trucking company. "When my father settled in Bridgeport [a Philadelphia suburb], he was a peddler with a pack on his back," said Tose. "Then he had a horse and wagon. He saved enough money to buy one truck. When he died, he had 10 trucks." The ambitious son and his mother kept expanding the fleet of Tose Trucking, Inc. until it numbered 700 trucks. The annual gross revenues soon hit $20 million. "Sometimes I had to drive a truck myself," said Tose. "I would drive tractor-trailers up to Scranton and Wilkes-Barre. Sometimes it got so icy that you'd see the trailer coming up to meet the cab."

After the remarkable growth of his family's trucking company, Tose's lifestyle became very expensive and very fast. Yet, something was missing. So when Wolman sank into deep debt, Tose saw the Eagles as the perfect venture. He would join the world's most exclusive ownership club. He would spend autumn Sundays in his Veterans Stadium luxury box, scotch in hand (Dewar's and Perrier with a twist). He would ride in a tan, chauffeur-driven Rolls Royce. Or, if pressed for time, he would fly in a $150,000 helicopter painted Eagles green. On social trips, Tose would be accompanied by gorgeous women, four of whom he eventually married.

While Tose was enjoying life in the fast lane, the Eagles were falling to the bottom of their division. Tose's first coach was Jerry Williams, who had guided Calgary to a Grey Cup appearance in Canada. Williams had also coached the Eagles secondary that held the Green Bay Packers to one touchdown in the 1960 title game. He designed a scheme involving the use of extra backs, a tactic that evolved into today's nickel defense for which George Allen took credit.

Williams had been a World War II hero, flying P-38s in the Pacific theater. "I flew 26 missions and came back on every one," he said.

Williams brought his star Canadian quarterback, Pete Liske, with him. But Liske proved to be a scattershot passer, hitting one and missing one, partially because the Eagles had no running game. After going 4–9–1 and then 3–10–1 in his first two seasons, Williams was fired after three straight losses to start the 1971 season. His replacement was Eddie Khayat, a big bear of a man with a southern drawl and a hard-knocks style of coaching.

The day after he was fired, Williams openly wept in the booth of a South Philadelphia diner, where he gave his farewell interview. He was a fine, decent man. But he was in a cold sport where the sharks swim and where fine, decent men are often dismissed by the mistakes of others. As former Dallas general manager Tex Schramm once said, "You remember the defeats longer than the triumphs." And the memories of failure can leave a grown man, even a heroic fighter pilot, in tears.

Soon after his hiring, Khayat announced a ban on facial hair. "It was not a big deal," Khayat said later. "It was not the first time that had been done. I had talked to some of our veteran players the day before. Too many of our guys wanted to do their own thing. I wanted them to all get alike very quickly. [Kansas City coach] Hank Stram had the same rules. Lombardi had the same rules. I knew I needed to shake things up a little bit." Some black players who desired facial hair disagreed with Khayat's directive and said so publicly. Khayat said those stories "were blown out of proportion. A lot of teams operated exactly the same way."

Surprisingly, the Eagles won six of their final 11 games under Khayat, a starting defensive tackle on the 1960 championship team. All of the wins came against losing teams, including three against the last-place New York Giants and Denver Broncos. A year later, however, the injury-riddled Eagles finished 2–11–1. It could have been 0–14 except for an 18–17 win over Houston, a 1–13 last-place team; a 21–20 squeaker over Kansas City; and a 6–6 tie with St. Louis, in which the Cardinals missed a 27-yard field goal with 17 seconds to play.

The most devastating defeat of Khayat's 25-game head coaching career was a 62–10 pounding by the New York Giants on November 26, 1972. The night before, the coach had invited me to share a beer at a cozy bar near Central Park in New York. A patron recognized Khayat and introduced himself.

"Do you think we've got a chance tomorrow?" Khayat asked.

"Sure, Coach," the fan said.

"Good," Khayat smiled. "That makes two of us."

The next day, the Giants rolled up and down the field, piling up 503 offensive yards and dealing the Eagles their worst defeat since a crushing 56–0 loss in their very first NFL game in 1933. "Everybody tried to run and hide in the Yankee Stadium clubhouse after the game," recalled rookie linebacker John Bunting. Khayat was furious. "All but my three 'Billys' quit on me," he kept screaming in that Mississippi drawl. "Billy Bradley, Billy Walik, and Wild Bill Cody. They didn't quit on me. The rest of you, if your ass was on fire, I wouldn't piss on it."

Predictably, the Eagles fired Khayat and began a serious search for a quality head coach. Tose called this author soon after the 1972 season ended with a 24–23 loss to the dreadful St. Louis Cardinals. He asked about potential candidates, and the name of Mike McCormack was offered. McCormack was coaching the offensive line for the Washington Redskins, a team headed for the Super Bowl. He had been a great offensive tackle for the Cleveland Browns during the Jim Brown era. Under McCormack, the Redskins' line had given up only 11 sacks and opened enough lanes for Larry Brown, Charlie Harraway, and the other Redskins backs to rush for 2,082 yards, or 149 yards per game.

Tose was an impatient man. He thought about some other choices: Howard Schnellenberger, Chuck Fairbanks, Don Coryell, Chuck Knox, and that old collegiate favorite of his, Joe Paterno. It would not be the last time he tried to lure Paterno away from the Penn State campus. But now, Tose decided to wait until after the Super Bowl and talk to McCormack.

The Redskins lost Super Bowl VII to the unbeaten Miami Dolphins and didn't score a single offensive touchdown. Washington's ineptitude wasn't McCormack's fault; Redskins coach George Allen had given his team its game plan 10 days before the kickoff. So the Redskins appeared flat on Super Bowl Sunday. To cope with Brown's cutback runs, the Dolphins applied a clever defensive tactic, hitting the center-guard gaps and mixing in blitzes against slow-footed quarterback Billy Kilmer.

Underrated tackle Manny Fernandez, hitting those gaps, finished with 11 solo tackles and six assists. Coach Don Shula reasoned that Allen would play it conservatively, relying heavily on the run. Shula was right. The Redskins threw 28 passes, but most of them were on third down. Kilmer's longest completion was for 15 yards. Moreover, three of his attempts were intercepted by an aggressive Dolphins defense. Brown's longest run against Miami's "No-Name" defense was 12 yards.

Mike McCormack returned to Washington and met with Tose. The owner had already heard from Paul Brown, who had coached McCormack. "Paul's recommendation was so strong that I had to wonder whether there wasn't a blood relationship there," said Tose. "I looked for a man with class, one who was associated with winning football. A good organizer. A guy who got along with players, and a man with leadership qualities."

It never worked out for Mike McCormack and the struggling Eagles for a couple of reasons. For one thing, the Eagles never stabilized their defense. They trailed in 12 of the 14 games during McCormack's first year, a 5–8–1 season. As a result, quarterback Roman Gabriel was forced to throw 460 times because the team was always behind. Gabriel was brilliant, passing for 3,219 yards and 23 touchdowns and making the Eagles the top passing team in the league. However, the punting and field-goal teams were weak. The Eagles also were hit with 61 penalties, 20 times in two defeats alone. McCormack's team was also one of the worst-conditioned teams in the league. More than anything else, the casual attitude toward conditioning and the constant penalties reflected a lack of discipline that would eventually bring McCormack down.

In McCormack's second year, Gabriel started the first 11 games, throwing to a group of receivers that came to be known as the "Fire High Gang" because of their stature. Harold Carmichael, the team's best receiver, stood 6'8". Tight end Charles Young, the No. 1 pick in a great 1973 draft, was 6'4½". Flanker

Don Zimmerman was 6'3½". Carmichael, who would break most of the team's receiving records (589 career catches, 8,978 yards, 79 touchdowns), had modest speed (he ran a 4.6-second 40-yard dash). But he had a 39-inch wingspan and enormous hands. From the base of his hand to the tip of his middle finger measured 9½ inches.

Thus, the Eagles were at least entertaining. But they couldn't reach the playoffs even in the weak NFC East. McCormack tried shuffling personnel, using young John Reaves, the No. 1 pick in 1972, and then rookie Mike Boryla, a notorious in-and-outer, at quarterback. McCormack was obviously seeking his quarterback of the future, when really he had no future. The Eagles finished 7–7, sweeping Green Bay, the Giants, and Detroit with Boryla starting and finishing the last three games. Yet, the Eagles were a divided team. There had been a preseason players' strike. Gabriel, the offensive leader, and linebacker Bill Bergey, the heart of the defense, were among 20 veterans who crossed the picket line at Widener College, the team's training camp site.

"[The strike] did hurt a little bit," said Gabriel, reflecting on a year of turmoil. "I don't like to think about some of the things that were done and said. But see, that was the end of my career, too, and I was dealing with my knee and my arm. Dr. [Vincent J.] DiStefano decided I needed to work out, so when the strike broke, I came in. I came in to be ready for the season. I had to work on my arm and my leg. It ended up being a bad move on my part because it created a lot of resentment."

The strike was called by union head Ed Garvey in an effort to win free agency in the *Mackey v. National Football League* case. Early on, McCormack gathered his team for a unity meeting at a South Philadelphia hotel. "I told them whatever they decided to do, they'd better stay together," said McCormack. Tose, the owner, had also called a team meeting. As the owner of a trucking company, Tose was used to the union game of hardball and couldn't understand why his players were angry. "Leonard's meeting wasn't good," said McCormack. "A lot of things were said, back and forth. And it kind of split our team for a while." When the numbers were counted, there were 28 strikers and 20 strikebreakers.

"They were the two lightning rods," said McCormack of Gabriel and Bergey, the strikebreakers who slipped into camp under cover of darkness. "Gabe and Bergey were the stars. A lot of guys resented that they had gone to Mexico in the off-season with Leonard."

When the Eagles arrived at the stadium for their first preseason game against Atlanta, they were jeered by striking teammates and members of the NFL Players Association waving signs that read, "We Are the Game." McCormack remembers meeting Falcons coach Norm Van Brocklin during the warm-ups. "We talked about how crazy it all was," said McCormack.

Crazy, indeed. One of the Eagles was a 288-pound offensive tackle named Willie Raines. During camp, Raines would lug a boom box around the Widener campus. "I do what a Funkman do," Raines would explain, his head tilted toward his box. He actually played in the Atlanta game before returning to the Gold Coast Barracudas, a semipro team in Florida. The Falcons easily won the exhibition game 23–7. Later, the equipment managers noted that some jittery starters on McCormack's patchwork team had handed in damp jockstraps.

Strikers have long memories. Besides, Philadelphia was a strong union town, so the organized workers never let McCormack's strikebreakers forget about what they had done. The Eagles finished with a 7–7 record in the strike year; their record easily could have been 10–4. Tight end Charles Young stepped out of the end zone, nullifying a touchdown that would have beaten New Orleans. Marion Reeves, a rookie, fumbled away a punt, setting up a decisive touchdown for the Cowboys in another loss. And against Washington, the Eagles suffered a blocked punt and a crucial fumble by Gabriel that gave the Redskins a 27–20 victory.

McCormack's last Eagles team finished 4–10, losing seven of its first eight games. One of the worst defeats in club history, and certainly the most humiliating, was a 42–3 drubbing by the Los Angeles Rams on national television. It wasn't as lopsided as that 52-point loss to the Giants in Khayat's last year. But this crusher happened on *Monday Night Football*, with a national television audience watching and laughing as the home team came apart.

"It's going to be short and sweet, gentlemen," McCormack said in his postgame address. "We had our butts kicked by a very good football team. They did everything they wanted to and we couldn't seem to do anything against them." James Harris, an average quarterback, twice beat Eagles corners Johnny Outlaw and Cliff Brooks for touchdowns. Both were caught by fleet-footed Harold Jackson, a former Eagle. Later, free-spirited defensive end Fred Dryer grabbed a fumble by Gabriel and ran 20 yards for another score. Linebacker Isiah Robertson intercepted backup Mike Boryla and ran 76 yards for the final Rams touchdown. On one possession, the Eagles played a laughable game of chasing fumbles and ended up in a third-and-46 hole at their own 11-yard line.

"It wasn't any fun," said Dryer, with a laugh. "It was too easy. Some of them just quit and some didn't."

Watching his team perform this slapstick routine turned Leonard Tose into a bitter man. All the more bitter when he saw fans batting inflatable dog bones around the stands like balloons and tossing real dog biscuits onto the field. Others waved "ALPO" signs while making funny faces for the television cameras. Indeed, the Rams had the Eagles and their fans on a leash all night.

Tom Brookshier, a former Pro Bowl cornerback who went on to become a national sportscaster, remembers an exchange with McCormack two weeks before the loss to the Rams. The Eagles had been routed by St. Louis 31–20, giving up 278 rushing yards to Jim Otis (116), a power back, and Terry Metcalf (81), a quick back with a little wiggle. Another reporter had raised the issue of character with the previous question.

"Mike was sort of an outspoken guy," said Brookshier. "So I asked him, 'Mike, how many dogs do you have on the team?' He said, 'Two, two dogs.' This was near the end of the press conference, but everybody whipped out their pens and wrote it down, 'Two dogs.' Now everybody was going crazy, trying to figure out who were the dogs."

The following Sunday, the fans moved a doghouse under the Veterans Stadium press box. "They pushed a big dog bone out on the field," recalled Brookshier. "They called it 'The Dog Bone Bowl.'" Predictably, the Eagles lost to Dallas 20–17, giving up a 21-yard Roger Staubach–to–Drew Pearson touchdown pass and a 42-yard field goal by Toni Fritsch in the fourth quarter.

"Mike didn't make it," said Brookshier. "Mike really trusted the players. You know, he was an old-time Cleveland Browns guy, and his coach, Paul Brown, really trusted his players. McCormack trusted them right down to the end. And that's when the 'dog' thing came up. With the strike and everything, it was really tough to figure out who was loyal, and sometimes, who wasn't."

Brookshier recalled that one of the players, an unnamed "dog," had held a good-bye party in South Philadelphia. There were rumors that it was a drug party. "I had heard that," said Brookshier. "And once in a while, the players would do some strange things, jumping offside, things like that, at the wrong time. I think those kinds of things wore McCormack out. Because if a player told him he'd do something, he believed it. I think he might have been taken over the edge a little bit, you know?"

The Eagles, dogs or not, didn't really have a stockpile of talent in the McCormack years. The coach even admitted it. "When I took over, I didn't investigate it that much," McCormack said. "But we only had two people who had even been drafted in the top round of the draft: John Reaves, the quarterback, and Steve Zabel, the linebacker. The next year we had two No. 1s and drafted Charles Young, the tight end, and Jerry Sisemore, the offensive tackle." The Eagles also drafted two more starters, center Guy Morriss and strong safety Randy Logan.

McCormack also had to execute a quarterback shuffle. He cut Pete Liske, made a costly blockbuster trade with the Rams for Roman Gabriel (in exchange for two No. 1 picks, a No. 3 pick, plus Pro Bowl receiver Harold Jackson and fullback Tony Baker), traded for Mike Boryla, and used Reaves in mop-up duty until he, too, was traded.

"You know, John Reaves had to start [as a No. 1 pick]," said McCormack. "He started his first year and was a little shell shocked. I think he set a record for the number of sacks [38]. And so we traded and brought Roman Gabriel in and he had a real good year. I remember we beat Dallas on *Monday Night Football* [13–10] and they had gone out to Los Angeles and the Rams beat them [37–31 the previous year]. I remember Tex Schramm saying that the only team that suffered in that trade was the Dallas Cowboys. That's because Harold Jackson caught the winning touchdown pass in the Rams win."

Gabriel played brilliantly and courageously in his brief Eagles career. "Both shoulders were about gone," he said. "And the arthritis in the knees started to go at that time. I was having my knees aspirated about once every two weeks. And probably the only reason I was able to do what I was doing was a little guy named Dr. DiStefano [the team physician]. He really helped me with his surgery and the things he prescribed to Otho Davis, our trainer." Leaving nothing to chance, Gabriel also used an anti-inflammatory balm produced from a secret formula by a woman in Manhattan.

"Right now," said Gabriel, "I'm not able to throw anything overhand. Underhand, I can throw about 20 yards. I have this orthopedic surgeon in Wilmington [North Carolina] who keeps a running record on me. He said one day, 'You know, Roman, we need to redo your knees. We need to redo your hip. We need to do your shoulder. And we need to do your upper back.'"

Gabriel says he told the doctor, "I'm going to keep going to the gym and keep doing my acupuncture and taking my vitamins. But when I die, you can do it all, and put on my tombstone that you did it all. That way, I don't have to waste my time rehabilitating because I'm enjoying life too much."

There were constant rumors of drug problems on the Eagles during the McCormack years. Gabriel heard the stories but never could substantiate them. "I can't rule out anything about any drug problem," he said. "We had enough problems just getting guys to work out. Mike was such a great player and then a great assistant coach. And he felt like men should be men. I'm not going to say he was lax, but he felt we were being paid to do a job and you should feel fortunate to be playing in the NFL. Apparently, some guys didn't feel that way."

Tose, the owner, said it was an easy decision to fire McCormack, who left with a 16–25–1 record, six of the losses by four or fewer points. "Mike had told me that in three years, we'd have a representative team," said Tose. "I construed that to mean a winning team, and we didn't have it. Our team didn't have any character. I thought we needed a new coach."

Jim Murray, the general manager and Tose's traveling partner, agreed with his boss. "Let's face it, we had morale problems," said Murray. "We had guys who packed it in after we lost our first two games. The weeks went by and we watched players go through the motions."

"We were in the middle of the water without a captain," said defensive tackle Bill Dunstan.

* * *

So how did Tose and Murray begin their quest for a coach to lead the Eagles out of the dismal period that featured just 31 wins in seven seasons? The typical Eagles fan has always appreciated tough, grinding football. The heroes of an older generation were Steve Van Buren, a great back with power, speed, and a nasty attitude, and Chuck Bednarik, known as Concrete Charley for his punishing style of play as a linebacker/center. Bednarik was the last of the two-way players. He was voted to the Pro Bowl eight times and is regarded as one of the 50 greatest players in NFL history.

Fans with long memories can still remember Van Buren slashing through the snowflakes for the score that beat the Chicago Cardinals in the 1948 title game. "He ran over a lot of guys and knocked them coo-coo," said teammate and tackle Al Wistert. But Van Buren paid a price for his smashing style. "The last two years I played with 10-12 shots of Novocaine in every game," Van Buren once told me. "At one time, I'd get it in my toe, ankle, and ribs, all on the same side. Other teams knew I was hurt. Sometimes I was groaning so much after a tackle that the other guys felt sorry for me."

Bednarik approached the game with the same reckless attitude. His most famous tackle came at the end of the 1960 championship game against Green Bay. The Eagles were leading 17–13 on Ted Dean's five-yard run. But quarterback Bart Starr had driven the Packers to the Eagles' 22-yard line.

"Starr went back to throw," said Bednarik. "There were only like 20 seconds left to play. Everybody was covered by our defensive backs [using one of Jerry Williams' creative extra-back coverages]. When Jimmy Taylor swung out of the backfield, I took off. A couple of our defensive backs came up and tried to knock him down. I came up and wrapped myself around him. I could see the clock above the east stands. It went six...five...four...three...two...one. He was trying to get up. When it hit zero, I said to Taylor, 'You can get up now. This [bleeping] game is over.'"

Actually, a second-string safety named Bobby Jackson, deployed as an extra back, was the first tackler to reach Taylor. "I hit him low and kept him from cutting to the outside," said Jackson. "Then Chuck came in and sat on top of him. There were about seven seconds left and the game was over." Jackson rarely is mentioned when old timers reflect on one of the league's greatest playoff games and the only playoff defeat of Vince Lombardi's career.

"I was in on the tackle but Chuck deserves all the credit," said Jackson. "He was the greatest football player who ever lived. It was just an honor for me to help out on that tackle."

The Eagles' present-day heroes were also known for their bruising style of play: Bill Bergey, the tough middle linebacker; Tom Woodeshick, the fullback who used to throw his forearm against parking meters to get them stuck in his adventurous college years at West Virginia; Ike Kelley, the special teams banger who captained the kick and coverage units known as Kelley's Killers; and Tim Rossovich, a linebacker with floppy hair who played on the wild side. Bednarik loved Rosso's style but not his long hair. "Hair like that belongs to people who carry guitars or are laying around the beaches in California," Bednarik said. "The rest of it, he's a superman."

Leonard Tose and Jim Murray knew their pro football history. They knew they needed a unique coach who was much more than just a screamer who drove his players mercilessly. Eddie Khayat had tried that, once returning at 2:00 AM from a road loss to Washington, then getting his players up for a 9:00 AM goal-line scrimmage the next day. They knew the Eagles needed more than a coach who felt his players should be self-motivated. Mike McCormack had tried that approach. Tose, a man who knew where to gamble, where to dine and drink, and where to get his hair styled, wasn't so sure about where he would find his next coach.

Tose and Murray would work their way through the list. They would fly to Miami Beach and Beverly Hills, two of the owner's favorite places for sun, scotch, and good times. But now Tose and Murray were searching for a very special coach. They would eventually find their man, far from Philadelphia and far down on their all-star list. Actually, it was more of a hunch than anything else that led them to Dick Vermeil, the coach that swept Leonard Tose out of his $1,200 Italian-crafted shoes. Said Jim Murray, "He reminded me of a young James Cagney."

Chapter 3

The Search

The outlook was grim. The Eagles had traded away a windfall of draft choices in the mid-'70s: four No. 1s, two No. 2s, two No. 3s, and one No. 4. They also had traded away Harold Jackson, their fastest receiver.

Owner Leonard Tose and Jim Murray, his bubbly, storytelling general manager, knew they needed a head coach who could mold a winner despite a shortage of talent. The Eagles simply didn't have enough game breakers on offense, and they lacked the run-stoppers and pass defenders to shut down opposing offenses.

The next head coach would have to sit on his hands during the early stages of the 1976 and 1977 drafts. Tose and Murray, of course, would never reveal their predicament to the coaches they interviewed. Murray, in particular, preferred to rave about the faithful fans and the great tradition of his sports-crazy city.

"The first name that came up was Norm Van Brocklin," recalled Murray. "He had been a great Eagles quarterback and had been promised the job in 1961 after Buck Shaw retired. But the Irish guy [general manager Vince McNally] didn't give it to him." Instead, the Eagles hired Nick Skorich.

"Obviously, we needed somebody who was a disciplinarian," said Murray. "I think the fact that we interviewed [Van Brocklin] sparked interest in some of our guys. But we owed him that. The only problem was that he was the first one. I told him, 'Look, you have to understand something. We're going to see other coaches. We have a list.'"

Tose and Murray next sought out Hank Stram, who had won a Super Bowl with the Kansas City Chiefs six years earlier. The Chiefs, a 13-point underdog, had used Stram's brilliant strategy to dominate the Minnesota Vikings. Stram called on Len Dawson's short, snappy passing game ("It's like stealing," he said of the loose coverage), and used his odd-front defense—with 6'7", 280-pound Buck Buchanan often playing over 237-pound center Mick Tingelhoff—to hold the Vikings' ground game to just 67 yards.

But then the Chiefs got old. Stram was fired and replaced by Paul Wiggin, who was 40, the same age as Dawson, the Chiefs' Hall of Fame quarterback. There was age across the defensive unit, too. Bobby Bell and Buchanan were in their mid-thirties. Yet, Hank Stram remained a popular coach known for his innovation and colorful sideline demeanor.

"Hank Stram was working for CBS, doing the Super Bowl in Miami," said Murray. "Al Michaels asked us if we had a limo. Sure, we had a limo. As Don Rickles used to say, 'Leonard Tose doesn't go to the bathroom without a limo.' Once he heard that, Stram agreed to talk to us."

Unknown to Tose or Murray, Stram had already made a commitment to the New Orleans Saints, a team in worse shape than the Eagles. Were the Eagles guilty of tampering? Probably. But nobody complained. These teams were desperate losers; the Saints had hired and fired four coaches in six years. Stram, it turned out, was playing the old money game, using a casual interest from the Eagles to pressure the Saints for a better contract.

"He just wanted to check us out," said Murray. "We took the limo down to Joe's Stone Crab House. I think we sent stone crabs to every person that Hank knew in the house. It was a tradition with Leonard."

The next interview was far more serious. Tose and Murray met Joe Paterno at the Madison Hotel in Washington, D.C. "A CIA-type meeting," said Murray. "A lot of people didn't know about it. Joe Paterno, of course, was a very good candidate for our job. He was so beloved here and definitely at the top of our list."

Tose reserved a hotel suite for Paterno. In his own mind, Tose sensed the Eagles were on the verge of running all of those pre-bicentennial stories off the front pages of the Philadelphia newspapers. The interview lasted close to five hours. It covered salary, roster control, fringe benefits, and a rough outline of the team's talent.

"I'll see you in the morning," said Paterno.

Early the next day, Tose ordered breakfast in his suite for all the guests, including Paterno, who arrived with several legal-sized pages in his hand. Paterno carried the pages in a prominent manner, like a lawyer approaching the bench with his briefs. The pages contained a single-spaced, handwritten list of Paterno's demands.

With his morning orange juice in hand, Tose scanned the list and quickly returned it to the coach.

"Anything else, Coach?" he said.

Paterno shook his head. Murray, sensing that they were closing in on a deal, asked to see the list. "Joe was very professorial," said Murray. "There were some real issues with that list. But Leonard would have given him anything. What is it they call in horseshoes? I think he was a leaner. I think it was closer than most people know. But Joe Paterno was a serious, serious candidate for that job."

It wasn't the first time that Paterno had flirted with a pro football job. He seemed to enjoy the dance, rushing to the interview before tiptoeing away. In 1969, Paterno had agreed to coach the Pittsburgh Steelers before the club interviewed Chuck Noll. Paterno was friendly with the Rooney family that owned the team. But when he told his wife Sue they would be living in Pittsburgh, she broke into tears. Paterno then reversed himself, telling family patriarch Art Rooney that he had changed his mind.

Four years later, Paterno appeared ready to move up and coach the struggling New England Patriots. Owner Billy Sullivan had offered Paterno a sweetheart deal, $1 million over five years and total control of the football operation. Again, Sue Paterno didn't like the idea of leaving Penn State and let her husband know it. Paterno slept on the decision and changed his mind in the morning. Sullivan was just getting out of the shower when Paterno called and said he was staying with Penn State.

In the end, Paterno tiptoed away from the Eagles job, too. Although Paterno's base salary at Penn State was modest, there were too many perks to ignore. And there was that college atmosphere that Sue Paterno and their five children loved. Besides, Paterno usually had his team in a nationally televised bowl game every year, an appearance that recruiters used often to seal the deal with prospective collegiate stars.

Undeterred, Tose and Murray kept moving and talking. They even interviewed Allie Sherman, the New York Giants' coach of the 1960s, who had been a second-string quarterback for the Eagles during the war years. Sherman was a heady player who actually threw nine touchdown passes as a backup for Tommy Thompson, a championship quarterback who was legally blind in one eye. Sherman was better known as a smart game-day coach who led the Giants to three conference titles, but couldn't finish the drives off, losing to Green Bay (twice) and Chicago in the NFL title games.

Sherman was a little left-hander from Brooklyn who played at Brooklyn College. On the bench, he was never far from Earle "Greasy" Neale, the Eagles' head coach. And when Sherman persuaded Neale to let him play, the coach's final words were always the same: "Give the ball to Steve," meaning Steve Van Buren, the great back.

"We had a dynamic interview with Allie Sherman," recalled Murray. "A lot of people didn't realize that he quarterbacked the Eagles at the old Municipal Stadium." Sherman was sharp and very interested in coming back to coach. But Tose wasn't feeling well, and everything was put on hold.

Tose, now weary from too many hotel nights and too many phone calls, returned home to interview one more prospect before he and Murray headed for the West Coast. The unlikely candidate was the king of the Ivy League coaches, Harvard's Joe Restic.

The interview went so well that Tose told Jim Gallagher, the club's public relations director, to make arrangements for a press conference. Gallagher had to scuffle to find some background material on Restic, who had coached in Canada and was regarded as an offensive genius within the Ivy League.

"He had the job," said Murray. "Leonard was just tired of it all."

"That's it," said Tose. "I'm taking this guy. I like him."

"Look," said Murray, "this guy was a successful coach at Harvard. But there aren't too many Harvard graduates in this league. This guy had this multiple offense and he coached in Canada. But the only reason I put him on the list was because he once interviewed for the Villanova job." Murray, it turns out, was manager of the Villanova baseball team and was familiar with Restic.

"He was just a beautiful man," said Murray. "I remember one of his big conditions [at Villanova] was that he wanted a mimeograph machine. After his second interview with us, he went in and negotiated with Sidney [club vice president Sid Forstater] about a salary, the whole thing. Then he said he wanted to call his wife and wanted time to notify the Harvard people."

When Tose heard about Restic's slow pace, he became uneasy, then angry. When that happened, the owner's lower lip would curl and he would reach for a cigarette.

"Get the California tickets," he told Murray.

To this day, Joe Restic insists the job was his if he had been more aggressive in his response. "There's no doubt in my mind about that," he said. "I got a call from Leonard Tose. He said to come right down, that the opportunity was mine. But there was no way I could project a 'yes' to them that day [after his second interview]. I had to go back and talk to my wife, to the school. You get the type of person who's willing to take a job on that basis and he's not going to be the type of person who's going to turn it around for you."

The Eagles called off a scheduled afternoon press conference, and Jim Gallagher stopped searching for something, anything, on Joe Restic to fill out his press release.

Tose and Murray were staying at the Doral Hotel in Miami Beach during January and throughout Super Bowl week. Although the tourists had started to migrate north to trendy Fort Lauderdale and its upscale Las Olas Boulevard, Tose preferred the Doral at 5900 Collins Avenue, where the palm fronds swayed in the warm winter breezes.

The Doral was easily recognizable to passers-by, with its glowing Starlight Room on the top floor. Tose knew all the clerks and bellhops and always got preferential treatment. He was a generous tipper, often handing out $100 bills for personal services. In a tight situation, he could also reach into his suit pocket for extra Super Bowl tickets. The Doral also supplied him with a sleek boat to cruise the nearby Intracoastal Waterway. Tose's other favorite properties were the Sherry-Netherlands in New York City and the Beverly Hills Hotel in Beverly Hills, California.

On January 1, Tose had risen late, relaxing in his bathrobe and enjoying his breakfast and the sun that streamed in his windows at the Doral. Late that afternoon, he and Murray began watching the Rose Bowl game. Ohio State, the top-rated team in all the college polls, was a 17-point favorite to bury UCLA in the season's second game between the two teams. (Earlier in the year, the Buckeyes had coasted to a 41–20 win, dominating UCLA's undersized defense.)

> *"I still remember watching him walk off the field that day UCLA beat Ohio State in the Rose Bowl. There was something in his manner that suggested the kind of strength we were looking for."*
>
> LEONARD TOSE, FORMER EAGLES OWNER

Tose's interest in the Rose Bowl was kindled by the first half. Ohio State held the ball for 21 of the 30 minutes, yet only scored once on a 42-yard field goal for a 3–0 lead. In the second half, the UCLA coach, Dick Vermeil, switched tactics. The Bruins began throwing the ball and eventually pulled off a 23–10 shocker, perhaps the biggest upset in Rose Bowl history. And when it ended, Tose and Murray saw Vermeil, a little guy who appeared smaller in the midst of his muscular players, race across the Rose Bowl field, yelling and whooping and dancing.

"I'll never forget it," said Murray. "He came running out and they kept showing tight shots of him. It looked like he just jumped off a Corn Flakes box. He and his wife and his kids, they were all running around the field in celebration. Dick was like a BMW. He was flying. And all of them were all-world huggers."

Tose and Murray looked at each other. "Leonard, let's get this guy on our list," said Murray.

Tose eventually would call Al Davis, the owner of the Oakland Raiders and an old friend, to inquire about Dick Vermeil's qualifications. Davis gave Vermeil a rousing endorsement and offered two other names from the college ranks: Mike White of California–Berkeley and Darryl Rogers of San Jose State.

So an unlikely trio—Tose, the 60-year-old playboy, Murray, the engaging confidante, and Sam Procopio, Tose's administrative assistant—headed for Los Angeles where they hoped to meet the man who would be their savior. There were still other coaches on their dwindling list, but Tose and Murray couldn't shake the feeling that Dick Vermeil, the little guy who had produced the shocker of all Rose Bowl shockers, was going to be their next head coach. And if Tose and Murray had known what happened on the UCLA campus *before* the Rose Bowl, they would have hired Dick Vermeil without the formality of an interview.

* * *

UCLA and California had tied for the Pacific-8 title, but the Bruins earned the Rose Bowl bid by beating Cal 28–14 in their seventh game. This would be the first bowl game for all of the UCLA players, as well as for Vermeil. The Bruins had worked endless hours to finish with an 8–2–1 record, so the players figured there was time for a day or two of fun before Vermeil resumed his long, fast-tempo workouts in full pads. After all, didn't every Rose Bowl team visit Disneyland? Didn't the team captains always pose with Mickey Mouse and Snow White, laughing in the California sun?

John Sciarra, the team captain and option quarterback, talked to the team's 10-man executive committee that had been formed by Vermeil to deal with off-the-field disputes. There had been some rumbling in the ranks about the need for Vermeil to "back off" on his workouts. The dissidents felt the team deserved a reward for achieving UCLA's first bowl appearance in 10 years. The Bruins players had heard that the Ohio State team planned to visit Disneyland before its first bowl practice in California.

Sciarra and nine other committee members headed for Vermeil's office with the demand.

"We got up there and he happened to be walking down the hall," said Sciarra. "He was totally stunned when he saw us."

Informed that the committee had a gripe, Vermeil invited its members into his office.

"What's this all about?" the coach asked.

"Well, Coach, a lot of the guys think we're working a little too hard," said Sciarra. "We beat Southern Cal and went right into preparations for the Rose Bowl. The guys think we should be enjoying it a little bit more instead of going right into double-days."

Vermeil looked at Sciarra. "What do you think?" he asked the team captain.

"Coach, you know I'm chairman of the executive committee," said Sciarra. "I'm just delivering the message."

"No," said Vermeil. "What do you think personally?"

"Coach, I'm fine with whatever you want to do," Sciarra said.

"Okay, okay, enough," said Vermeil. "Randy [Cross], what do you think?"

"Well, Coach," said Cross, "like John says, we came up here to tell you we've been working kind of hard. Maybe we ought to back it off a little bit."

Some of the other players shook their heads in agreement. "We're going to be too tired," one of them said.

Vermeil stood up and walked behind his desk. The coach put his hand on his head and looked at his players. The room grew quiet. All of a sudden, Vermeil slammed his hand on the desk.

"Damn!" he shouted. "I'm going to tell you something right now. You'd better get your asses back into that locker room. You'd better get ready in 10 minutes because we're going out early. And if you're not ready, I'm going to walk the practice field and I'm going to start recruiting students who have tried and wanted to play for UCLA in a way it should be represented."

Now the players were edgy, eager to leave the site of the explosion. But Vermeil wasn't done talking.

"You know, your scholarships are on the line," he said. "You'd better get your act together right now. I'm tired of all this crap. I'm not going on national television and putting this institution in a position where it's going to be embarrassed. Get your asses back in the locker room and tell the guys to get their asses out there on the field in 10 minutes."

The stereo was playing and the players were dancing and yelling when members of the executive committee returned. "Hey, cut the jukebox down, turn it off," said Sciarra. "The only thing I can tell you is that the man is very pissed off. Now if you don't get your stuff on and get out there on the field, then everybody's scholarship might be in jeopardy."

A few moments later, the door opened. Vermeil entered, followed by the entire coaching staff.

"I don't know what this is all about," said Vermeil. "But I'll tell you right now, this is not the kind of team that I thought I was coaching. You know, you represent UCLA, and you're going to take pride in that when we walk on that field on New Year's Day. And I'm going to do my job to get you ready. This is what it takes to get ready and this is what it takes to beat Ohio State."

There were unsubstantiated rumors that the UCLA players were going to remain in the locker room and refuse to practice. But it never came to that. Not with Vermeil threatening to use replacement players and embarrass the school against the No. 1 team in the country.

So, the UCLA players resumed their workouts in quiet anger as Vermeil drove them. They worked on timing and precision. The UCLA players knew they would be a stronger team in the fourth quarter, based on their workload and dedication. But would they have the lead, or would it end in another rout as it had back on October 4? Vermeil kept reminding

"A lot of the players kind of resented the fact that he worked us so hard.... But at the end of the day, there was respect for Dick Vermeil, at least my respect, because he always worked harder than I did."

JOHN SCIARRA, FORMER UCLA BRUIN
AND PHILADELPHIA EAGLE

them of how Ohio State and Woody Hayes, its legendary coach, were beatable. Not only that, but Vermeil recalled a trip to New York's Waldorf-Astoria Hotel with Sciarra, the team captain, and UCLA chancellor Charles Young.

"There were only seven or eight bowls back then, and this was sort of ABC's kickoff to the bowl season," said Sciarra. "The captains and the coaches of all the bowl teams were there. They rolled out the MacArthur Bowl that went to the national champion. And the [ABC] people started saying that they should bring up the Ohio State reps and present the trophy right then instead of waiting until January 1."

As he listened to the buzz in the Waldorf-Astoria ballroom that night, Vermeil shook his head. Inside, his emotions were churning. If he had one wish, it was that he was out on the practice field, pushing his Bruins in full pads, then pushing some more.

"When he got back on campus," said Sciarra, "he was not a happy camper. That's when he worked our asses off. We went through almost double-day sessions. That was kind of his motivation."

And now it was New Year's Day, game day in Pasadena. UCLA and Ohio State were eager, as were the 105,464 fans who jammed the Rose Bowl that afternoon. Many had come to see the unbeaten Buckeyes, with two-time Heisman Trophy winner Archie Griffin and national scoring leader Pete Johnson in the backfield. The mighty Buckeyes defense featured safety Tim Fox, linebacker Bob Brudzinski, and end Aaron Brown. That defense, quick and punishing, had given up only 79 points all year, posting three shutouts.

Although Ohio State controlled the ball for 21 minutes and gained 174 yards in the first half, the Buckeyes led by only 3–0 on Tom Klaban's 42-yard field goal. Ohio State's defense, meanwhile, was controlling UCLA's option offense by jamming the line of scrimmage, daring the Bruins to pass. UCLA's offense, pressured by the Buckeyes that were seemingly everywhere, gained only 49 first-half yards.

"We had run the option on them in the first game and scored three touchdowns," said Sciarra. "Woody Hayes was no stupid guy. He watched us move the ball against them earlier, so he figured we were going to run the option again. All of a sudden I looked up and they've got eight guys on the line of scrimmage, a whole swarm of guys. We fumbled the pitch on our first series.

And they were shutting us down. We were in the game only because our defense was playing phenomenally."

At halftime, Vermeil decided to take the Ohio State dare. "He made the point that we had softened them up in the first half," said Randy Cross, the All-American guard. "So now it was a game for the team with the will and the coach with a second-half plan."

"Okay, guys, forget the attack with the option right now," Vermeil told his players. "We're coming out throwing the ball. It's all [man-to-man] coverage, so this is going to be easy." Vermeil reminded his receivers, Wally Henry and Norm Andersen, to "stick 'em hard, make your breaks. John is going to throw you the ball. It's going to be simple. This isn't complicated." And Vermeil reminded his blockers, too. "You're going to block on your guy and block your asses off each time we get the ball," the coach said.

Vermeil was right. The safeties, Tim Fox and Ray Griffin, were being used for run support. It was simple, a pitch-and-catch game, as the Buckeyes remained in their run-stopping formation, fearing the UCLA option.

"We came out, boom, an out to Norm Andersen, first down," recalled Sciarra. "Boom, another out to Wally Henry, first down. Boom, down the middle to Ricky Walker, first down. Then I threw a 16-yard touchdown pass to Hollywood Henry."

Sciarra would hit on nine of 13 second-half passes for 173 yards. Henry put a little wiggle move on his defender and turned another Sciarra pass into a 67-yard score and a 16–3 UCLA lead after three quarters. After the Buckeyes closed to within 16–10, Wendell Tyler cut loose on a 54-yard run and it was all over.

On Tyler's run, he ran behind his tight end to the strong side. After Sciarra faked an inside handoff, he sprinted to the outside with Tyler as a trailer. This drew the outside linebacker and the safety. Tyler took Sciarra's pitch and raced into the end zone, just the way the play was drawn up in Vermeil's blackboard sessions.

"They started backing off their defense in the middle of our second drive," said Sciarra. "So we just started running the option again. We just kind of dominated them in the second half. There were some deep balls in the first half that I did not hit and probably should have."

And then it was over. The noise that cascaded from the Rose Bowl stands kept coming in tumultuous waves. There was Dick Vermeil, sprinting and pumping the air like a victorious boxer. And all of those old UCLA grads who remembered the war years, which were the bad years, felt giddy and young again.

It had been 10 years since UCLA had won its first Rose Bowl after five straight defeats. Like Dick Vermeil's obsessed team, the 1965 Bruins upset top-ranked and unbeaten Michigan State 14–12. It was a mirror of Vermeil's season; Michigan State had beaten those Bruins in an earlier game 13–3.

Ohio State guard Ron Ayers came right out with it. "We had beaten UCLA earlier in the season," Ayers said. "The coaches wanted to change up the game plan, but Woody believed that since we had beaten them once doing it his way, we could do it again. Dick Vermeil outcoached him that day. UCLA knew everything about us. They knew our formations, our tendencies, where the ball was going on every play."

In the days that followed one of the greatest victories in UCLA football history, Vermeil never sat still. He was quickly out on the recruiting trail, up and down the state with a new goal: winning a national championship. The Bruins had been crowned champions by United Press International in 1954. The Associated Press had ranked them second.

* * *

Southern California was still basking in the thrill of UCLA's unexpected Rose Bowl victory when the Eagles' traveling party arrived in Los Angeles. Dick Vermeil, the coach who had thrilled Tose and Murray as they watched intently in their penthouse suite at the Doral Hotel, was already working on the next season. He was on a recruiting trip, that necessary part of college football that involves selling your school and your program to high school stars.

In recruiting, the sharks of the game promise everything: a starting position in your sophomore year; trips to major bowls; introductions to prominent alumni boosters; and appearances on prime-time television.

"I got my first dose of Dick Vermeil in recruiting," said Randy Cross. "Terry Donahue was my offensive line coach. Terry was a legend himself. So between him and Dick, you really had no shot [to go elsewhere]. Once your parents met [Vermeil], you were toast. You were going to UCLA."

While Vermeil was meeting parents and prospects, Tose, Murray, and Procopio were headed for the swank Beverly Hills Hotel. This was Tose's favorite haunt. The guests stayed in two- and three-bedroom bungalows. There were huge Hollywood deals talked about and finalized there. And it was here that Tose expected to close his own deal on a head coach.

"I don't think [Vermeil] knew I was interviewing, and I sure as heck didn't know he was interviewing," said Mike White, the California–Berkeley coach. "I remember the hotel was an older place, with those cabanas, or bungalows. It was basically one of the first interviews I had been through. I thought it went pretty good. It was about what makes you tick. You know, my philosophy and just being honest about what I could bring to the table. But I guess I lost out."

As White sat there and listened to Tose's questions, he found himself in awe of the man. It was late morning, and Tose was still in his bathrobe.

"He knew a lot about me," said White. "To be honest with you, it was a helluva experience for me. You're really in the presence of someone who is so strong in the league and had such a tremendous reputation. I was almost in awe of the situation, just because of the fact that he was such an imposing figure and had such an impressive personality. I was proud that I was asked. Then I was through and gone. And obviously, Dick got the job."

Darryl Rogers, who had built a strong program at San Jose State, appeared with the recommendation of Al Davis, Oakland's maverick owner. Rogers was an impressive coach. He had been a standout receiver and had earned a master's degree at Fresno State. Rogers was among a group of California coaches who dominated the college scene in the 1970s, along with Bill Walsh, John Ralston, Mike White, Tommy Prothro, and Dick Vermeil.

"He was a fine interview," said Murray. "It wasn't that he wasn't an impressive coach. It's just that we got the perfect fit. We got a coach from God." Rogers eventually moved up in the college ranks, coaching at Michigan State and

Arizona State. In 1985, he was hired by the Detroit Lions, a team that always seemed to be changing quarterbacks and finishing with a mediocre record.

While Tose and Murray waited, Vermeil was out of his office, visiting California's best prep athletes. Murray, one of the game's true dreamers, kept thinking about the Rose Bowl and what he had seen that afternoon on the television screen at the Doral.

"It was one of those moments you never forget," he said. "Here's UCLA pulling off the upset of the century. And when the cameras zoom in for a tight shot of Dick Vermeil, here's this young, good-looking California guy, so intense that sparks are shooting through the tube at us."

Murray finally reached Vermeil at his UCLA office. He introduced himself and told Vermeil he would like to arrange a meeting with Tose at his bungalow in Beverly Hills.

Vermeil quickly told Murray that he wasn't interested in coaching the Eagles. "I'm recruiting players," Vermeil said. "I want to win another Rose Bowl and coach a national championship team at UCLA. So I'm not interested."

"Geez," fumed Murray after the call had ended, "he's not even interested in talking."

Tose's lip curled as it always did when he was upset. "Jimmy, you certainly picked a fine guy. How bright can he be? He's five minutes from our hotel and he won't even walk across the street to talk about the opportunity," he said.

Murray swallowed hard. He thought about the man next to him and how Tose almost always succeeded in whatever he tried to do. Tose always traveled with a zipper bag that was packed with $100 bills. The waiters at Tose's favorite restaurants would line up to serve him, knowing that each of them would be rewarded with one of Tose's bills.

But this was a far different circumstance. Tose, the king of the Philadelphia Eagles, felt like he did after one of those comical Sundays when his team was outhit, outplayed, and outscored.

A half-hour later, the phone rang. Murray answered. The voice sounded like Tose's barber, so Murray handed Tose the phone. The caller turned out to be Vermeil, who said he had changed his mind.

"I'd have to be crazy not to listen to an offer," he told Tose. "I'll be right over."

Now the mood had changed. In football parlance, Tose and Murray were at their opponent's 6-yard line rather than punting out of their own end zone. And they had the perfect plan—and the money—to lure Dick Vermeil off the California recruiting trail and away from the gorgeous UCLA campus.

> *"I encouraged Leonard Tose to hire him, and I encouraged Dick not to pass up the opportunity. I told Leonard, 'If you hire him, you'll never regret it.'"*
>
> GEORGE ALLEN,
> FORMER RAMS HEAD COACH

In a matter of minutes, Vermeil was at the door. "He was driving a powder-blue Mustang, the UCLA colors," recalled Murray. "Dick got over here in about eight minutes."

The interview lasted several hours and, according to Murray, "was very intense." At one point, Vermeil asked Murray, "Why would I want to come to Philadelphia?"

"What the heck does that mean?" Murray asked.

"Well, the fans. I've been in there with the Rams," Vermeil said.

"I'm going to tell you two things," Murray said. "No. 1, our team is so bad, if you win a game for our fans, you'll get a standing ovation. Listen, if you win the coin toss, you'll get a standing ovation. That's how bad our team is."

Now Jim Murray was on his Eagles pulpit. "You level with our fans, not only will they embrace you, you'll move your family here. You'll raise your kids here, and you'll become a household name," he said.

Vermeil promised he'd be back for a second interview. The meeting with Tose and Murray had gone exceedingly well. Vermeil had talked to George Allen and Chuck Knox, two highly successful NFL coaches. Each had given him the same advice: seize the opportunity in Philadelphia.

All the while, Vermeil must have wondered whether he could turn around a faltering franchise that had not made the playoffs in 15 years. Fifteen years?

That was 1960, the year he was coaching football and swimming at tiny Hillsdale High School in San Mateo, California.

As Tose waited for Vermeil's return, Jim Murray kept thinking how impressive the coach had been in their meeting. Vermeil was a little guy, perhaps 5'8", with the trim body of a marathoner. His most prominent feature was his jaw, one that seemed to jut out like Don Shula's. He had allowed his thick, light-brown hair to grow fashionably long, the California-cool look of the 1970s. His coaching style was all about boot-camp discipline and extremely long, punishing workouts.

"To say he's direct is an understatement. To say he's intense is putting it mildly," Murray said. "Look, this wasn't any snap decision on our part. Leonard had missed on three other coaches. He was like a bettor down to his last two bucks at the track. This choice had to be the right one. But after talking with Dick, Leonard was certain he was our guy. 'The man is just what we need to turn our team around,' he said."

Before Vermeil could return for a second interview, Tose and Murray had to survive the Beverly Hills Hotel's attempt to eject them after they had overstayed their reservation and caused complications for the establishment's previously booked guest: unknown to the Eagles party, Yitzhak Rabin, the Israeli prime minister, had reserved Tose's bungalow. Rabin showed up, accompanied by several of his guards carrying Uzis and dressed in camouflage.

"We've got squatters' rights," said Tose, as night fell on the popular hotel. "Tell them I won't buy any more Israeli war bonds. I'm staying until we get a coach." Eventually Murray passed out enough $100 bills to extend their stay.

After talking with his family, Vermeil returned for a second interview. There had been a family vote against moving to the East Coast. Dick's wife Carol and their three children, all teenagers by then, had all opposed the move. David had already attended two different high schools. Besides, Vermeil had purchased a new home not far from the UCLA campus. And he had promised them he wasn't going to leave Southern California. Vermeil had also checked out Tose's character and whether he was a true competitor or just another rich owner.

"Dick wasn't positive he was ready," said Eagles quarterback Roman Gabriel, who was called by Vermeil, his former position coach with the Rams. "I felt he was. I knew he coached on all levels and was a winning coach at all levels. One year with the Rams, he had the best special teams in football."

Vermeil, buoyed by what Gabriel and former Rams coach George Allen had told him, decided to accept Tose's generous offer.

The following day, on February 7, 1976, the parties adjourned to the office of E. Gregory Hookstratten, Vermeil's agent as well as an attorney for the Rams. ("I used to call him the West Coast commissioner," said Murray.) Vermeil signed a unique five-year contract. It contained a clause in which the coach would get paid a 50 percent bonus for any money that he deferred. There were also more perks: country club privileges, a new car, a life insurance policy, and performance bonuses.

"Whatever it was, it was short money," Murray said later. "We thought at the time it was high fare. That's the way we used to look at people's contracts. Looking back, he probably should have gotten more."

Carol Vermeil knew all along her husband would accept Tose's offer. "He can't turn his back on a challenge," she said.

"She's right," said Vermeil. "I never would have left UCLA to take over a winning program like the Rams or the Steelers. What could a coach prove there?"

> *"I don't want to make him sound like he's selfish, or inconsiderate.... It's just that he's completely involved in his work during the football season. That's the way it is."*
>
> CAROL VERMEIL

So Dick Vermeil headed back to his new home, which soon would become his former home. The contract had made him a future millionaire. And in the middle of a bitter Philadelphia winter, he would begin to tackle the biggest challenge of his life.

Chapter 4

"We're Launching a Crusade"

The only noise was the sound of the winter wind that swirled through Veterans Stadium in the kind of crazy patterns that field-goal kickers despise. But inside the Vet, the more familiar name for the five-year-old South Philadelphia facility, reporters and television crews mingled with office staffers of the Philadelphia Eagles in anticipation of a major news event. This was the day that Dick Vermeil, the team's new head coach, would appear and talk about his plans to turn around a losing franchise.

Vermeil had taken the red-eye from Los Angeles after a speaking engagement in San Diego. He had signed a five-year contract to coach one of the worst teams in pro football. Yet, he had spoken positively about his new job, almost as if he was going to coach in Dallas, where the Super Bowl trophy was on display.

"There's no secret to winning," Vermeil had told reporters the day before from Los Angeles. "You've got to have good football players. They've got to be disciplined, motivated. I'm a player-oriented coach."

Attorney E. Gregory Hookstratten, who negotiated Vermeil's contract, knew what motivated his client. "Dick likes a challenge," said Hookstratten. "He's one of those guys who is perpetually coming out of the chute."

Eventually Vermeil entered the room. The television lights flooded his entrance while veteran sports reporters tried to size up the man most of them had never seen before. Flanking Vermeil were Leonard Tose, the beaming owner, and Jim Murray, his general manager and confidante.

"This is a happy day for the Eagles organization and for me personally," said Tose. "And, I hope, for the Eagles fans. In Dick Vermeil, we've added a young, dynamic, and imaginative coach. There were many quality people who sought the head coaching job with the Eagles. But no one impressed us as much as Dick Vermeil. And now it gives me great pleasure to present the new coach of the Philadelphia Eagles."

Vermeil knew that the Eagles had won only four games the previous season and scored only 225 points. He also knew the Eagles had mortgaged their future on two quarterbacks, 14-year veteran Roman Gabriel and young Mike Boryla. And he certainly knew that his new team lacked a workhorse running back, the staple of every offense that Vermeil had ever coached. Yet, the little guy at the microphone put a positive spin on his situation.

"I do believe there are lots of football players here in Philadelphia's program who have not played as good as they are physically capable of playing," Vermeil said. "And I think that is part of my responsibility. It'll take some time. But I didn't come here with the idea that five years from now, we'll be successful. Five years from now, if we're not successful, I won't be here."

That was an off-season unlike any other. Including the Eagles, nine losing teams had hired new head coaches. The two expansion teams, Seattle and Tampa Bay, would begin play with their own rookie coaches. Thus, Vermeil would be among 11 new head coaches, or nearly 40 percent of the league, who would be trying to make winners out of teams considered years away from seriously competing.

At UCLA, Vermeil had assembled—or inherited, according to his predecessor Pepper Rodgers—a talented group of assistant coaches. Yet because of his relatively late hiring, he was able to sign only one member off his college staff, receivers coach Carl Peterson. Vermeil's two UCLA secretaries, sisters Helen and Betty Jurgenson, also followed their boss. So did a Beverly Hills character named Wojtkiewicz S. Wojchiechowicz, known around the football office at UCLA as Bow Wow. He answered the phone and brought back coffee for the Bruins coaches while endearing himself to Vermeil.

"During the season, he acts as a valet for me," said Vermeil. "When things get a little grim, he can make me smile."

In the off-season, Bow Wow would return to the glittering world of Hollywood and Beverly Hills, showing up at parties and telling everybody he was a Polish prince. Bow Wow also claimed that he had been married to gossip columnist Sheila Graham. He passed around a business card that listed a number in Trancas Beach, north of Malibu. But when you tried to dial the number—Hollywood 9-125—it was one digit short.

Vermeil eventually rounded up a decent staff that included defensive line coach Chuck Clausen, who was on the Ohio State staff in the 1976 Rose Bowl; receivers coach Dick Coury, who coached under Tommy Prothro, a Vermeil favorite, at San Diego; and running backs coach Johnny Roland, signed off the Notre Dame staff. Vermeil retained offensive coordinator John Idzik and defensive coordinator John Mazur from Mike McCormack's staff as "bridge" coaches. Both were released a year later, when Vermeil took over the offense and Marion Campbell, a former Eagles star, replaced Mazur.

Vermeil's first draft was close to a complete bust. The Eagles had traded away their first four picks. Of their 15 middle and low-round choices, nine never played a minute in the NFL. The top pick, fourth-rounder Mike Smith, a speed rusher from Miami, never flashed his collegiate form and was cut. Most of the training-camp stories about Smith involved his daring rescue of a little girl who was drowning while he was in college. Smith's heroic feat happened on the morning of a big game against California. Smith then sacked Steve Bartkowski three times, sparking a Hurricanes win.

The Eagles, who had the 111th pick after a trade with Miami, could have drafted offensive tackle Dan Jiggetts (the 161st player taken); guard Tom Rafferty (119); or either of two linebackers, Carl Ekern (128) or Woody Lowe (131). All four players became solid starters and enjoyed lengthy NFL careers. Indeed, Rafferty played 14 seasons for the Dallas Cowboys, appearing in two Super Bowls.

What saved the draft for the Eagles was an obscure defensive end named Carl Hairston from an obscure school called Maryland–Eastern Shore. Hairston was shooting pool in Martinsville, Virginia, when a man named Sam Trott approached him. Trott was an alumnus of Maryland–Eastern Shore and a volunteer recruiter. All Trott knew was that Hairston was a big man and if he was shooting pool, he could handle himself on a football field, given the reputation of Martinsville pool players.

Hairston was employed as a truck driver for a furniture company, working the Martinsville–New York turnaround for $250 per week. "I had just come off the road and went across the street to the pool hall," recalled Hairston. "Sam asked me if I played football. I weighed about 275 and had gotten out of high school and been working for two years. Sam and I talked and two weeks later, he told me I had been accepted at Maryland–Eastern Shore."

They soon began calling him "Hurricane" Hairston for his devastating pass rush. He blew away blockers with that quick first step that all great rushers possess. Scouts call it "the burst." Although Hairston became a star, Maryland–Eastern Shore went winless in his final season. Yet, the late Jackie Graves, then an Eagles scout, liked Hairston's quickness and size.

The Eagles took Hairston with their seventh pick, marking the start of an extraordinary career in pro football. He played in 224 games over 15 seasons and totaled over 100 tackles for five straight years (1977–81). Over the years, his nickname changed to "Big Daddy," reflecting a warm, caring individual.

*　*　*

The Eagles headed for Vermeil's first training camp with a collection of 97 players, only 27 of them from Mike McCormack's last 4–10 team and 49 of them draftees or rookie free agents.

"The two weaknesses we have are on the defensive and offensive lines," said Vermeil. "I've been a coach for 17 years and you would never know any coach who thought his players were good enough. What I found out is that coaches can worry too much about players they don't have rather than the players they already have. We need more work than anybody in the league. We need the time. We need the opportunity. If these guys didn't need that much work, they wouldn't have the kind of record they did. But I don't want to hear the term 'rebuilding.' I'm not here to rebuild. I'm here to compete."

As he has ever since his first coaching job in 1960 at tiny Hillsdale High School in California, Vermeil believed that hard work was the key to any successful football program. Work those long hours. Bang each other around on the practice field. Watch game films until 3:00 or 4:00 AM, seeking any kind of edge from the tapes. The hell with the cold coffee. Yet, what Vermeil quickly learned was that tough players and dedicated coaches can carry a program only so far. Talent has to take over if a team is to dominate its division and, hopefully, its playoffs.

So, what kind of team did Dick Vermeil take to his first training camp at Widener College in Chester, Pennsylvania? The Eagles offense had finished 21st in the league the year before, scoring only 225 points and rushing for only three touchdowns, a league low. The defense was just as bad. It ranked 16th, giving up an average of 159.5 rushing yards per game and 302 points. Aside from being pushed around in the trenches by bigger, quicker drive blockers, there was another glaring weakness: the pass rush. The Eagles had none. Bill Dunstan, a defensive tackle noted more for his muscle than his burst, had five of the team's 17 sacks.

The year before, McCormack had seemed confident with his talent. "Our first 22 are set," McCormack gushed. "All we're trying to do is fill in behind them." Later that season, however, McCormack admitted the Eagles needed to improve at least eight positions. The big need was for a strong, durable running back.

Everywhere Vermeil looked, there was temptation. On October 22, 1975, the struggling World Football League folded, turning loose some familiar backs: Larry Csonka, Calvin Hill, and Jim Kiick. Another formidable runner, John Riggins of the New York Jets, declared himself a free agent, open to all offers. Not only didn't the Eagles sign any of those veteran backs, but three of them— Riggins (Washington), Hill (Dallas), and Csonka (New York Giants)—ended up on the roster of NFC East rivals. (Kiick signed with Denver.)

"We could have spent a million dollars to get Csonka or Riggins," said Vermeil. "We didn't. It all goes back to our basic philosophy of not starting out by throwing all that money to one guy and creating an attitude problem on a team that already had an attitude problem. I didn't want Csonka to come in there simply because Leonard Tose had offered him $5 million. Hell, it disgusts me that these guys, the free agents, are running around selling themselves like some hookers on Locust Street."

Then Vermeil returned to the subject of work ethic. "You don't talk about running the football," he said. "You work to do it. Running the football is physical, and you work to be physical. There's very little finesse to it."

"He'd go on a vacation to Acapulco that was supposed to be for 10 days. After four days, he was ready to go home. His wife would say, 'Let's stay.' Dick would say, 'I've got to get back to work.'"

LEONARD TOSE

As the date approached for the opening of Vermeil's first training camp, Philadelphia was preparing to celebrate the bicentennial. There would be parades, wagon trains rolling into historic Valley Forge, an air show at the Willow Grove Naval Air Station, an address at Independence Hall by President Gerald Ford, and, of course, countless displays of fireworks.

Meanwhile, Dick Vermeil was preparing to open the earliest training camp in league history for rookies at Widener College in suburban Chester. "To me, the Fourth of July is just another square on the calendar," Vermeil told Jim Murray, his general manager. "Winners have luxuries like holidays; losers don't."

Forty-seven rookies reported to Widener on July 3; the veterans would follow a week later. The next night, Vermeil gave his players a little precamp speech about hard work, dedication, and purpose. "Gentlemen, we're not starting a season, we're launching a crusade," the coach said. "That's why I wasn't interested in signing all of those free agents: Csonka, Riggins, and Hill. We have to develop a pride from within the Eagles, a pride in wearing the green-and-white uniform. Pride is something you can't buy."

As Vermeil was talking, loud bursts filtered into the meeting room, making it difficult to hear. The noise continued, seemingly getting louder. Between the bursts, there was the unmistakable sound of cheers.

"Carl, what's that?" Vermeil asked his assistant coach. "What's going on out there?"

"I forgot to tell you, Coach, that there's a fireworks display going on at Widener Stadium," said Peterson. "It's the Fourth of July, the 200th birthday of our country."

"I don't care whose birthday it is," snapped Vermeil. "Go outside and tell them to hold the noise down."

A week later, the veterans appeared at Widener, wondering what Vermeil's first camp was going to be like. There was Roman Gabriel, the 36-year-old gun-slinging quarterback trying to come back from off-season knee surgery. There was Harold Carmichael, the 6'8" receiver who had caught 172 passes over the past three seasons. There was Bill Bergey, a fullback at Arkansas State who had been converted to a run-stuffing linebacker by a wise coach named Benny Ellender. And there were offensive tackle Jerry Sisemore; tight end Charles Young; center Guy Morriss; and strong safety Randy Logan, drafted by Mike McCormack in 1973. (Several years later, Vermeil would send McCormack a thank-you note for achieving one of the best drafts in Eagles history.)

But where were Vermeil's running backs? Sure, the coach had said that running the football is all about hard work and nerve and dedication. The Eagles brought 11 backs to camp, five of them rookies. Within five years, all of them would be gone.

The veterans were Tom Sullivan, a lightweight runner with a little wiggle who had led the team in 1975 with 632 yards but not a single touchdown; Art Malone, a plugger and lead blocker obtained from Atlanta; George Amundson, a former No. 1 draft pick of the Houston Oilers who had ranked 106th in rushing in 1974 with 138 yards; James McAlister, one of those World Football League nomads, who had gained 335 yards for the Eagles in a spot role the year before; and Ron "Po" James, a four-year veteran who had led the Eagles in rushing (565 yards) as a free-spirited rookie in 1972.

Vermeil also had acquired some new backfield talent: Herb Lusk, the "Pray-ing Tailback" from Long Beach State; Steve Campassi, a little kick returner from Kentucky; Mike Hogan, an injury-plagued slasher from Tennessee

(Chattanooga); and journeyman Marv Kendricks, who had experience with the Toronto Argos in Canada and the Portland Storm of the WFL, where he was coached by Dick Coury, Vermeil's receivers coach.

So, what Vermeil lacked in quality he had in quantity. And until he could find a true 1,000-yard back, Vermeil was going to do what he had always done as a coach: work his players until they were exhausted, then outwork all of them himself until he, too, was exhausted. The weak would quit on him and leave camp. The slow-footed prospects would be sent packing. The men who remained, the ones who made it through six weeks of the most intense training any of them would ever experience, would become Eagles.

"The day he came in was like a nightmare," said linebacker Bill Bergey. "It was all that college crap. He started laying down his rules. No hats in the meeting rooms. Helmets had to be worn at all times on the practice field. Chin straps must be buckled. I thought, *What's this crap?* I mean, I was in my eighth NFL season. I didn't need all this Harry High School stuff. And most of the guys felt the same way. We were professionals and we thought Dick was treating us like a bunch of kids."

As the weeks unfolded, however, Bergey changed his mind. He had been there during the Mike McCormack years, when veteran players made their own rules and took a play off now and then. "It became clear what [Vermeil] was doing," said Bergey. "He was setting a mood of discipline, which was needed. Things got out of hand the previous year that hurt us. Dick let us know right off that he wasn't going to stand for it."

"I think bringing Dick Vermeil to Philadelphia was one of the greatest things that I had a part in. Because Dick Vermeil became Philly, and Philly became Dick Vermeil..."

JIM MURRAY, FORMER EAGLES GENERAL MANAGER

Vermeil's practices lasted two and a half hours in the morning, and three hours in the afternoon. He had two-a-day practices scheduled right up until the final preseason game on September 5. John Jacobi, a 6'6" rookie offensive tackle from West Texas State, and Kirk Johnson, another rookie tackle, were rewarded with chilled bottles of imported beer for "strenuous practice without backup relief." Several days later, however, Jacobi and Johnson decided they had lost their heart for the game and left camp.

Meanwhile, there was a coaching friend 2,375 miles away who knew exactly what was happening at the Eagles' camp because he knew Vermeil's style. "He's a smart, sound fundamentalist, who emphasizes the muscle-strengthening exercises you need to play football," said Tommy Prothro, the San Diego coach. "With your knees bent, that's the best way to play any game. Second, he's a master at putting together the daily practice program. He asks each assistant to sit down and tell him what he wants to accomplish. That means that his coaches have to be organized and thinking in long-range terms."

Chuck Knox, another coach for whom Vermeil worked, knew the Eagles would be doing plenty of hitting. "He never lets his team forget that football is a contact sport," said Knox. "One of his favorite expressions is 'Screw on the Ree-dell!' That's the way he pronounced Riddell, the name of the helmet company. He means, be ready to hit. His approach to football is that you're not going to fool the other guy; you've got to take them on."

Take them on. That was Vermeil's approach to the game, and also the battle cry of a 30-year-old rookie receiver named Vince Papale.

* * *

All through camp, the unheralded Vince Papale led with his body, checking anybody who moved on Vermeil's kick coverage and return teams. The media guide listed his college as St. Joseph's—a school that didn't field a football team.

It turns out that Papale had learned his trade with the Philadelphia Bell of the defunct World Football League. He learned from Ron Holliday, a little 5'9" pass catcher, who taught him how to run clean, hard routes, and from former Denver Bronco Marvin Frazier, who counseled him about the proper way to use his hands. Joe Gardi, a Bell coach, stayed after practice to help Papale polish his moves.

"You're a great athlete, you've got a lot of heart," Gardi told Papale, who had been a running, jumping, tossing decathlon star at St. Joseph's. "But as a wide receiver, you suck."

Papale, however, impressed Vermeil with the way he hustled and banged others around, never shying away from a collision. In pro hockey, he would have been known as an enforcer.

"I love hitting people," said Papale. "I made a lot of noise. And I knew I had to keep my head on a swivel, hoping I wouldn't get taken out. A lot of guys would take you out because I was taking them out. Geez, you always had to watch out. They could take you out at the knees back then."

Papale was always counting heads; he knew whether or not he made the team was largely a numbers game. "When Dick made the final cut from 50 to 45, I knew I was up against it," Papale said. "I was never really told that I had made the team. So, when we got out on the field and I was counting around, I figured if I was going to be on the roster, I'd be the 45th guy."

It was getting late in camp and Papale was still counting heads. Then, as the Eagles were doing their knee bends, Vermeil appeared. Papale stiffened at the sight of the head coach. He was contemplating his life, still unsure of whether he was going to be a football player, a bartender, or a teacher of accounting, business law, and consumer economics at Interboro High School, his alma mater.

"Congratulations, old man," said Vermeil. "You're a Philadelphia Eagle."

Papale was stunned. "Coach," he stammered, "can I be excused for five minutes? I've got to make a phone call."

"What's the deal?" asked Vermeil. "Who are you calling, *Sports Illustrated*, CBS, and all those people?"

"No, Coach," said Papale. "I just want to call my dad and all the guys at the Westinghouse plant down here in Essington."

Vermeil waved him in to the nearest phone. Frank Papale, known as "King-ee" to his fellow workers, had been operating a burner for a lifetime at Westinghouse, working with large acetylene torches. "I called the foreman and said, 'Tell King-ee that his son's a Philadelphia Eagle,'" said Papale. "I heard him yell out, and then the whole wing, the 'E' wing at Westinghouse, just exploded. My dad got on the phone. He was crying. I was crying, too. We partied for 48 hours."

Years later, the fascinating story of Vince Papale would become the inspirational Disney movie called *Invincible*. Mark Wahlberg, a fine actor, played Papale. In real life, Papale would catch only one pass in three seasons. It was a 15-yarder from Roman Gabriel, the last completion in Gabriel's impressive 16-year career. Papale's real role was covering kickoffs and punts, flying downfield and dodging forearms, elbows, and everything else. For his mayhem, he was paid $21,000 as a rookie, plus a $2,000 roster bonus.

Papale became a football version of Rocky Balboa, the city's fictional boxing hero. He had a rugged, handsome face and had that long track stride that carried him into the action. For three seasons, he was Rocky in pads, running downfield and knocking aside blockers. The city's faithful fans, who have always appreciated good, smashmouth football, idolized him.

Dennis Smelser was another rookie who played on the wild side. A free-agent tackle from Texas A&M, Smelser had a raw-edge philosophy. "If you're going to knock people on their rumps," Smelser said, "you've got to hate them."

Unlike some other coaches who feared injuries, Vermeil held daily "nutcracker" drills in which a ball carrier and a blocker were matched against a tackler, with all the action confined to a narrow chute. Smelser was very active in the nutcracker, knocking tacklers on their backs. "I'm from a wishbone team," he explained. "Just comin' off and hittin' people, that's nothing new to me. That was our bread-and-butter at A&M. We called it a 'shotgun alley.' It's kill or be killed out there. And I guess you have to have some hate involved."

On the seventh day of training, Dennis Smelser unexpectedly walked out of camp, never to be seen again. "I'm disappointed that he left," said Vermeil. "He has a lot of talent, and it really hurts when a kid has the talent and can't get a chance. It's a dumb thing to do. Evidently, he got a lot of pressure from home." Vermeil was referring to Smelser's wife, Debra Ann, who was seven months' pregnant.

Bill Capraun, an injury-plagued offensive tackle, also left camp for the second straight year. Vermeil said Capraun, who missed the entire 1975 season with a knee injury, left his playbook and this discouraging note: "Knee trouble; what a bleeping drag."

When the preseason games started, Vermeil shuffled players in and out, sizing up his talent and focusing on two areas: running the ball and stopping the run. Gabriel was still recovering from the fourth operation on his right knee and didn't play. The quarterback work was divided among Boryla; free agent Johnnie Walton, a World Football League star; and Steve Joachim, a local quarterback from Temple who had been cut by the Baltimore Colts and signed as a free agent on July 4, 1976, the day Vermeil heard those celebratory fireworks.

They say that preseason games are meaningless, but Vermeil drew some fast conclusions after the Eagles lost all six of their games and scored only 70 points. Vermeil knew he needed a big-play quarterback. Gabriel was 36 and had limited mobility because of his injured knee. Boryla threw nine interceptions and only three touchdown passes during the winless summer games and wasn't considered an NFL-caliber quarterback. Walton, a late signing, had played in four different leagues, including a stint with the semipro Columbus Barons, but displayed a powerful arm.

Walton was also bidding to become the Eagles' first African American quarterback. "I'm only a player," he said. "The establishment atmosphere is different in different places. And it's up to the establishment whether I make it. I do know I feel comfortable in this camp. Management is beautiful. I'm sure only the strong will survive."

Vermeil also knew he needed a productive runner, preferably a back with speed and moves. In six preseason games, the Eagles rushed for only 630 yards and a lowly 3.3 yards-per-carry average. Hogan, a fullback type, showed promise, averaging 4.8 yards per rush. Yet, Vermeil needed speed more than muscle.

As camp ended, Vermeil settled on his roster, a collection of journeymen, middle-round draft picks, overachievers, a once-great but now-injured quarterback, and a handful of quality players. But they were the best conditioned athletes in the league. They had a nasty edge to their attitude, driven to that state of mind by their coach, the little whip of a man who was determined to outwork the other 27 coaches in the league. And now they were starting the regular season in the toughest of all divisions, the NFC East.

Jon Gruden, who would later win a Super Bowl as head coach of the Tampa Bay Buccaneers, was the league's youngest offensive coordinator with the Eagles in 1995. "It was always a square-fist-in-the-mouth type of game," said Gruden. "Physical football games. The weather played a factor late in the year. Defensive-minded teams. Struggles, intense physical struggles are what I remember about the NFC East."

Vermeil relished the challenge. He wanted to build a winner in the league's strongest division, just as badly as he had wanted to upset Ohio State with his intense, superbly conditioned UCLA team. And Vermeil didn't even mind the season opener: playing the Cowboys on the road in the September heat of Dallas, Texas.

The Cowboys ruined Vermeil's debut. Their offense rolled up 445 yards and Dallas coasted to a 27–7 win that could have been a lot worse—the Cowboys blew four scoring chances inside the 10-yard line. "Damn," swore defensive tackle Pete Lazetich, "it seemed as though they had a helluva offensive game plan. It seemed like they hit us just as we were changing something and it went right for them."

Boryla, who struggled through a 14-for-31, two-interception game, said the biggest factor was in the minds of the losers. "I don't mean to sound like a psychologist," Boryla said, "but I've played on teams where you just knew you were going to score. I don't know how to get it. The thing is, we're waiting for something to happen, something to go wrong. That's understandable because we haven't had success yet. When we have some success, we'll play loose."

It was the 12th consecutive season-opening win for the Cowboys, who defeated the Eagles for the 11th straight time at home. The only Philadelphia score came with 3:24 left in the game when Boryla flicked a 20-yard pass to halfback Tom Sullivan off a fake end-around. The Eagles rushed for 136 yards, just 37 more yards than in their 1975 opener for Mike McCormack. And there was a dark footnote: McAlister had lost three fumbles.

"Guys, we've got to do a better job coaching these guys," said Vermeil, "and they've got to do a better job of playing. I'm disappointed for the players. I thought we'd play 'em tougher than we did, and if they beat us, it would be by a closer score. I think we can run successfully this year. But we can't fumble the damn thing. And I'll tell you why we fumbled it. It's anxiety."

The following week, Vermeil's defense held the hapless New York Giants to 82 yards rushing and forced five fumbles in a 20–7 win, Vermeil's first as a pro coach. Vince Papale, the storybook special teams hitter, set up one touchdown by recovering a muffed punt at the 3-yard line. The Eagles also flashed a punishing ground game, shoving around the Giants in the trenches to pile up 211 yards.

However, Vermeil's "better job of coaching" mantra would be repeated almost every week the rest of the season. Except for a 14–13 win over Atlanta that tackle Bill Dunstan saved with a blocked field goal, the Eagles lost four games over the next five weeks. Then, after Bill Bergey led a scuffling defense in a 10–0 shutout of the poor Giants, the Eagles dropped five more in a row by a combined 86 points. During that swoon, the offense scored 31 points and only four touchdowns, just one of them on the ground.

The most frustrating loss was to St. Louis, a 17–14 struggle the Eagles simply gave away. Just as the Eagles were poised to upset the high-scoring Cardinals, halfback Dave Hampton fumbled away Boryla's pass at the 15-yard line with 27 seconds left to play. Horst Muhlmann was loosening up his kicking leg when Hampton was stripped of the ball by linebacker Mark Arneson. Hampton had been a productive back with Atlanta, but had lost 11 fumbles in two seasons and ended up with Vermeil, a man with an eye for backs.

"What's really sad is that we played damn good football this afternoon, and we still lost," said Bergey. "I'm damn proud of the guys I'm associated with around here. I'm proud because I sincerely believe these guys are going to turn this around."

Two weeks later, there was no optimistic chatter in the loser's dressing room. Instead, the talk was all about the Oakland Raiders, the eventual Super Bowl champions, after they rolled up 250 rushing yards in a 26–7 rout. The Raiders were so physical, so dominating, that they turned the Eagles defense into a collection of flailing amateurs. Dunstan was yanked early and replaced by rookie Carl Hairston and, later, by Pete Lazetich.

"They were very basic," said linebacker Frank LeMaster. "Power sweeps, power up the middle. No tricks today. They just bring it at you. You've got to play tough, hard-nosed football against them."

Gabriel, starting his first game, took the Eagles on an early 67-yard drive, hitting Carmichael with a one-yard pass for a 7–0 lead. It was the 200th scoring pass of Gabriel's career. The Raiders dominated the rest of the game with that mammoth offensive line that included future Hall of Famers Gene Upshaw and Art Shell. The Eagles suffered five fumbles and left Vermeil shaking his head in disgust. Gabriel fumbled three exchanges with center Guy Morriss and also fumbled twice more under pressure. Meanwhile, long snapper Dennis Franks kept delivering wild snaps to his punter. Two of the wayward snaps led to blocked punts by Ted Hendricks.

The Eagles lost two more division games to the Redskins (24–0) and Cowboys (26–7), scoring only once on Gabriel's 20-yard pass to Charlie Smith. In the season finale, the Eagles rushed for 270 yards in the kind of game Vermeil loves and trounced the Seattle Seahawks 27–10. All Gabriel did was hand off to Mike Hogan inside and Tom

"He encouraged high standards. No bad habits. No sloughing off…ever. In training camp, you'd wake up and you didn't know if it was Monday, Wednesday, or Friday."

JOHN SPAGNOLA,
FORMER EAGLES TIGHT END

Sullivan outside. The final run-pass ratio was Vermeil's dream game plan: 72.9 percent runs, 28.1 percent passes. Sullivan rushed for 121 yards and Hogan for 104. Vermeil, however, wasn't deceived by what happened in that offensive display against a young expansion team. After all, the Seahawks defense had given up 140 points in losing its previous four games.

Vermeil's first season ended with a 4–10 record, matching Mike McCormack's record the year before. Yet, there was a good feeling among Vermeil's players, the ones who had survived and bought into his exhausting program. Vermeil drew two conclusions from his first season. First, he needed a new quarterback. And second, he needed a runner tough enough to slash inside the tackles and fast enough to dip outside the ends in his one-back offense.

A few days after the season ended, the little guy from Calistoga probably broke open a bottle of Napa Valley wine and began thinking about the 1977 season. In short order, he would find himself with a strong-armed new quarterback and a quiet rookie kick returner; together, they would give Vermeil the two weapons he needed to get the Eagles back on track.

Chapter 5

Jaws and Wilbert

The most important part of any pro football puzzle is always the quarterback. It's been that way since the late 1970s, when the NFL owners changed the rules to open up the passing game. In 1977, they voted to limit the contact that defenders could make with receivers to one bump. A year later, they limited the area of contact to five yards, further freeing the receivers. The owners also approved a new, more lenient style of pass blocking. Remember the old folded-arms technique? The new rule allowed offensive linemen to extend their arms and block or jam with their hands open.

The changes were in response to complaints from the television networks, who felt there were too many drab 13–7 games that only a defensive purist could love. Indeed, the Miami Dolphins won back-to-back Super Bowls, beating the Washington Redskins 14–7 and the Minnesota Vikings 24–7, by running the ball 90 times and throwing only 18 passes. Super Bowl VIII between the Dolphins and the Vikings saw Miami quarterback Bob Griese hand the ball off 51 times and carry two other times himself on sneaks. The game took less than two and a half hours to play, providing far less time for commercials than the television moguls wanted.

In Philadelphia, the rule changes only put more pressure on Dick Vermeil to find a new quarterback. Entering the 1977 season, he had given up on young Mike Boryla. Vermeil saw Boryla as a smug, scattershot quarterback without a future.

Vermeil also suspected that Gabriel's age (he would turn 37 on August 5) would make him a serious risk, especially against the stingy defenses in the NFC East.

Meanwhile, the Los Angeles Rams were involved in another of their quarterback controversies. This one involved James Harris, a Buffalo Bills castoff; Pat Haden, a seventh-round pick in a solid 1975 Rams draft; and Ron Jaworski, a surprise second-round pick in the 1973 draft from Youngstown State. Vermeil had once worked for Rams coach Chuck Knox, so the details of Knox's stew were well known back in Philadelphia. "It was almost spooky," said defensive end Jack Youngblood regarding the Rams' quarterback shuffle. "In all my years of football, I've never heard of such a merry-go-round."

Jaworski was a spot player in his first four seasons, but he had always talked and acted like a starter. "I'm sorry, but I'm going to be the Rams' starter," Jaworski would say to Harris, who happened to be his roommate. Sometimes Jaworski would be more emphatic. "There's a spot reserved for me in the Hall of Fame," he would tell reporters who always flocked to his locker for lively quotes.

Ken Meyer, the Rams quarterback coach, couldn't quite believe that Jaworski was even a legitimate prospect. At Youngstown State, Jaworski had been a frail, 170-pound quarterback playing in a so-called side-saddle offense. He would set up several yards behind the center and run a multitude of plays in the unconventional scheme.

"I took one look at this hollow-chested kid and I said, 'This can't be a quarterback,'" said Meyer. "But he's so coachable and so enthusiastic. He gets so hyped up that my biggest problem is calming him down."

Jaworski dominated the other two Rams quarterbacks in at least two aspects of the game. He possessed one of the most powerful arms in the league, far stronger than either Harris or Haden. Seeing that wicked 18-yard sideline pass, reporters began calling him the Polish Rifle. Jaworski also could outtalk either Harris or Haden, the latter a Rhodes Scholar from Southern Cal. Later, in Philadelphia, he would earn a new nickname: "Jaws."

When in a playful mood, Jaworski would warm up his arm by winding up and simulating a baseball pitcher. His receiver, usually a second-stringer, would squat like a catcher.

"Strik-k-k-k-e-e-e," the receiver would bellow.

Jaworski would pump his fist and go into his windup again.

"The way he acted at first bothered some of the older guys," said veteran guard Tom Mack. "They weren't sure whether he was for real or not. It was as if they were saying, 'If you're so good, hotshot, why don't you show us what you can do?'"

Whenever he got the chance, Jaworski would fire that fastball, responding to Mack's gibe. And whenever he engaged in conversation, he would pull the trigger on his machine-gun mouth, giggling and bragging and joking. His listeners found him different and amusing.

"We've come to understand the things Ronnie says," said veteran offensive tackle John Williams. "We've accepted him for what he is. He's loquacious and effervescent. But you don't try to smother him, or you destroy him as a person."

Jaworski always had an explanation for his act: it relieved the pressure of playing quarterback, the toughest job in all of sports. "Hell, pressure is what you put on yourself," he said. "I don't guess the coaches like some of the clowning I do, but it keeps everybody loose. If I kept things inside of me, I'd go crazy. So I'll say whatever's on my mind on the spur of the moment, even if it gets me in trouble sometimes."

In 1975, Jaworski replaced an injured Harris and won the final two games, including an upset of the Super Bowl champion Pittsburgh Steelers. Jaworski actually scored the only touchdown in the 10–3 win, executing a nifty quarterback draw. A week later, the Rams got a solid passing game from Jaworski and 202 rushing yards from Lawrence McCutcheon to bury St. Louis 35–23 in their NFC divisional playoff game.

Yet, Harris started the conference championship game, which the Rams lost to Dallas in a 37–7 rout. Harris threw only two passes before he was yanked, but by then it was already too late; the Cowboys had built a 21–0 lead.

The same script continued in 1976. Jaworski replaced the injured Harris and started the season against Atlanta. Then he broke his shoulder bone in the third quarter while diving into the end zone. Jaworski returned five weeks later, replacing an injured Haden and leading the Rams to a 20–12 win over Chicago. Then he was benched after the Rams lost to New Orleans 16–10.

Jaworski has several theories on why he was in and out of the Rams' lineup. One idea has to do with marketing. "Management knows there has to be people in the stands," he said. "And fans want to be able to identify with the players. You had James Harris, a black quarterback; Ron Jaworski, a Polish kid from New York; and Pat Haden, a native son of Southern California. Management figured that all things being equal, they could win with any one of us. So they'd go with the most marketable package. And eventually that was Haden."

"Pat Haden is more marketable," agreed tackle John Williams. "He'll sell more tickets than Ron Jaworski. Ron Jaworski is more marketable than James Harris. People in Beverly Hills can relate to Haden before Jaworski and Jaworski before Harris. It's that simple."

The hard-core Rams fans, however, grew to adore Jaworski. "That's because I was a different kind of commodity," Jaworski said. "They were used to seeing cool, level-headed quarterbacks, and here I came, very excitable and jumping around all the time. I was something new."

There were also persistent rumors that Rams owner Carroll Rosenbloom favored Haden, the home-grown quarterback. Jaworski heard the rumors and believed them. "I knew his starting wasn't Coach Knox's decision, and I have to say it to live with myself," he said. "There's no way that kid was a better quarterback than I was."

Jaworski says that after his shoulder healed in 1976, he worked with the first team in preparation for the Chicago game. Two days before the kickoff, however, Knox told Jaworski that Haden was his starting quarterback. "I was really burned up," said Jaworski. "Then he told me it was out of his hands. I knew right then it wasn't his decision."

Haden had heard the rumors, too. "I heard that some players thought Rosenbloom put pressure on Coach Knox, but he never told me that," said Haden. "So I don't want to make a bigger deal of it than it is." Rosenbloom said simply that "there's no way I would tell Chuck who to play," and let it go at that.

On March 10, 1977, at precisely 6:14 PM EST, all of those boastful lines from the mouth of Ron Jaworski ended with a major trade of two of the league's best talkers. The Rams finally gave up on Jaworski and dealt him to the Eagles for Charles Young, a gifted but unhappy pass-catching tight end.

Jaworski and Young were both playing out their options, meaning the Eagles and Rams actually obtained rights to each player, including the right to match another team's salary offer. Only days before the trade, the Eagles said Young rejected a three-year, $750,000 guaranteed contract.

Vermeil was thrilled by the trade. "He has a very strong, or what we call live arm," the coach said about his new quarterback. "He can fire the football...throw darts. And he has tremendous poise. He's not an accomplished quarterback yet. Very few quarterbacks are after they have only played [three seasons]. But I think he's one we can build around."

Minutes after the trade had been officially made, general manager Jim Murray reached his owner, who was vacationing in Acapulco. Murray sounded the words that Leonard Tose had been waiting to hear after months of squabbling with Young over his contract demands.

"When you make mistakes, everybody in the stadium knows it. The same thing when you make great plays. I'd just gotten to the point where I really didn't give a damn about what people were going to say."

RON JAWORSKI,
FORMER EAGLES QUARTERBACK

"It is done," Murray told his boss.

The trade, it turns out, also ended Mike Boryla's career as an Eagle. Boryla had produced a number of exciting victories for Mike McCormack at the end of the 1975 season. A year later, however, he became involved in a silent feud with Roman Gabriel over the starting spot. Boryla brooded for months over his backup status. Seeking his own answer, he blamed the coaches for his demotion. Two days before the final game with Seattle, Boryla went into Vermeil's office and asked to be traded.

"Basically, I think I was badly coached this year," Boryla said. "I just feel the coaching I received was very poor. The sooner I'm traded, the better."

Gabriel, on the other hand, proved to be a classy competitor. Soon after Jaworski arrived, Gabriel concluded that he would start the season on the bench. The thought of opening a 16th season as a backup can play horrible tricks with a 37-year-old man's ego. But Gabriel surrendered to the reality of Vermeil's new direction.

The last time Gabriel had watched from the sideline was in his early years with the Rams under George Allen. "It might be a little difficult if I went away from my philosophy of keeping busy," he said. "I always spend a lot of time working at the game. I'm still competing out there and it all comes down to how well the team is doing. And with Ron, it will be a bit easier. He's a tremendous competitor and he's going to be a good football player."

The presence of Jaworski, throwing darts on the field and keeping it loose in the locker room, put Vermeil in an anxious mood. "I'm going to do everything possible within my ability to improve the Eagles organization," he said before the start of his second training camp. "Last year, I did what I wanted to do, and that was to give every football player that was here an opportunity to prove to me that he could, or couldn't, make it."

Earlier, Vermeil had summed up his talent. "Every NFL team is playing with average players at certain positions," the coach said. "But the great teams have some 'super supers' at the other positions. These are the guys who come up with the big plays; the great catch, the great linebacker play, or the great defensive line play. I'm not degrading our personnel. But I think they are good enough to win more than four games in this league."

It didn't take long for Jaworski to bond with his coach, an important part of any team's program. "When I lost my father at the age of 19," said Jaworski, "I lost the direction and discipline that a young man needs. But thanks to the coach, that void was filled."

Vermeil soon found he shared striking similarities with Jaworski. His new quarterback was the son of a lumberyard worker from Lackawanna, New York (population: 19,064), a steel town south of Buffalo. They both were raised in small towns by strong-willed fathers. They both played several sports in high school (Jaworski was such a promising catcher that he once was considered a major league prospect). They both worked at jobs where you got your hands dirty (Jaworski worked in the steel mills in Lackawanna and Youngstown through his senior year in college). They both married hometown girls. And, of course, they both approached football with the fortitude of two mountain climbers.

"When he does everything mechanically right," said Vermeil, "getting back, setting up, delivering…I don't know if it's possible to zing it any better. It's just a tight spiral. It comes off like a shot. Ron has the kind of arm to throw any kind of pass you need thrown. There are some people you can't have try the deep slants and the stuff coming back against zone defenses, but he can."

> *"I can say unequivocally that any success I've had as a father, as a player, as a husband, and as a businessperson is directly attributable to Dick Vermeil."*
>
> RON JAWORSKI

The Eagles struggled through a 3–3 preseason in 1977 that proved two things: first, that Jaworski was an inexperienced quarterback who needed more talent around him; and second, that most of Vermeil's running backs were either a step too slow or too light to take the pounding of the NFL.

Meanwhile, Vermeil began pushing himself harder than he pushed his players. His office at Veterans Stadium was without windows, like the casinos in Atlantic City, so he could easily forget about how many hours he had been there. Vermeil relied on Bow Wow, the character from Beverly Hills, to remind him that it was 3:00 AM—time to shut off the projector. Bow Wow would convert the sofa into a pullout bed and Vermeil would reluctantly try to sleep.

"We all get wrapped up in this thing," said Marion Campbell, Vermeil's creative defensive coordinator. "But there's a point where you've got to say, 'Hey, I've got to shut the projector off.' I don't know what it was about Dick. That man didn't get turned on till the night. Then he went into high gear."

Jaworski, who liked to predict excitement and then produce it, promised a high-scoring offense. The Eagles had scored only 11 touchdowns through the air the previous season. Their notoriously slow offense had totaled only 165 points, second lowest in the league. But Jaworski vowed to personally thrill the home fans with his rifle arm that would, of course, produce the Eagles' first 30-point game in three years. A lot of them, in fact.

"The big problem last year was not putting enough points on the board," he said. "And I know I can put points on the board. I really believe I'm a big-play quarterback. If I see a 'Wanda' [weak-side] blitz coming, I'm not going to try to get a five-yard gain. I'm going to try to get six points. That's why I say I'm a big-play quarterback. This is the start of something good here. But before we say we're going to run, we've got to crawl. Then we're going to walk, then run. I think the crawling stage was last year."

> *"Before Dick came, our games were almost always decided in the first quarter. If we got behind, you could see three or four guys here and there giving up."*
>
> JOHN BUNTING,
> FORMER EAGLES LINEBACKER

In the off-season, Vermeil visited his old friend, Bill Walsh, who had been pulled out of the pro ranks and hired to coach at Stanford. Vermeil asked a lot of questions about the passing game. Walsh, of course, was an offensive genius. His success was built around quick, rhythmic passing and the willingness to throw on early downs when the defense was playing its best run-stoppers. Walsh also liked running backs who could catch and slash for first downs; smaller offensive linemen who could pull; and tall, long-striding receivers.

Vermeil listened intently to Walsh in their chat sessions, jotting down notes. This was his custom, dating back to the years when he attended clinics as a high school coach, driving to all corners of California. Vermeil favored a different kind of offense than his old friend. He liked to establish the run, then mix in play-action passes when the defense began crowding the line of scrimmage with extra defenders. Walsh always ran from a two-back set. Vermeil was a one-back coach all the way, sometimes loading up with a two-back I formation. Vermeil took what he could from Walsh, knowing he lacked a fast, physical back and enough quick offensive linemen. He also knew that Jaworski wasn't a fit for Walsh's fast-paced scheme, even if he had installed the so-called

West Coast offense. Jaworski had the quick release that was necessary in Walsh's system, but he wasn't mobile enough to play Walsh's game of throwing on early downs, often off quarterback movement.

So Vermeil clung to his one-back system, despite the fact that he didn't have a featured back. If his second season was marked by progress, it didn't show up in the bottom line. The Eagles won only five games and tied the Giants for last place in the NFC East with a 5–9 record. All five of the Eagles' wins came against last-place teams. Dallas, Vermeil's bitter rival, swept the series, but only by scores of 16–10 and 24–14. The year before, the Cowboys swept by 27–7 and 26–7, behind those "super supers," as Vermeil called their star players.

"Dallas can come in here and win playing an average game, with people like Too-Tall Jones and Harvey Martin," said Vermeil. "We can't do that. I don't have the luxury of guys week to week fluctuating their play. A good percentage of our roster has been cut from someone else. For example, [cornerback] John Outlaw doesn't have good hands. We have a rally and start a bonfire whenever he makes an interception on the practice field. That's why John was cut from New England, because he couldn't come up with interceptions, not because he couldn't cover or play football."

Down the stretch, the Eagles lost four straight games, scoring only 50 points. They blew a 16–0 lead and lost to St. Louis 21–16. A week later, Jaworski was sacked eight times in a 14–6 loss to New England. At one point, Vermeil's offense failed to score in three tries from the Patriots' 1-yard line. Then kicker Ove Johansson, a replacement for struggling Horst Muhlmann, had his 19-yard field goal blocked.

Vermeil was crushed by the late-season slump. His feeling was that if the Eagles had followed his rigid off-season program, they should have controlled the fourth quarter in tight games. Vowing to work even harder, he pulled himself together and sounded an optimistic note.

"I'm not saying we're a great team," the coach began. "But the attitude on the squad, how they're working, how they're accepting the coaching, is really on the plus side. And I think it has a lot to do with the way we established things last year. Hell, we were on the field for three hours yesterday, working the whole time, and I didn't hear one complaint. And I know so much more about what we have, and so much more about what we need. Last year, I just had opinions to go on."

* * *

If there was another silver lining to the 1977 season, it came with two games left when Vermeil began thinking about his shy rookie running back, Wilbert Montgomery. In two previous games, the Eagles had gotten a grand total of 150 yards on 60 rushes, an average of 2.5 yards per carry. At the time, Vermeil was a desperate coach with a slumping 3–9 team. The next game was with the New York Giants, a rowdy bunch with some tough run-stoppers, including linebackers Brad

> *"Dick always said, 'If you guys weren't bitching, I wasn't working you hard enough.'"*
>
> RON JAWORSKI

Van Pelt and Harry Carson and tackle John Mendenhall. Vermeil initially decided to keep Montgomery on the bench until the final game with the New York Jets.

Then, after Montgomery raced 99 yards to score with the second-half kickoff against New York, Vermeil waved him in to face those nasty Giants. Montgomery responded, using his speed and quickness to rush for 59 yards in a spot role. The Eagles prevailed 17–14 as Jaworski took the offense on a 14-play, 63-yard game-winning drive. The next week, Montgomery started and dazzled the Jets with a 103-yard, two-touchdown game.

"Those were tough times for me," said Montgomery. "I just couldn't learn the system. Every night I studied harder and all I got was more confused. I'd sit in meetings and they would be using terms I'd never heard before. I was afraid to ask questions. I was afraid they'd think I was dumb."

"We couldn't get him to line up right, with all the formations and motion," said Vermeil. "We could have cut him. On the basis of the number of mistakes he made, we should have sent him home. But you can't do that in the Eagles organization. You see innate talent and you tell yourself you've got to have time."

Montgomery roomed with Cleveland Franklin, another rookie back from Baylor. "The two of us would try to hide so we wouldn't get picked to run during the seven-on-seven drills," Montgomery said. "When [Vermeil] did pick me, I'd freeze."

> *"First and foremost, he respected the game as a coach and he wanted the players to respect the game the way he did."*
>
> WILBERT MONTGOMERY,
> FORMER EAGLES RUNNING BACK

Vermeil admitted that the Eagles came close to cutting Montgomery several times not just because of his mental lapses; he also suffered from a nagging college injury. At Abilene Christian—where he scored 76 touchdowns, 37 of them as a 19-year-old freshman—Montgomery had absorbed a vicious blow to his thigh from somebody's helmet. His leg was in a cast for six weeks. By the 1977 NFL Draft, Montgomery had dropped out of the top 50 prospects because of a calcium deposit that had formed on his injured left thigh.

The New England Patriots, a team desperate for a halfback to team with power runner Sam Cunningham, had ranked Montgomery among the top five college backs. Two days before the draft, Patriots coach Chuck Fairbanks asked Montgomery to come to Boston for a physical exam. Fairbanks also wanted Montgomery to run a 40-yard dash and perform other agility drills. Those tests would determine whether he had recovered from the whack he got at Abilene.

Montgomery's time in the 40 was 4.5 seconds, decent for a back but slower than his previous sprinter's time of 4.4 seconds. He passed the agility phase, but the Patriots doctors took a dim view of his thigh injury. "They said it was worse than they had been led to believe," said Montgomery. "The doctor told Fairbanks I'd probably have to undergo surgery and miss the entire season."

Montgomery was shaken by the diagnosis and the fact that he had flunked the club's physical. He sat outside of the coaches' office with tears in his eyes. Montgomery figured that all 28 teams would pass him over, costing him a pro career. "I knew Fairbanks wouldn't take me," Montgomery said. "I figured once the word got out that nobody would take me."

Vermeil, however, decided to take a chance when the Eagles' second of three sixth-round choices came up. Maybe it was scout Bill Baker's glowing report. Maybe it was a hunch. Whatever the reason, long after the Patriots had taken Oklahoma back Horace Ivory in the second round, Vermeil selected Montgomery. (Ivory had a brief career as a Patriots backup, starting 12 games in five years and then drifting out of the league after a brief stop in Seattle.)

The tale of Montgomery's remarkable career created a feel-good story that was retold whenever old scouts gathered in those little college towns. At Abilene Christian University, Montgomery's alma mater, details of his career were passed down to a new class of footballers the way fine jewelry is passed down within a family.

At Greenville (Mississippi) High School, Montgomery had developed into an all-state back. He purposely shrouded his fame in secrecy. His mother Gladys, a woman of good sense, feared that Wilbert would suffer a serious injury, just like his older brother Alfred, who separated both shoulders playing in junior college. The younger Montgomery pretended to be visiting friends on Friday game nights. He told his mother he was sleeping over at a friend's house whenever Greenville High played on the coast in Gulfport or Biloxi and had to stay overnight.

"Of all my children, I was probably closest to Wilbert," said Gladys Montgomery. "He stayed around the house more than the others. He'd sit with me while I cooked the dinner. He was a wonderful influence on his younger brothers. I still remember the day he left for Abilene. Lord, how the two of us cried."

Wilbert was anything but a mama's boy, however. During his second pro season, there was a rumble along Pattison Avenue, not far from the Vet. Montgomery and teammates Billy Campfield and Oren Middlebrook were driving home from a Phillies baseball playoff game. "There were seven guys in the other car," said Montgomery. "They began throwing beer cans at us. We came to a stoplight and one of the guys jumped on the back of our car and started beating on the trunk."

Montgomery decked two of the bullies. Campfield and Middlebrook got involved, too, before the police arrived to halt the fighting. "Everybody looks at Wilbert and thinks he's too small," said the late Eagles scout Jackie Graves. "He's short, not small. He's well put together. He's got great strength in his legs and upper body."

Fred Washington, the Greenville High coach, knew that Montgomery was a special back. "In gym class, he ran past the other kids like they were standing still," said Washington. "He could run a 9.6 100-yard dash, and he set the school record in the long jump of 25 feet, six inches."

When Wilbert began scoring touchdowns in bunches, drawing the scouts and media types, he finally confessed to his mother. "He sat right there in the chair with his head down," Gladys Montgomery told Philadelphia sportswriter Ray Didinger. "He said his conscience was bothering him. I know football must have meant a whole lot to him because he never lied to me before. But what could I say? I had already said 'no' and that didn't stop him. I never liked football."

Wilbert, however, convinced her that absorbing the bumps and bruises of the game was a way to earn a college education. "All right," she said. "Just don't come running to me when you get hurt."

Montgomery had a great career at Abilene Christian, marred only by that major thigh injury that limited his final season to eight games, 108 carries, and 597 yards, all career lows. It also dropped him at least four rounds in the draft. He wound up as the 154th player and the 27th back chosen.

"The guy had scored 76 touchdowns in four years," said Vermeil. "We figured he must have something."

By playing at Abilene Christian rather than Jackson State, where he could have succeeded Walter Payton, Montgomery was able to start as a freshman. Besides, the discipline (no swearing or drinking was tolerated) allowed him to easily buy into Vermeil's program, which was also focused on discipline.

Montgomery turned out to be, in trainer Otho Davis' words, "one of the finest, most successful cases I've ever had." It was Davis and his able assistant, Ron O'Neil, who brought Montgomery back to glowing health during a three-month rehabilitation period.

"I thought he could play," said Davis. "I remember he was very shy and timid. He was in here twice a day, every day, in the off-season. We made Wilbert a special Fiberglas pad. He did pretty well with it. I guess it cost all of $2.98. The main thing was getting his strength built up and getting confidence in himself."

So now Vermeil had found the two keys to his ball-control offense: Jaworski, a gritty, giddy, strong-armed quarterback; and Montgomery, a quick, strong, elusive running back. The fact that Jaworski roused his teammates with his bubbly personality was seen as a bonus.

The third key member of Vermeil's improving offense was already in place when the coach arrived. Harold Carmichael, who stood 6'8" with 39-inch-long arms and huge hands, had already emerged as the Eagles' featured receiver. But it had taken some intense instruction by Tom Fears and Boyd Dowler, his position coaches.

Carmichael had been a seventh-round pick—and the only starter—in a disappointing 1971 Eagles draft. At Southern University, the only school to offer him a scholarship, Carmichael caught 86 passes, 16 for touchdowns. Yet he was regarded as a marginal prospect because of his poor route running and the level of competition he faced. During his rookie training camp, Carmichael was routinely handled by much smaller cornerbacks.

"They owned him," said Fears. "He'd telegraph his moves, just like a boxer telegraphs his punches. Hell, they'd beat him to the spot, and I mean some of the guys that didn't make our club."

Carmichael's biggest problem was cutting. Dowler, his next coach, studied endless game films and found that Carmichael was often slipping at the time of his break. The problem was eventually corrected and Carmichael made the Pro Bowl in his third year, a 67-catch, nine-touchdown season. "I never had things broken down to me, never given a reason why I was doing things like I was," said Carmichael. "They found I wasn't keeping my weight over my feet, and that was causing me to slip."

Mike McCormack said Carmichael used to pout on the field whenever he dropped a pass. "I hope that maybe he can grow up," said McCormack, who once benched Carmichael in favor of backup Don Zimmerman. "He doesn't mean to hotdog it out there. But after he drops one, I wish he would quit the theatrics and get back to the huddle."

Off the field, Carmichael was a flamboyant figure, driving a red Coupe deVille with windows the shape of a football. His end-zone celebrations were just as flashy. Carmichael would spin a football, and then he and Charlie "Home Boy" Smith and Don Zimmerman would extend their hands, as if rolling dice. On another occasion, Carmichael nearly beheaded New York Giants safety Spider Lockhart with a monster spike.

"He can stand flat-footed and eat apples off a tree without using his hands," said former quarterback Norm Van Brocklin after watching Carmichael catch six passes in a game.

During his career, Carmichael played with five different quarterbacks: John Reaves, Pete Liske, Mike Boryla, Roman Gabriel, and Ron Jaworski. His big years came as a member of Roman Gabriel's "Fire High Gang" (the three receivers were the 6'8" Carmichael, the 6'4½" Charlie Young, and 6'3½" Don Zimmerman). In those years, Carmichael achieved a new level of fame, that of an exciting, game-breaking star.

When Vermeil arrived with his ball-control offense, Carmichael became a dedicated receiver, less interested in dice rolls and flame-red cars than in contributing to his team. He became a true professional, catching, blocking, and acting as a decoy with consistent excellence. "When you see a guy competing like he does, it's great," said Jaworski. "He's just super as a receiver, too. For a guy his height, he's not just a tall guy. He's got flexibility, quick feet. And he can make catches behind him that a quick, 5'8" guy can't."

At last, Vermeil had some offensive firepower in his ranks. Keith Krepfle, an underrated tight end, would replace Charles Young. Guard Jerry Sisemore, the team's best blocker, would develop and eventually move outside to tackle; Woody Peoples, a 49ers castoff, would replace him. There were still some holes in the defensive unit. The arrival of Marion Campbell as the new coordinator and Fred Bruney as the new secondary coach helped limit the weaknesses. Together, Campbell and Bruney took the Eagles into a new defensive era, highlighted by the development of a tough linebacking corps that bonded like brothers and spent many long nights studying game films, like their coaches.

*   *   *

Vermeil's starting units were a unique mix consisting of a few high-round draft picks, many more middle- and low-rounders, and a number of free-agent pickups from the castoff heap. High, low, or in between, these Eagles shared a common trait. They were "tough ol' birds," as Keith Krepfle liked to say.

All NFL players like to think of themselves as muscle-flexing, chest-bumping performers. Yet, these Eagles could lay claim to being the toughest of them all in a tough league. It's safe to say that none of them would have made Vermeil's team without showing that he was a fighter, a scrapper, a tough ol' bird. But that was the only edge that Vermeil's collection of overachievers would have.

Even before training camp opened for the 1977 season, Vermeil had sent each player a 146-page off-season conditioning manual. Starting on February 15 and continuing through July 18, players were encouraged to follow a demanding five-days-a-week program. Vermeil's objective: increase a player's strength, flexibility, endurance, and, as a by-product, his speed. The Eagles were previously regarded as one of the worst-conditioned teams in the league, mostly because of player indifference.

Vermeil's manual included 23 different exercises. "Our edge has to come from outworking our opponents in every phase of the game and this certainly includes off-season conditioning," Vermeil said in his cover letter. "The program is in your hands.... If you are self-motivated and dedicated, you will go to work immediately. We are going to win in Philadelphia. It is just a matter of being persistent. Go to work. The job you save may be your own."

In a sense, Vermeil was guaranteeing, at least to his players, that he would turn the Eagles into a winner. Four years before that, Mike McCormack had made a similar pledge. "I think the days of building programs are gone," McCormack had said shortly after being hired in 1973. "You've got to show results on the field. I'm planning on winning next season, if it's humanly possible." The McCormack Eagles, however, went 5–8–1, 7–7, and 4–10 before he was fired.

The only guarantee that Vermeil could feel safe about related to conditioning. Assuming his players followed his program, the Eagles would be stronger, tougher, and faster. The manual was divided into four sections: Flexibility; Strength and Power; Heart, Lungs, and Legs; and Diet and Rest. There was also a long list of food items and their caloric content (malted milk shake, 502 calories; beer, one glass, 114 calories; cottage cheese, one tablespoon, 27 calories).

The last section of Vermeil's manual was a personal diary to keep track of individual workouts. On May 10, for example, a player was supposed to record the time it took to recover (a pulse rate down to 90 beats per minute) from eight 110-yard runs, each clocked at 20 seconds. The next day, May 11, the player focused on strength and power training: bench presses, squats, and power cleans.

As Vermeil was unleashing his motivational skills on the Eagles, a negative report surfaced that caught the coach by surprise. Despite sellout crowds at the Vet and the excitement of a new Vermeil era, the team was projected to lose $1.2 million in 1977. The Eagles, it seemed, had always been burdened by substantial interest payments on loans from major banks. Business manager Jim Borden said the club would have lost money, even without a $16 million loan from Crocker National of California.

Why the huge loan? "The players here are well paid," said Borden, "and we have spent it on the scouting side, the medical side, and for facilities."

Indeed, one of the first requests that Vermeil made was for the purchase of round tables at Widener University, the training camp site. "We're not very good," conceded Vermeil, "but we're going to be a family and we're going to talk to one another. So we need these round tables in camp, so we get to look each other in the eye."

Vermeil never allowed himself to become entangled in his owner's shaky finances and his addiction to the gaming tables in Atlantic City and Las Vegas.

He just kept adding new players and new coaches and kept working those crazy hours. At the end of another 18-hour day, Vermeil would stop to take a deep breath and remember what his old friend, Bill Walsh, said about coaching in the NFL.

> *"Dick was famous for taking the players to dinner and having them over for barbecues. He went way out of his way, far beyond what other coaches would have done."*
>
> BILL WALSH,
> FORMER 49ERS HEAD COACH

"This season will be a challenge unique in itself, and that's one of the attractions of coaching that many highly successful businessmen envy," said Walsh. "We always have exciting things happen to us. We conclude one experience and begin another one anew as a given season. So many men I know envy that kind of life. It gives life a lot of meaning because from year to year, there is anticipation. That's the exciting part of coaching. Now, there is certainly a downside…"

For Dick Vermeil, and later, for Bill Walsh himself, those concluding words would become frighteningly prophetic.

Chapter 6

"This Is Family"

With the approach of his third season in 1978, Dick Vermeil thought the Eagles had improved on both sides of the football. "There isn't any comparison between the two squads," he said after the Eagles had finished with a 5–9 record in 1977. "This squad is totally committed to working together and getting better. Nobody is grumbling to go anyplace else and nobody is mad at this coach and that coach. We have the foundation. It'll just take time."

Vermeil's foundation included Ron Jaworski, his young, gunslinging quarterback; Wilbert Montgomery, his younger, elusive running back; Harold Carmichael, a towering, more mature wide receiver; Herm Edwards, a heady free-agent cornerback; a fine linebacking crew that included Bill Bergey, John Bunting, and Frank LeMaster; two speed pass rushers, Carl Hairston and Lem Burnham; and a vastly improved blocking unit that included future Pro Bowl tackles Jerry Sisemore and Stan Walters.

Vermeil had also upgraded his coaching staff. John Ralston was lured out of retirement to coach the offense. Bill McPherson, who had been on Vermeil's staff at UCLA, was hired to coach the linebackers, the heart and soul of Marion Campbell's 3-4 base defense. McPherson also was responsible for the defensive phases of Vermeil's special teams (field goal, kickoff, and punt coverage). Ken Iman, the offensive line coach, was also assigned to coach the offensive phases (punt and kickoff returns).

The special teams coaching arrangement seemed awkward, even foolish, especially since Vermeil himself had been one of the first special teams coaches with the Los Angeles Rams in 1969 under George Allen, a special teams guru.

> *"There aren't too many people who could call me up and say they had a flat on the Pennsylvania Turnpike, and I'd find a way to get there. But I'd get there for Dick Vermeil."*
>
> STAN WALTERS,
> FORMER EAGLES OFFENSIVE TACKLE

Yet, Vermeil felt comfortable enough with McPherson and Iman sharing the duties, even though neither had coached special teams before.

The year before, Vermeil's special units had been outstanding, limiting opponents to an average of 20 yards on kickoffs and 5.4 yards on punt returns. Sure-handed Larry Marshall had helped the Eagles average 10.4 yards on punt returns, and Montgomery averaged 26.9 yards on kickoff returns, including that 99-yarder against the Giants.

Field goals, unfortunately, were another matter. Horst Muhlmann had missed five of eight tries, costing the Eagles at least one win. Replacement Ove Johansson missed three out of his four tries. Both were cut. However, Vermeil liked a local kid, Temple's Nick Mike-Mayer, who made all three of his field goals and seven extra points in the final three games.

The only lingering special teams issue was punting. Spike Jones, who punted 255 times and had five blocked in three seasons for the Eagles, had averaged only 37.2 yards in 1977. Vermeil brought him to camp the next year, but Jones never punted again for the Eagles. In his search for a replacement with a younger, livelier foot, Vermeil invited four other punters to camp, including another local star, Tim Mazzetti, who once kicked a 54-yard field goal for Penn.

Vermeil, sensing this could be a breakthrough season, began working even longer hours than before. Vermeil began pushing himself harder than in the 1976 and 1977 seasons.

"Dick was right in there working with us," said Chuck Clausen, the defensive line coach. "I mean, that offensive staff would sometimes go until 4:00 or 4:30 in the morning, and Dick, he'd be right there working with them. Dick would go to bed in his office, lay down on the couch, go to sleep for an hour and a half, and go again the next day. Dick had more energy and could drive himself harder than any person I've ever seen, and he drove us that way. I was in my late thirties when I went to work for Dick. I had the energy then, so I could take it. But I wasn't so sure about working for him when I'm 55."

Clausen said he turned down several coaching opportunities to stay with Vermeil and work the night shift. "I never considered leaving," Clausen said. "I felt a sense of loyalty to Dick. He worked hard to get good players. The other thing about the Dick Vermeil player, he wasn't a problem. He was a good guy. Not only a good football player, but he was a good human being, honest and dependable. He wasn't a showboat."

Jim Murray, the general manager, used an analogy to describe Vermeil's driving style. "Dick's not the kind of guy who looks for the easy way out," said Murray. "His wake will spill and force people out of the boat. But that's the way he wants it. If he was a fullback, he'd never go around end. Every carry would be right up the middle."

Since he started coaching at little Hillsdale High in 1960, Vermeil always believed that the way a coach treated his players was just as important, maybe more important, than clocked times in the 40-yard dash and clever game plans.

> *"He taught me more about living my life and treating other people than he did about playing the game, and he taught me an incredible amount about how to play the game."*
>
> RON JAWORSKI

"I think you can win in this league if you have one gift, and nothing else," Vermeil said. "That's the gift of projecting an air of warmth and sincerity. Football is so difficult. It's hard to remember that players are persons. It's important to feel a deep sense of concern for them as individuals and transmit it."

* * *

Around the NFC East, rival coaches sensed that the Eagles were no longer pushovers. The other four division teams had won 12 of the 14 games in

Vermeil's first two seasons, but six of the Eagles' losses had been by six points or fewer.

"The Eagles have a different mental attitude now," said Dallas' Tom Landry. "[Vermeil] has convinced them that they can win."

"Of the 250 million Americans today, nobody is better equipped than Dick Vermeil to be a winning football coach," said Redskins coach George Allen. "Present company excepted, of course."

Mike White, a longtime friend, said Vermeil has always had a belief that he could win with hard work and a special coach-to-player relationship. "You want to give back to him what he gives to you," said White. "It's an intensity formula that fits everywhere he's been."

"He genuinely loves his players and he wins them over. His loyalty is impeccable."

MIKE WHITE,
FORMER RAMS ASSISTANT COACH

White said Vermeil used the same style when he coached the swimming team at Hillsdale High. "Carol [Vermeil] was involved, too," said White. "She'd bring cakes and desserts to the pool. Dick didn't know the first thing about it. I'm not even sure he knew how to swim. But he turned the program around. I think one kid might have even gone to the Olympics."

Yet, the old-time Vermeil formula—long, hard working hours and honesty from the head coach's office—couldn't prevent the 1978 training camp from becoming a summer of comical mistakes. Vermeil's major problem continued to be the punting game. While the Eagles won four of their five preseason games, Vermeil was vehemently disappointed in his newest punter, Mitch Hoopes. He was so disappointed that he brought in a journeyman named Rick Engles to offer Hoopes some competition. This was seen as a puzzling move, given Engles' mediocre average of under 38 yards in two seasons of flip-flopping between Seattle and Pittsburgh.

And then the merry-go-round began. The Eagles cut Hoopes on August 15. They cut Engles on August 22 and brought back Hoopes. They cut Hoopes on August 28 and brought back Engles. They cut Engles on September 25 and re-signed Hoopes. Finally, with weak punts still in the air, they cut Hoopes one more time after the fourth game on September 30. Then Vermeil hurriedly dispatched an aide to Chicago, where Engles signed a contract just before the 4:00 PM deadline on Saturday, the day before the Eagles played in Baltimore.

"I remember we were going to a game in Washington, and I think he fired the kicker on Saturday morning before we got on the bus," recalled linebackers coach Bill McPherson. "I tell people that and they say, 'Are you kidding me?'"

As the farce unfolded, there undoubtedly were laughs in the front office in Dallas, where Hoopes used to punt. And maybe in Seattle and Pittsburgh, the two teams that had cut Engles a total of three times.

As an Eagle, Engles punted in six games. His moments with the football ranged from surprising to scary. On his own authority, Engles ran out of a punt formation in the opener against the Rams. Then he threw a pass that lost two yards in the fifth game against the Colts. Now angry and frustrated by his own blunders, Vermeil signed yet another punter, Mike Michel, a free agent who had been cut by Miami.

That wasn't to be the last time the Eagles heard from Engles. Later that season, Engles claimed that he and Hoopes had been "stashed," or hidden, against league rules in a local hotel after being waived during the punting follies. "I've lost my wife and I'm broke," said Engles. "She took all of the money and filed for divorce." Engles said that after he was cut, the Eagles paid all of his expenses, including room, food, laundry, and phone bills. "Mitch told me he rang up about a $500 bill," said Engles. "He really lived it up."

Indeed, it turned out that the Eagles had shuffled Engles from one hotel to another, once registering him under the name of Rick Bengels. This author remembers Engles sitting next to him at the counter of a Ramada Inn. Engles ordered a breakfast of steak and eggs two days after being waived.

Asked how long he planned to stay in the area, Engles smiled. "Oh, I'm going to hang around here for a while," he said. "It's a long drive to Oklahoma, and I'm in no hurry."

Vermeil later admitted the Eagles had indeed stashed his punter. "What we were guilty of was paying his expenses for one week when he was not on our roster," said Vermeil. "I lost confidence in the guys here. I couldn't get anybody better. My players didn't have any confidence in him. When I got a chance to get somebody better, I got him."

The move that Vermeil made didn't come until after the sixth game, when the Eagles were 3–3 and Engles had made every punt an adventure. The Eagles signed Mike Michel, a onetime Stanford punter who had been released by Miami. Meanwhile, the NFL eventually confirmed that Engles indeed had been stashed and took away Vermeil's third-round choice in the 1980 draft. The Eagles that year could have drafted wide receiver Carlos Carson, who caught 353 passes for the Kansas City Chiefs in a superb career that included a Pro Bowl appearance.

After a 4–4 start, the Eagles lost a heartbreaking 16–10 squeaker to the St. Louis Cardinals when injuries depleted their backfield. "I started the game with four running backs and ended with none," said Vermeil. "I've never had that experience before. And I'll tell you, it was a terrible experience."

Jim "Boom-Boom" Betterson went out with a knee problem. Cleveland Franklin suffered a pinched shoulder nerve covering a punt. Wilbert Montgomery was finished after only three carries with a knee injury. And Billy Campfield was left "glassy-eyed and not really into the game," according to quarterback Ron Jaworski, after some hard knocks on special teams.

"I didn't have any running backs left," said Vermeil after Franklin and Campfield had lost fourth-quarter fumbles. "I didn't know who to play. It completely shot our running game. The second half we were going with two kids who couldn't hold on to the ball."

The next two weeks, however, the Eagles won with their fast-flowing defense. Herm Edwards, the new right corner, saved a 10–3 win over Green Bay with an interception near the goal line with 1:16 left to play. The next week, the Eagles forced four turnovers and edged the New York Jets 17–9 to up their record to 6–5.

Then Vermeil and his gritty Eagles got a big, big break. They were losing to the Giants 17–12 with only seconds to play. All the Giants needed was for quarterback Joe Pisarcik, who had thrown two first-quarter touchdown passes for an early 14–0 lead, to take a knee and run out the clock. Instead, Giants offensive coordinator Bob Gibson inexplicably called for a running play. The hurried handoff glanced off Larry Csonka's hip and took a nice bounce right into the hands of Herm Edwards, who danced 26 yards into the end zone for the winning touchdown with just 31 seconds left.

The Eagles' shocking 19–17 victory came to be known as the Miracle at the Meadowlands. All the Giants coaches were fired for their part in the debacle. Except for Pisarcik, the names of the cast involved in the miracle game have been forgotten. Pisarcik emerged as a punching bag for long-suffering Giants fans (the Giants would lose 15 of 16 games to the Eagles from 1973 to 1981) and anyone else who wanted a laugh whenever the two teams squared off. (Ironically, Pisarcik would later be signed by Vermeil to serve as Jaworski's backup.)

One man who didn't see the amazing finish in person was Eagles owner Leonard Tose. Instead, he was 1,338 miles away in a private room at the Texas Heart Institute in Houston, where he underwent heart surgery. Dr. Denton Cooley, the famed surgeon, performed the operation, which involved replacing Tose's aortic valve. Minutes after the game, Vermeil and Murray were on the phone with their thrilled owner.

"What did that do to your new valve?" Vermeil asked Tose. Vermeil then gave the owner a play-by-play review of the bizarre win. Unknown to the coach, Tose already knew all the details.

"Dick, I had a broadcast of the game piped into my room here," said Tose.

"Oh, you heard it, huh?" said Vermeil.

They both laughed, the laughter of one becoming the laughter of the other. Then Murray told reporters that the surgery had been "very successful" and that Tose "would be on injured reserve until the Dallas game in three weeks."

After losing that game to the Cowboys 31–13 and allowing Jaworski to absorb an eight-sack pounding, the Eagles entered the final week of the season with a rare chance to reach the playoffs. In their way were the last-place Giants and their vilified quarterback, Joe Pisarcik.

Just before the Eagles ran down the tunnel and into the gale-force winds that howled around the Vet, Vermeil gave them a final pep talk.

"Twelve years, guys," said Vermeil. "Twelve years. That's how long it's been since the Eagles were winners. Well, you can be winners today. You've worked for it, and you deserve it, and I'm proud of each and every one of you."

This time it would take no miracle, no favorable bounce of the ball, no prancing touchdown return by Herm Edwards. As swirling winds wreaked havoc inside the stadium, the Eagles played like a playoff team and the Giants played like a team that knew John McVay, their head coach, was going to be fired. It ended in a 20–3 romp in which the Eagles had an overwhelming edge in the offensive and defensive trenches. So physical were the Eagles that the defense knocked both Giants quarterbacks, Pisarcik and Randy Dean, out of the game. In addition to sending two quarterbacks to the sideline, the defense notched three interceptions (two by Herm Edwards) and four sacks while allowing just 48 rushing yards.

As Vermeil came off the field, there were hugs and pounding of backs and shrieks of joy. In a rare response to the moment, stadium officials allowed the fans to race onto the field as the final seconds ticked down. "I know it's against regulations and all that," said Jim Murray, "but it's just a great moment in sports. It's a neighborhood team and it's a neighborhood town. It was that kind of win."

Once inside, Vermeil came face-to-face with Tose. The coach threw his arms around his owner, pressing his head against Tose's Pierre Cardin tie. Suddenly, Vermeil began sobbing. As Tose patted his coach on the back, Vermeil let it all out. "This one was for you," he said, his tears flowing. "That was for you."

Moments earlier, Vermeil had stood in the middle of the locker room, surrounded by the players, most of them middle- or low-round draft picks or unwanted free agents. They had bonded in another of Vermeil's exhausting camps, and now they were winners headed for a new experience: a wild-card playoff game against Atlanta.

"The Eagles are now winners," a teary-eyed Vermeil said. "The coaches are winners. It's a great, great feeling. It's a feeling I've talked about for a long, long time."

The jubilant players talked about Vermeil's double–tight end set that confused the Giants, and about the swarming defense that forced five turnovers. They talked about a 1-2 running punch of Montgomery (130 yards) and fullback

Mike Hogan (100 yards). And they looked at Vermeil, their driven coach, who now had tears in his eyes.

Montgomery's big day gave him 1,220 yards for the season, breaking Steve Van Buren's club record of 1,146 yards. "We knew what it would take to win," said a giddy Jaworski. "Just take the ball and stuff it on them. The first two series, [the offensive line] came out and they were awesome. We couldn't get to the line of scrimmage fast enough. The Giants, they were just trying to find something. The 3-4 they used usually gets you a flow to the ball, but nothing they did was really effective." Jaworski called it the best full game of blocking the team had produced that season.

"I think the guys relaxed," said Edwards. "They told themselves, 'Why are we getting so tight? Everybody go out and have some fun.' That's what we did. Dean, he got shook up. He got knocked out. Same thing with Pisarcik."

In response to the familiar postgame question, "What was working, Wilbert?" Montgomery suggested that everything seemed to be working. "The cutbacks were there," he said. "The off-tackles were there. You just ran hard till you met something."

Bill Bergey, the run-stuffing linebacker, tried to put the win into perspective. "This was really a championship game for us," Bergey said. "We blew some coverages and there were some breakdowns. But we made up for it with aggressive play."

Charlie Johnson, the nose tackle, wore that playoff grin that had been conspicuously absent from the Eagles locker room for 18 years. "Hey, I don't know what happened to those quarterbacks," Johnson said. "All I know is that we were runnin' and gunnin'. All I wanted to do was get to the ball."

"We played it as if it was the last game of the season," said Edwards. "You had to do that. It was just guys using all the ability they have and believing in each other. This is family. We're just a big family."

* * *

Now it was on to face Atlanta, a team the Eagles had edged 14–13 on a blocked field goal in Vermeil's first season. The Falcons had lost three of their last five games, struggling offensively with a weak running game and a cold quarterback. Their leading rusher, Bubba Bean, had averaged only 3.7 yards per carry. Steve Bartkowski, their veteran quarterback, had thrown 18 interceptions—one for every 20 attempts—in a scattershot season. But the Falcons had some terrific defenders: linemen Jeff Merrow and Mike Lewis; linebacker Fulton Kuykendall; and a ballhawking corner, Rolland Lawrence, who had six interceptions.

The Eagles were healthy, prepared, and peaking emotionally. After beating the Giants, they had presented the game ball to Tose, their colorful owner. The presentation was captured in a four-color photograph that Vermeil had signed: "Leonard, you've been a winner for a long time, but now it shows in the won-lost column. Thank you for the opportunity to be a part of your first winning season. Sincerely, Dick."

There was one nagging and familiar issue on Vermeil's mind as the Eagles prepared for an expected physical struggle with the host Falcons. Six weeks earlier, kicker Nick Mike-Mayer had broken two ribs. Vermeil, who had been through the agony of a kicking change earlier in the season, had turned to Mike Michel, his punter, to handle both duties. And now Michel would be both the kicker and punter in the biggest game of his and Vermeil's careers.

The Eagles broke on top when Jaworski threw to Carmichael, who slanted inside defender Rolland Lawrence, for a 13-yard touchdown. Then it became a defensive struggle as predicted until Jaworski drove the offense 60 yards for a third-quarter score and a 13–0 lead. Montgomery, held to 19 yards by some terrific pursuit by the Falcons and a soggy field, got the score on a one-yard dive over left guard.

Michel, who had missed the first extra point, converted this time on a kick that caromed through the uprights after striking a leaping Falcon. The Eagles had other chances, but Mike Hogan lost one fumble at the Atlanta 15-yard line and Billy Campfield lost another at the Atlanta 38.

Yet, despite the turnovers, the Eagles seemed in command with a 13–0 lead and the home fans jeering Bartkowski. Then Hogan's first-down fumble with 8:16 left to play started the Eagles' collapse. Bartkowski threw an apparent interception to free safety Deac Sanders, but somehow split end Wallace Francis smuggled the ball away for a 49-yard gain. Bartkowski looked left, then swung back to the right and found Jim Mitchell for a 20-yard touchdown. Tim Mazzetti, once one of Vermeil's kickers, added the PAT and it was 13–7.

The Eagles controlled the ball until 1:56 was left and Michel was in the game to punt. Another special teams breakdown, this time a 15-yard face-mask penalty, gave the Falcons the ball at midfield. Bartkowski took the offense in from there, whipping a 37-yard scoring toss to Francis with 1:39 left.

Jaworski wasn't going down without a fight, however. He barely missed a scoring bomb to Oren Middlebrook when the ball glanced off the rookie's hands at the goal line. But Jaworski completed four other passes, reaching the 16-yard line and giving the Eagles a chance at a 34-yard field goal with 17 seconds to go.

Michel, who had never kicked a field goal in a regular-season game, hit his try strongly after a perfect snap from center Guy Morriss and a perfect hold by John Sciarra. But his kick sailed off to the right, creating what Michel would later admit was the lowest point of his two-year pro career. (He also had been short on an earlier 42-yarder.)

Mazzetti, the former Penn and Eagles camp kicker and onetime Philadelphia bartender, made the difference with his two conversions as Atlanta won 14–13.

"They did a good job," said a weary Vermeil, "but we allowed it to happen. When you fumble a simple running play when it's nut-cutting time, you're allowing them to come back."

Michel hung quietly in the silent Eagles dressing room. "I'm disappointed in myself," he said softly. "I let my teammates down. I thought I hit it good enough, but I didn't follow through enough." Later, there was an unconfirmed report that Vermeil kept Michel from boarding the team's charter flight.

The other Eagles tried to be kind to poor Mike Michel. "Mike is a punter who was sort of transposed to kicker," said linebacker Frank LeMaster. "He did all he could. I think he did an adequate job. I'd be more upset if it was his job and it came down to that. I know Mike feels terrible. It came down to the point where he could have been the villain or the hero, and he missed being the hero by three or four inches."

Vermeil, now burning inside, was in high gear following the defeat. Some members of the traveling party, including several coaches, were with their families. Marion Campbell had a son, Scott, who was a player with the Georgia Bulldogs. Vermeil, however, wanted to leave as soon as he could, as if Fulton County Stadium, Hartsfield Airport, and the Georgia pines were all reminders of the defeat. Vermeil promptly told his coaches they would meet in his office at 8:00 AM the next morning.

A meeting on Christmas morning while the church bells were pealing?

Several staffers approached one of Vermeil's friends, an assistant coach who wanted to remain anonymous. "Can you talk to him?" one of them asked.

"Dick, a lot of the guys have families and it's a holiday," said the assistant. "Do we really have to meet tomorrow?"

"Damn," swore Vermeil, still brooding about the fumbles and the missed field goal that cost the Eagles a one-point game. "That's all you guys think about, your kids and this and that."

Five minutes later, he walked back to the assistant and said, "Tell all the coaches that we're not meeting tomorrow."

"Then he called me the next day and invited me over for Christmas dinner," the assistant said. "Unbelievable."

*　*　*

Even with that terrible experience in Atlanta, the Eagles proved that they were a much better team than the collection of castoffs, low-round draft picks, and marginal free agents that formed the nucleus of Vermeil's first team in 1976. The weaknesses, of course, were obvious, even to the ballboys. The Eagles had no dependable kickers or punters. In three seasons, the three Eagles punters averaged 36.6 yards, 37.2 yards, and 37.2 yards again, among the lowest averages in the league. Their five field-goal kickers made 26 of 48 attempts, or 54.1 percent, the worst accuracy rate in the league.

"I've worked for seven NFL coaches and there's not a genius in the group," said Vermeil. "I know how they do things. I've seen them do it. I've been with them when they did it. I've helped them do it, and it's all basically organization. There ain't no secrets. You've got to have a plan and stick with it."

Vermeil faced another challenge aside from the struggles of his kickers. Actually, it was an ongoing problem from the Mike McCormack years: the drug scene of the 1970s had spread to the locker rooms of professional sports. This was especially true of pro football, where the games were spaced a week apart and emotions ran to peaks and valleys.

"For me and for the majority of the team, the drug problems were not talked about openly," said Stan Walters, the Pro Bowl offensive tackle. "If anybody was using drugs, they certainly wouldn't say it around me or certain other people. I heard the rumors, probably the same ones everybody else did. I made a statement one time that if somebody was smoking marijuana or some other stuff, and we were going into a game, we were going to have a talk with Coach Vermeil. I didn't want some guy in Disneyland when we were trying to win a football game."

According to newspaper reports, former Eagles quarterback Roman Gabriel gave an interview to the *Christian Science Monitor* in which he said he had heard that Vermeil cut two players in his first season "who were selling drugs right under the coach's nose." Gabriel later said he couldn't remember the interview. "The only thing I ever said was that half the team wasn't following the conditioning program scheduled by Mike McCormack," Gabriel said. In his defense, Vermeil said, "I really don't know if they were [selling drugs] or not. I cut some players I was concerned about. I went on past rumors. Players know a lot more about what's happening in the locker room than the coaches. I was made aware of the situation but I had no proof of it."

Linebacker Frank LeMaster later confirmed there once was a drug presence. "The team had 'undesirables' involved in drugs who cut themselves," LeMaster said. "They were guys who were here today and gone tomorrow. You have to understand, before Dick came here, it was like Grand Central Station the way they were bringing in players. Some guys were obvious. They'd be late to meetings. They looked like they had been through hell. They looked like they had been dragged in off the street. But that was a long time ago."

Vermeil would enter his fourth year with the Eagles, aware that eight of the 11 NFL head coaches hired in 1976 had already resigned or been fired. Only Seattle's Jack Patera and Tampa Bay's John McKay, the two expansion team coaches, had retained their jobs.

Lou Holtz resigned from the New York Jets after 13 games, claiming, "I hate the cold." Monte Clark (San Francisco) lasted one season. Jim Ringo and Tommy Hudspeth (midseason replacements in Buffalo and Detroit), and Hank Stram (New Orleans) coached for two seasons. Pat Peppler, who replaced Marion Campbell in Atlanta, was replaced himself after coaching nine games. Excluding the expansion coaches and Vermeil, the coach with the longest tenure of those hired in 1976 was Bill Johnson of the Bengals, who lasted three seasons. John McVay of the Giants, who replaced Bill Arnsparger after seven games in 1976, coached the remainder of that season and lasted through 1978.

The Eagles, now winners, were making solid progress. But the long hours and the enormous pressure were taking a terrible toll on Vermeil, who would come to be known as "the Little Dictator." He would never deny that the nickname fit.

Chapter 7

A Matter of Life and Death

Even though the Eagles had faced six of the worst pass defenses in the league, their own passing game had struggled through most of the 1978 season. In games against the Los Angeles Rams (80 yards), Washington Redskins (82 yards), Green Bay Packers (97 yards), and New York Giants (64 yards), it was little more than a pop-gun operation.

The year before, the NFL owners had opened up the passing game by approving two major rule changes: limiting defenders to a five-yard zone within which they could bump receivers, and allowing blockers to jam pass rushers by extending their arms and punching, like a boxer delivering a stiff jab.

Vermeil had other things on his mind during his first three seasons. But now he knew the Eagles had to open up their passing game if they were going to compete in the NFC East, a tough division with big-play quarterbacks such as Roger Staubach, Jim Hart, and Joe Theismann. Besides, Vermeil had seen how Pittsburgh had won two Super Bowls by taking advantage of the jazzed-up rules. In 1978, the Steelers averaged 168.7 passing yards per game and scored 28 touchdowns, 31.4 yards per game and 12 touchdowns more than the Eagles.

Vermeil was a stats coach all the way, using trends and figures provided by Bud Goode, an old California friend and early computer whiz. He also knew where to go to upgrade his pass offense. Vermeil hired 67-year-old retiree Sid

Gillman, a legendary coach and old friend, who had studied the passing game like Picasso had studied life with a brush in hand.

"One of my weaknesses is the lack of depth in the background of pro football," Vermeil admitted. "The people who have been in the game for years have a depth of thinking that I can't have yet. Based on more years of experience, adding a Sid Gillman to my staff helps me in that area. It gives you depth in your offensive thinking. It'll show even more next year. I think we got a little too stereotyped at times from an offensive standpoint."

In 1977, only four teams scored more than 300 points. A year later, under the new rules, 11 teams topped the 300-point barrier. The Steelers were the first team to take advantage of the liberalized rules, scoring 356 and 416 points and winning back-to-back Super Bowls in 1978 and 1979. Vermeil brought in Gillman as a spark, not only for the offense but also for the head coach himself.

"When you don't have enough horsepower, you put a different kind of cam shaft, or use two carburetors, on a high-compression head," said Vermeil, using an automotive analogy to point out the need to revamp his offense.

Off the field, Gillman was never far from a film projector. He had used his imagination to develop the sophisticated pass offense that is such a big part of pro football in the 21st century. Extra receivers. Comeback routes. Tailbacks running pass routes. These tactics are familiar today, but in the '60s, that kind of passing style was uniquely Gillmanesque.

The peak of Gillman's brilliant coaching career was with the original San Diego Chargers, an American Football League power. Using Gillman's passing scheme, the Chargers won five division titles and an AFL championship in 1963, routing the Boston Patriots 51–10 and racking up 610 offensive yards. San Diego averaged an amazing 10.2 yards for every offensive play.

"You know what football is to me?" Sid Gillman once said. "It's blood."

Gillman's contribution to Vermeil's offense was delayed because of open-heart surgery. But once Gillman and his personable wife Esther arrived, he began selling Vermeil on a more aggressive approach to passing. He didn't have to sell anything to Jaworski, who had been frustrated in the early years by Vermeil's predictable game plans.

Esther Gillman said her husband became interested in finding a projector to view football films when they were dating in the early 1930s. "We'd go to the theater where they would show those Grantland Rice sports reels before the movie," she said. "Something flashed through his brain, and he had his brother tell the projectionist to snip the football parts off the sports reels and send them to us. Before we left on our honeymoon, he was looking through the want ads and saw a 35-millimeter projector on sale for $15. He bought it and I gave him hell. I told him we couldn't afford to buy a projector when his first job [at Ohio State, his alma mater] was going to pay him $1,800 a year."

Gillman would pin a sheet on the wall and run the projector, using the primitive film clips that his brother would send him. Later he introduced the use of film to the college ranks. "He was way ahead of himself in the use of visual aids," said Esther.

As the start of training camp loomed in 1979, and Sid Gillman was undergoing heart surgery, the Eagles were rocked by the arrests of Mike Hogan and Jim Betterson on charges of being part of a South Jersey–Philadelphia cocaine conspiracy. Nineteen days later, both fullbacks were placed on the waiver list. Hogan, a three-year starter, was waived on July 18. Betterson, who was recovering from knee surgery, was placed on the reserve list. A grim-faced Vermeil said Betterson would be cut when his knee was healthy.

"Dick is so caught up in this thing about character," said Roman Gabriel. "I think in his mind he thought he had gotten rid of everyone involved in that. That's why what happened had to be a shocker."

"Dick's our man," said linebacker John Bunting. "We've got to stick by what he does. This won't hurt us because everyone respects Coach Vermeil so much. It might even make us stronger. We'll pull together."

Said Vermeil, "My policy with the Eagles is a little different. It may not be fair. But it's fair if you know what [the rules] are. Involvement, association, being accused in any way of drugs will not be tolerated. I'm probably a little old-fashioned about certain things. I'm not very tolerable. I'm not very liberal. I've checked with the league and there's nothing against having stricter rules than they do."

"Dick taught me about responsibility. Being responsible or accountable to admit your mistakes and not tell a lie. He felt that character would outlast athleticism."

JOHN SCIARRA

Eventually, Vermeil obtained Leroy Harris, a squat, 230-pound fullback, a week before the season opener. Harris became available for a fifth-round draft pick when Larry Csonka returned to the Dolphins after a brief fling with the New York Giants.

Vermeil had added some new talent, including some situational players, to give the Eagles more depth and versatility. The new talent included pass rusher Claude Humphrey, an 11-year veteran who had retired the previous season; John Sciarra, Vermeil's quarterback at UCLA who had been converted into a safety, and Louie Giammona, a 5'9" running back and special teams hitter (both joined the team in 1978); John Spagnola, an underrated tight end; and long snapper Mark Slater.

Humphrey was reunited with Marion Campbell, the man known as "Swamp Fox," who had coached him during his best years in Atlanta. The Falcons, a 3-4 team on defense like the Eagles, had wanted Humphrey to play over the tight end, thus minimizing his pass-rushing role. "He was like a pitcher for 13 years who is asked to play third base," Campbell said after Humphrey retired four games into the 1978 season. But now Humphrey was reenergized and ready to join Carl Hairston alongside nose tackle Charlie Johnson.

Johnson had been a military policeman in Vietnam. Hairston had driven a furniture truck before being recruited for college from a pool hall. Both were seventh-round picks. "I think this is the best defensive line I've ever played on," Humphrey would later say. "And that goes all the way back to the beginning."

Sciarra would emerge as a valuable utility player. He would come in as a nickel back on a young, aggressive secondary; hold for conversion and field-goal attempts; return punts when Wally Henry was injured; and even play quarterback when Vermeil called for a little razzle-dazzle option play on the goal line.

Giammona was the most controversial import. Vermeil, his teammates would soon learn, was his uncle. Giammona stood only 5'9", but he was fearless when he stepped onto the field, throwing his body around as he used to do at Calistoga High, Vermeil's old school.

"I was the nephew of the head coach, and I was a 5'9", 175-pound white back," said Giammona. "Everybody thought that to be able to run the ball, you had to be 6'2" and 275 pounds, run the 40 in 4.2, and lift up the planet." Giammona, however, would prove to be a great special teams banger and, a few years later, a valuable backup for Montgomery. Slater, a 12th-round choice in the 1978 draft, would snap on punts and join Giammona on special teams.

*   *   *

The Eagles didn't need any pep talks at the start of the 1979 season. They were more talented and deeper than they had ever been. The drug problem, more real than imagined, had been removed. Jaworski was entering his third season at the helm, and he had Sid Gillman alongside to critique his moves. Montgomery, the record-setting back, was coming off a 1,220-yard season. And, perhaps most importantly, Vermeil had found his kicker in Tony Franklin, a bare-footed, long-distance talent from Texas A&M, and, hopefully, his punter in Max Runager, who had only 14 of 61 long-hanging punts returned at South Carolina. Franklin and Runager were the Eagles' third and eighth draft picks in what would become Vermeil's best draft.

The Eagles won three of their first four games. Franklin kicked seven field goals, the special teams were devastating, and the 1-2 punch of Jaworski and Montgomery was very much in evidence.

The following week, the Eagles faced the Super Bowl champion Steelers. "They've played four teams," Vermeil said. "New England, with the best offensive line in football; Houston, with the best running back [Earl Campbell] in football; St. Louis, with the best young running back [Ottis "O.J." Anderson]; and Baltimore, a team that's still jelling. Those teams averaged 3.1 yards per snap. Well, we'll make more yards on them than those other people. They'll be hard yards, and Wilbert Montgomery will be sore when it's over."

Vermeil also warned his team "not to be intimidated" by the Steelers. "They've been doing it to people for a long time," he said. "We just can't allow it to happen. There's no pressure on the Eagles. Most of my people feel we're going to beat their asses. Look, I don't give a bleep if they're all-Italy. It will be a tight, flat-ass good football game."

At the offensive meeting to reveal the game plan, Vermeil talked for 65 minutes. "In Coach Gillman's day, when they wore leather helmets, they used to run the hell out of this play," said Vermeil. At one point in the game preparation, Vermeil had not been outdoors for 68 straight hours. His breakfast was usually a cup of coffee; his lunch, a Carnation bar.

And then the Eagles, with their fans screaming and chanting and punching the air, stunned the Steelers 17–14. That gave the Eagles a 4–1 record and an unfamiliar spot in the NFC East standings, tied for first place with their bitter rivals from Dallas.

"It always amazed me that [Vermeil] was involved with so many things. The second year he was here, I was looking at TV one day and he was out there with handicapped kids at the Special Olympics. I remember thinking, When does the guy have time to rest?"

HERMAN BALL, FORMER EAGLES
PERSONNEL DIRECTOR

Franklin, the bare-footed kicker, boomed a 48-yarder to break a 10–10 tie in the third quarter. Montgomery rushed for 98 "hard yards," as Vermeil had predicted. Montgomery also scored the clinching touchdown after linebacker John Bunting had returned an interception off Terry Bradshaw to the 2-yard line. Two other heroes were Edwards, the clever cornerback, who stole one of Bradshaw's passes in the end zone, and nose tackle Kenny Clarke, who recovered Franco Harris' goal-line fumble.

The Eagles won two more games with some awesome drive blocking that helped Montgomery rush for 127 yards in a 28–17 win over the Redskins, and 117 yards in a 24–20 win over St. Louis. Against the Cardinals, the Eagles totaled 249 return yards, most of them by Wally

Henry, Vermeil's old UCLA returner. Franklin also boomed a 51-yard field goal in that game, the third-longest in club history.

Just as suddenly, though, the Eagles hit a rut. They dropped consecutive games to the Redskins (17–7), Bengals, (37–13), and Browns (24–19). Jaworski threw five interceptions during the three-week swoon and the Eagles lost seven fumbles. With the 8–2 Cowboys next on the schedule—a nationally televised *Monday Night Football* game, no less—Dick Vermeil went into high gear.

> *"He was intense and demanding, but he was appreciative of everything you did."*
>
> MIKE DOUGHERTY,
> EAGLES VIDEO DIRECTOR

"I was the only one who could hang with Dick," said Jerry Wampfler, the offensive line coach. "I was sort of a night person, too. After practice, we ate there. Then we'd go over the practice film. Depending on what day of the week it was, we'd make adjustments in our offense, either in pass protection, or pass offense, or the running game. Early in the week, like on a Tuesday night, he would make more changes than later in the week, when we'd kind of fine-tune things and maybe adjust a formation, or a motion, or a shift. Then it was a matter of him asking, 'Are you getting done what you think you're getting done?'"

As the week wore on, Vermeil and his staff studied the Cowboys like generals plotting a surprise invasion. The coaches pored over game films, the Cowboys' and their own, until very late at night. "I'd be there on Monday night, working until 1:00 or 2:00 in the morning, doing editing," said Mike Dougherty, the team's film director. "You never even thought about time. Nobody really looked at the clock. It was just something that we did because he [Vermeil] did it. You wondered where he got all this energy."

According to receivers coach Dick Coury, Vermeil and most of his assistants worked until 4:00 AM as often as three days a week. "The main reason was that when Dick was calling plays and coordinating the offense, he'd get to see everything," said Coury. "He'd say, 'Jerry [Wampfler], go down and get the running game.' He'd bring it in about 10:00. The next night you'd almost have to start over so Dick could see what you were talking about."

Some of the assistants, including Coury, slept at a hotel across from the stadium at least twice a week. Some of the linebackers, including Bill Bergey, their leader, joined them. "When you worked for Dick," said Coury, "you're talking about getting in at 7:00 AM and going home sometimes around 4:00 AM. But we'd go to the hotel most of the time."

Wampfler, the offensive line coach, called Vermeil "the most organized coach I've ever worked with. He was organized in all phases, too. The only phase we weren't organized in was sleep."

"Dick would be right there, working with us," said Chuck Clausen, the defensive line coach. "Then he'd go into his office, lay down on his couch, and go to sleep for an hour and a half. Dick had more energy and could drive himself harder than any person I've ever seen, and he drove us that way."

"The thing I appreciated about Dick is that I never had to worry about my back. Later, I mentioned that I was living in my old hometown and we were raising money to refurbish the high school stadium and put artificial turf on the field. Dick came in here and spoke and helped raise the money."

JERRY WAMPFLER,
FORMER EAGLES ASSISTANT COACH

Vermeil wanted to win the Dallas game very badly. The Cowboys, it seemed, were always sniping at him. If they weren't snickering about his long hours in the office, they were mocking Jaworski, the talkative quarterback who had an opinion on everything. Moreover, the Eagles hadn't beaten the Cowboys in Dallas since 1965, a string of 13 straight losses.

At the time, the Cowboys' defense was designed to stop the run. They used Tom Landry's flex defense, and almost always brought their strong safety forward to bolster the run-stoppers and force everything back inside to the linebackers, always a Cowboys strength. Indeed, one of their earliest strong safeties was Mike Gaechter, and that spot became known as the "Gaechter position."

Vermeil remembered how the Cowboys defense had swarmed to Montgomery the previous season, so he and Sid Gillman, his offensive guru, put together a wide-open game plan that would stun the Cowboys and thrill the *Monday Night Football* audience across the country.

"We used the pass to set up the run, and that's a 360-degree turn for us," Jaworski was later to say. Jaworski, of course, meant 180 degrees, but who among the Eagles was counting?

Eleven of the Eagles' first 13 plays were passes signaled in by Vermeil. On fourth-and-1 from the Dallas 32-yard line, Jaworski froze the Cowboys defense with a run fake, then lofted his first of two scoring passes to Harold Carmichael.

Fearing mistakes, visiting teams had almost always played into the hands of the Cowboys by refusing to throw on early downs. But on this memorable night, the Eagles played gambling, almost reckless offense and won 31–21. With Vermeil calling plays, the Eagles threw 12 times on first down and 11 times on second down.

As in most unexpected triumphs, there were unlikely heroes. Johnnie Walton came off the bench when Jaworski injured his left wrist and threw a 29-yard touchdown pass to Charlie Smith. Rookie Tony Franklin, who missed three field goals, also boomed a 59-yarder. Backup center Mark Slater set up Smith's score by forcing a fumble on special teams.

Both Jaworski and Dallas quarterback Roger Staubach were knocked out of the game in the first half. Both returned, but it was Jaworski who threw a 13-yard scoring pass to Carmichael for a 24–7 lead in the third period. Jaws finished the game despite the injured wrist, the one with a tiny quarter-inch screw inside a fractured navicular bone. The Cowboys also tore some cartilage beneath Jaworski's left shoulder and left red welts all over his body.

After the Cowboys had closed to within 24–21 on two touchdown passes by Staubach, Vermeil refused to panic. On third-and-3 with 61 seconds left, Montgomery made a nifty inside-out move and raced 37 yards to the end zone for the clinching touchdown.

"On the offense, we were a little bit on the reckless side," said a teary-eyed Vermeil. "But sometimes you can be embarrassed doing that, too."

Including three sacks and one scramble, Vermeil sent in 39 pass plays and only 37 runs. When the Eagles had field position between the 40-yard lines, they had a pass-run ratio of 8-3 on first down, 5-4 on second down, and 7-3 on third down. Inside the Dallas 40, Vermeil called seven runs and six passes, including a daring fourth-and-1 scoring pass to Carmichael on which Benny Barnes bit on Jaworski's play fake.

"This is the most meaningful thing that's ever happened to me," said Vermeil, who got the game ball. "It started in the off-season, in training camp, and through a lot of tough days and nights, a lot of bitching and moaning."

Forty-two of the 45 Eagles had never won a game in Dallas. The three who had—Jaworski, defensive tackle Manny Sistrunk, and guard Woody Peoples— had done it with other teams.

Rookie linebacker Jerry Robinson, who was in on a dozen tackles, said he knew all about the bad blood that ran between the two division rivals. "Sure I knew there was a rivalry between the Eagles and Cowboys," he said. "I knew that when I heard Dick Vermeil talk about Dallas in training camp."

"Philadelphia played a good game," Landry said. "They were a very hungry football team. We made too many errors. We gave them the football and they took advantage of it."

Early the next day, Vermeil saw trainer Otho Davis at the Philadelphia airport and asked him for a sleeping pill. "I'm going to the office and I'm going to try to get some rest," Vermeil said. "I'm a little wound up." Davis gave the coach a pill. "I didn't know what it was," Vermeil said, "but I laid down at 5:20 AM and didn't wake up again until 12:30."

After his seven-hour nap, Vermeil walked downstairs to the field at Veterans Stadium. Some stadium workers were still celebrating the upset, whooping and cheering as they drove their carts.

"They probably deserved this win as much as the players," Vermeil said. "I've said it before, but it's amazing, the love this city has for the Eagles. I felt that from the middle of my second season here. I'm convinced that's why the fans get after me sometimes. I can understand how they lose patience with me. Days like this make it all very gratifying. I just hope today they are as excited as I am. I believe they are."

The Eagles received a congratulatory telegram the next day. "Congratulations," it said. "I wore my Eagles sweat suit to bed last night." It was signed by Don Rickles, the comedian and a friend of owner Leonard Tose from their days in Beverly Hills.

The Eagles won four of their last five games—losing only in a rematch with Dallas—to finish with an 11–5 record as Vermeil won most of the Coach of the Year awards. The Cowboys, however, won the division title because they had a better conference record (10–2 to 9–3). That meant the Eagles would be an NFC wild-card team, playing on the road.

Crazy things happened on that final weekend. The Cowboys rallied to knock the Redskins out of the playoffs in a wild 35–34 ping-pong match. Chicago, needing to beat St. Louis by at least 33 points to win a tiebreaker with the Redskins, routed the Cardinals 42–6 to earn a matchup with Vermeil's Eagles.

In the first round of the playoffs, Philadelphia staged a second-half rally and turned a 17–17 tie into a 27–17 win over the Bears to advance to the NFC divisional playoff. The latest hero was Billy Campfield, an obscure 11th-round pick from Vermeil's third draft. Jaworski fed him a pass in the flat, and Campfield turned it into a 63-yard touchdown that broke the tie. Franklin added a 34-yard field goal, his 23rd of the year. The Eagles defense, "flashing" to use Vermeil's favorite word, held Walter Payton to 67 yards and quarterback Mike Phipps to a drab 13-for-30, two-interception, 142-yard game.

But a week later, playing a fourth-year expansion team, the helpless Eagles fell behind 17–0 and eventually were upset by Tampa Bay 24–17. The Bucs kept lining up in a double–tight end formation and pulling both guards, leading into the power alley with their fullback and pitching the ball back to Ricky Bell, their magnificent tailback.

On their opening drive, the Bucs controlled the ball for nine minutes and 34 seconds, an eternity for Ron Jaworski, who kept shuffling his feet on the opposing sideline. Bell kept attacking the left side of the Eagles defense: end Claude Humphrey, linebacker John Bunting, and cornerback Bobby Howard. When it was over, Bell had rushed 38 times for 142 yards and two touchdowns, almost always beating the Eagles defenders to the corner, at least those who were still standing.

"If you're asking me where to put the blame, I don't know where to put it," said Humphrey. "I do know this. They've got a better football team. That's where to put some of the blame."

Jaworski had an up-and-down game, completing only 15 of 39 attempts. His key receivers, Carmichael and Smith, caught only six passes. Carmichael finally got loose for a 37-yard score with 3:36 left, cutting the Bucs' lead to 24–17. But with 2:11 left, Jaworski and his battered offense couldn't fashion a tying touchdown. The series ended in the final minute with Jaworski throwing three incompletions and having his fourth-down pass fly out of bounds as Carmichael broke inside.

"I was confident," Jaworski said of the final drive that ended at the Bucs' 45-yard line. "But I was also realistic, too. I realized you're limited in what you can do. You get down to no timeouts and you can't be going for five or six yards. And it's a risky thing when you throw downfield."

Howard, the cornerback, said the Bucs pulled away because of their flawless execution in the running game. "They had us down real well," he said. "They played super today. You could tell from the start. It was like they were caged and [the coaches] were letting them out."

* * *

So now Vermeil's fourth season had ended in a jarring defeat. The Eagles had been beaten by an expansion team that had scored 10 points in its last three games. The Eagles defense, ranked fourth against the run but looking leg-weary at the end, allowed an expansion team to rush 55 times for 186 yards.

The long season had taken a toll on Vermeil. He and his 10 assistants had worked those crazy hours, sitting beside projectors and drinking stale coffee, and seeking an edge, any kind of edge, to turn the next game their way. Vermeil would never admit it, but during the seven-month season, he placed coaching football ahead of his family. Yet, with the Super Bowl so tantalizingly close,

Vermeil would join Tose, the owner, for a brief vacation in Acapulco, and then plunge right back into preparing for a new season.

"To me, every day is a matter of life and death in coaching football," he said. "I've never been satisfied. If I do something, I want to do it better than anybody else. I've been fortunate in that at every level I've coached—high school, junior college, college, and professional—I've been successful. I've been fortunate enough to be named Coach of the Year at every level. Now I'm in a league with 27 other guys who are always among the best, and I want to be the best. I've always been like that. I don't know why."

Over the years, the adage has been that a football team reflects the personality of its head coach. Lombardi's Packers were always tough, grinding teams. Chuck Noll's Steelers were always big on fundamentals. Bill Parcells' New York Giants always featured great linebacking play (Parcells himself was a linebacker).

Vermeil's teams had certainly taken on his identity. In 1977, a devastating 17–13 loss to a weak Detroit team left many of the Eagles overcome with emotion. "I just don't feel like talking," tight end Keith Krepfle had said, tears welling in his eyes. "I can't talk now," linebacker John Bunting had said, openly crying in the embrace of Vermeil. "I just feel snakebitten," Jaworski had said after Tom Sullivan's last-minute fumble at the Lions' 13-yard line assured the outcome. "We've got a lot of young guys here. Sooner or later, we're going to come together and bust a lot of people."

Maybe Bill Bergey, the linebacker, said it best. "Dick's personality has rubbed off on us," Bergey said. "He talked about character. He talked about discipline, and paying the price, and he defined it better than anybody ever had with his actions. There's something very special about Dick Vermeil. As athletes, we all want to play but we want to achieve things, if only for ourselves. But with Dick, you go beyond that. You play for 'The Cause.' In the fourth quarter, we reach down for something that the other teams don't have."

In the earlier years, however, Vermeil was often overcome by his own emotions. This was particularly true after games in which momentary hope turned to defeat because of a mistake or two. "It got to the point where I couldn't eat or sleep," said Vermeil. "I was feeling damn near sick all the time."

Sometimes Vermeil couldn't bring himself to address the team. "So I had Leonard talk to them for me," he said. "I'm an emotional guy. Too emotional. Too intense most of the time."

Carol Vermeil, the coach's wife, also felt the strain. "It gets lonely and I get the blues," she said. "I wouldn't be human if I didn't. But as Dick progressed in his career, I resolved within myself that I had to share him with the team and the public. Dick and I have had our share of ups and downs. But we've never doubted our love for each other. As long as you have health and your family, you have no business complaining in that state of mind."

"It wouldn't do him any good, or me any good, if I demanded more of his time. After the season ends, when he has more regular hours, he'll get more involved with the kids and with the home. But then things happen. Problems come up and he isn't even aware of them."

CAROL VERMEIL

Before the December 29 divisional playoff game against the Bucs, Vermeil kept his staff working until just before midnight.

At about this time, owner Leonard Tose began to worry about Vermeil's health. He called Carol and asked her if there was anything he could do to change her husband's hard-charging style.

"I can't do it. I can't make him relax," she said. "I don't know if you can, either."

Marion Campbell, the defensive coordinator, gave it a try after another one of those marathon nights. "Dick, I'm going to speak my piece," he said. "You're killing yourself."

Vermeil's shrugged off Campbell's concern. "That's just what I believe in," he said. "I know I'm too emotional, too intense. I still feel I'm outcoached whenever the team loses. I've just got to be me. When we lost to Tampa, a lot of people said the team was flat. Well, I'm responsible for how we played."

Dick Vermeil was 37 years old when he left the Los Angeles Rams to become the head coach of the UCLA Bruins.

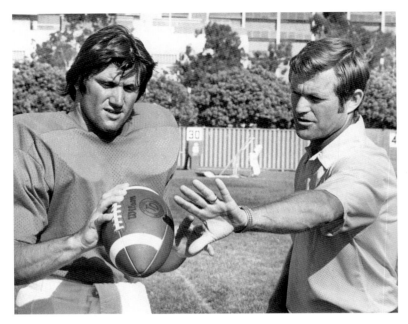

Vermeil's tutelage was instrumental in the development of Bruins quarterback John Sciarra.

Vermeil's Bruins won the Victory Bell in their matchup with rival USC in 1975, then followed it up by upsetting Ohio State in the Rose Bowl.

Seeking a head coach who could instill discipline in their team, the Eagles hired Vermeil as their head coach in 1976. Photo courtesy of the Philadelphia Eagles

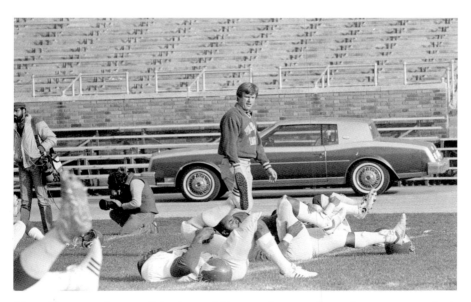

Vermeil's approach to conditioning and his marathon practice sessions came as a shock to many of the Philadelphia veterans.

Maxwell Club president Francis J. Bagnell, Dick Vermeil, and Ron Jaworski celebrate the quarterback's Maxwell Award in 1980. Acquiring Jaworski from the Rams gave the Eagles a much-needed leader on offense. Photo courtesy of the Philadelphia Eagles

In Vermeil's fifth season, he led the Eagles to Super Bowl XV, a game they lost 27–10 to the Oakland Raiders. Two years later, Vermeil resigned after pushing himself and his team to their limits.

Vermeil returned to coaching in 1997 at the request of St. Louis Rams owner Georgia Frontiere. In his third season, Vermeil won his first Super Bowl title.

Quarterback Kurt Warner led the Rams' explosive offense and was the MVP of Super Bowl XXXIV.

A tearful Vermeil resigned from coaching for a second time just days after winning his first Super Bowl.

Lured back to the sideline by a love for competition, Vermeil posted a 44–36 record in five seasons with the Kansas City Chiefs.

Vermeil said good-bye to the coaching world for the final time after leading the Chiefs to a 10–6 record in 2005.

Dick Vermeil was burning himself out. All of the symptoms were there.

"It affects your mood, it affects your attitude, and it affects your ability to sleep and to manage stress, and enjoy your relationships at home and with people," says Dr. John Trotta, a noted professor of clinical psychology from Scarsdale, New York. "You end up eating poorly on convenience foods to get things done. You end up in a time warp, squeezed from all angles."

There would be one more wonderful, memorable season for Dick Vermeil and the Eagles. And then the pace, the pressure, and the economics of the game would take over completely.

Chapter 8

Finally Super

After four exhausting seasons that most NFL players would have rebelled against, Dick Vermeil finally had assembled his kind of team. Tough. Disciplined. Opportunistic. Dedicated. Passionate. And, just as importantly, devoted to "The Cause." They had what linebacker Bill Bergey described as "that something extra that other teams don't have." Not that the Eagles were a super team. But there was a sense of unwavering optimism among the strange collection of talent that Vermeil and player personnel director Carl Peterson would send out for the 1980 season.

Position by position, the Eagles couldn't match up with the other top teams in the league: San Diego, Dallas, Oakland, Cleveland, and Los Angeles. Yet, like the champion Eagles in that wonderful season of 1960, Vermeil's fourth team had a special bond that excluded the divas, the malcontents, the braggarts, and the loners.

Consider Vermeil's starting lineup:

Offense
Receivers: Harold Carmichael, 7th rounder; Charlie Smith, free agent
Tackles: Stan Walters, 9th rounder; Jerry Sisemore, 1st rounder
Guards: Petey Perot, 2nd rounder; Woody Peoples, free agent
Center: Guy Morriss, 2nd rounder

Tight end: Keith Krepfle, 5th rounder

Quarterback: Ron Jaworski, 2nd rounder

Running backs: Wilbert Montgomery, 6th rounder; Leroy Harris, 5th rounder

Defense

Ends: Dennis Harrison, 4th rounder; Carl Hairston, 7th rounder

Nose tackle: Charlie Johnson, 7th rounder

Linebackers: Bill Bergey, 2nd rounder; Frank LeMaster, 4th rounder; John Bunting, 10th rounder; Jerry Robinson, 1st rounder

Cornerbacks: Herm Edwards, free agent; Roynell Young, 1st rounder

Safeties: Randy Logan, 3rd rounder; Brenard Wilson, free agent

Bill Davis, who coached the tight ends for Vermeil from 1976 to 1978 before leaving for Miami, was stunned as he followed the rise of the Eagles. "We [Dolphins] had second- and third-line players doing things every day that some of their first-stringers couldn't do," said Davis. "Now I know how good a coach Dick is."

By now, after four years of wielding the whip, Vermeil had earned his dubious nickname, "the Little Dictator." It was coined by Gary Smith, a beat writer for the *Philadelphia Daily News*. Surprisingly, Vermeil didn't object to the name.

"I don't mind," said Vermeil. "Hell, I was a dictator. I also like to have everything open. I believe you should always tell the media the truth. If you can't, then don't tell them anything. But don't bullshit them. It doesn't cost a dime to be honest."

Vermeil's attention to detail matched his honesty. He kept track of his tight schedule by dividing a legal pad into four lists. Each list was designated for a special person. One

"Lots of people work hard. But he's the most productive person I've ever been around. His motto is, 'A great occasion is worth to a man, what preparation has made it.'"

LYNN STILES,
FORMER EAGLES ASSISTANT COACH

was for Carol, his wife. Others were for Carl Peterson, his personnel guy, and Lynn Stiles, his administrative assistant and longtime friend. The fourth and longest list was for himself.

"He takes it everywhere he goes," Carol said. "I mean *everywhere*. I tell him, 'You're not bringing that thing are you?' He can't help himself."

Vermeil also carried a small tape recorder with him everywhere he went. If the idea for a new play crossed his mind, he dictated the details into the recorder. It was not unusual in the off-season for him to dictate ideas in the middle of the night. During the season, of course, Vermeil usually was awake most of the night.

Even though Vermeil had turned the Eagles into winners, he kept driving himself at the same frantic pace. The working hours remained long and hard on the mind, if not the body. Sid Gillman, who was 69, usually left the stadium about 9:30 PM. Campbell and Coury were both 51, far beyond their playing days. At the end of a working night that sometimes lasted until 4:30 AM, they felt 10 years older than that.

It was all part of Vermeil's master plan to reach the Super Bowl. He knew the Eagles weren't talented enough to win on Sundays if they came out flat. There were only four first-rounders on the entire roster, including defensive end Claude Humphrey, a 36-year-old castoff from Atlanta, and rookie corner-back Roynell Young. Vermeil's approach was the same he took with Napa Junior College, UCLA, or the Hillsdale High swim team. Outwork your opponents. Keep driving yourself. Will yourself to succeed.

Nickel back John Sciarra said Vermeil's relentless style reminded him of the movie *Gladiator*. "If you remember the movie, the gladiator was the general of the army," said Sciarra. "He was not sitting on the top of the hill, watching his troops fight. He was down there among them, fighting with them. And I think that's the respect that the players had for Dick Vermeil. Even though he worked us quite hard, I think he knew by getting the kind of character player that he wanted that they could endure that. Dick wasn't somebody who would drive around in a golf cart. He didn't go out and play golf while his assistants were working. Dick worked harder than anybody in the organization. So when you have a leader that's working harder than anybody else, then it's a little bit more palatable when you're the one being asked to do the work."

The season that followed reflected the true grit of a team that loved its general despite the heavy load it was asked to carry.

The Eagles got off to a spectacular start, winning four of their first five games and averaging 28.4 points. Wilbert Montgomery rushed for 169 yards in a 42–7 thrashing of Minnesota. The Eagles were so moved, so thrilled, that Charlie Johnson, the muscular nose tackle, carried Vermeil off the field. That little ceremony got a laugh from Tex Schramm, the Cowboys' president, who said he had never seen a coach carried off the field so early in the season.

Schramm had also made another cutting line. "It gets under my skin when [Vermeil] talks about sleeping in the stadium and working 60 hours, and all of that stuff," said Schramm. "I know how hard other coaches work, and they don't talk about it that way."

"I didn't read all that stuff," shot back Vermeil. "But Tex Schramm can stick it in his you-know-what."

Vermeil's next game was with the New York Giants, a rebuilding team that lost to the Eagles 35–3 in Week 3 on a day Jaworski threw three touchdown passes. Indeed, Jaworski was the league's hottest quarterback over the first five weeks with a 60 percent completion rate, 1,174 yards, and 11 touchdown passes.

But then the Eagles stood around in the rematch and let the Giants outhit them and outscore them 16–3 in the first half. The gloating, finger-waving Giants, a 1–4 team, danced into their dressing room with a 13-point lead.

"I've seen a lot of stupid things in my life," said Bill Bergey, "but that puts them right up there with rolling the football like a pair of dice, like this team used to do."

The Eagles reacted to their first-half slumber party with a flurry of four straight touchdowns in the span of 18 minutes, 32 seconds. Given field position by the awakened defense, Jaworski took Vermeil's offense on scoring drives of 61, 39, 47, and 55 yards. Louie Giammona, subbing for the injured Montgomery, contributed a lot more than just firing up the special teams.

Little Louie handled the ball 14 times on the four drives, rushing for 24 yards and catching four passes for 52 yards. He caught a 26-yarder on third-and-1, a favorite passing down with the gambling Eagles, to set up one of his two touchdowns.

At one point in the first half, the Giants stopped Leroy Harris on fourth-and-one at their own 36. Their defensive unit, led by Gary Jeter and Bud Hebert, pranced off the field after the hit on Harris, swirling their index fingers in the air and slapping hands. "I felt the game swung around at halftime here, in this locker room," said a jubilant Vermeil in a raspy voice. "[The Giants] were waving their hands in circles. We said we were going to come out in the second half and make them stick that finger where it belongs."

Beasley Reece, referring to the Giants' early 13–0 lead, paid the Eagles the ultimate compliment. "Against most teams in the league, we would have won this one easily," the Giants safety said. "But the Eagles didn't quit on themselves. They didn't throw bomb after bomb. They held together and came back."

A week later, the Eagles took over first place in the NFC East. The 17–10 win over Dallas wasn't easy. The two division rivals banged and shoved and collided in a game that was fought along the lines of a back-alley brawl. Both star backs, Montgomery and Dallas' Tony Dorsett, were forced out of the game, Montgomery with a knee sprain and Dorsett with a cracked rib.

The individual battles within the war didn't end until Roynell Young, a rookie cornerback, knocked down Danny White's fourth-down pass from the Eagles' 8-yard line in the final minute. Tony Hill and Drew Pearson ran crossing patterns that took Hill, the intended receiver, into the left corner on a fade pattern. Young clawed the ball loose and he and Hill tumbled out of the shadow-covered end zone. Hill got up looking for a flag that never came. "I thought it was a clean play," said Young.

Just when the teams seemed ready to drag themselves on weary legs and aching bodies into overtime, a tipped pass fell into the hands of Charlie Johnson, the nose tackle, at the Dallas 20 with 5:53 left. Out of that turnover, the Eagles scored the decisive touchdown, a 15-yard slant pass to flanker Charlie Smith.

It was that kind of grim, scuffling game, and the Cowboys were a combative opponent. Under those conditions, against that foe, it was the kind of game that played on the emotions of grown men.

"We gave everyone who suited up a game ball," said Vermeil. "How could you give it to any one person?"

The Eagles kept winning with each game, it seemed, featuring a different script. The heroes of a 17–14 win over Chicago were Joe Pisarcik, the backup quarterback, and Giammona, the special teams captain. With Jaworski woozy from a concussion, Pisarcik took the Eagles on a 70-yard drive, setting up Tony Franklin's winning 18-yard field goal with 2:02 left. Giammona, subbing for Montgomery, did it all: 79 rushing yards, four catches, and a 27-yard completion to Krepfle on a rarely used halfback option pass.

The following week, third-down specialist Billy Campfield caught the winning pass against Seattle in a 27–20 comeback win. It ended an 84-yard drive that Jaworski (8-of-9 on the march) called "maybe the best drive I've ever been involved in with the Eagles." Dick Coury, the receivers coach, agreed. "That's as fine a drive as a quarterback can have," Coury said.

Two more wins over the winless New Orleans Saints and the inconsistent Redskins gave the Eagles a 10–1 record, their best in 31 years. And now the streaking Oakland Raiders were next. The Raiders had struggled in September, but then their defense, led by linebacker Ted "the Stork" Hendricks and cornerback Lester "the Molester" Hayes, carried them to six straight wins.

When it was finally over, when the two bruised teams had limped to the hot showers, the Eagles had prevailed 10–7. The difference was a creative game plan put in by Eagles defensive coordinator Marion Campbell and Chuck Clausen, his line coach.

"Our offense was not really clicking early in the season," said Tom Flores, the Oakland coach. "We just weren't as good an offensive team as we were later on. We were a big-play team, but we had some problems with them. We weren't able to come up with any big plays. And, of course, that pass rush killed us."

Philadelphia's pass rushers produced eight total sacks and numerous hurries against quarterback Jim Plunkett. The Raiders, with their great offensive line, figured that their two All-Pros, Gene Upshaw and Art Shell, could handle any-thing. Campbell, however, had his rushers looping and blitzing, and the Raiders couldn't handle the surprise tactic.

"We came up with a pass-rushing scheme that we had never used before," said Clausen. "It was just one of those things we came up with in practice. I worked with my guys on the field and we did some things that they had no reason to practice against. We got into the game and they worked as well as they ever worked. They couldn't pick it up, and they couldn't adjust. And we had enough different variations, so if they adjusted, we had something else."

The key offensive play for the Eagles was just as unusual. What started out as a bootleg play ended up with Jaworski shaking off blitzer Randy McClanahan and lofting a 43-yard pass to an unlikely receiver, fullback Leroy Harris. Harris momentarily lost the ball in the lights, but made a basket catch like a center fielder and rumbled all the way to the Raiders' 28-yard line. Montgomery eventually scored the game-turning touchdown on a three-yard sweep past free safety Burgess Owens and linebacker Matt Millen.

"It was amazing that he caught it," said Vermeil. "Leroy is like a volleyball player on the practice field."

How vicious was the hitting? "That was the hardest-fought, physical foot-ball game I ever played in," said Stan Walters, the Eagles' left tackle. "Just two teams smacking the hell out of each other. The offenses couldn't move because the defenses were hitting. It was probably the best game I ever played in."

The pounding seemed to take something out of the Eagles; they lost their next two games, 22–21 to San Diego and 20–17 to Atlanta. In both losses, the usually strong running game was missing.

A week later, Campbell's defense returned to its dominating style, holding the run-happy St. Louis Cardinals to 67 yards rushing and 126 net yards in a 17–3 win. That left the Eagles at 12–3 and the Cowboys at 11–4 in the two-team NFC East race. The other three division teams, the Redskins, Cardinals, and Giants, would all finish with losing records.

On that crazy final weekend, the Eagles faced the Cowboys in Texas Stadium, the site of so many of their emotional losses but also one of their greatest wins, the 31–21 *Monday Night Football* shocker in 1979. With a Cowboys win, the two teams would be tied in four of the five tiebreaker categories. The fifth tiebreaker involved net divisional points; the Cowboys, Vermeil was told, needed to win by at least 25 points to clinch the division.

Dallas, knowing it needed fast touchdowns, jumped out to a 21–0 halftime lead. That margin grew to 35–10, as Franklin missed two field goals and an angry Vermeil kept protesting some debatable holding calls. The Eagles' predicament left Jaworski "in a state of shock."

During the Dallas surge, trainer Otho Davis shuttled on and off the field. The Eagles lost receivers Carmichael and Smith, linebacker Bill Bergey, defensive end Carl Hairston, and special teams hitter/holder John Sciarra to various injuries. That's why the furious comeback, in which the Eagles cut the final score to 35–27, featured a number of obscure backups including receivers Scott Fitzkee and Rodney Parker, linebacker Al Chesley, and pass rusher Tom Brown.

A 25-point or greater rout would have given the Cowboys 68 net divisional points to the Eagles' 66 and therefore the NFC East crown. Instead, the most bizarre scene in Texas Stadium history unfolded in the loser's dressing room. Jaworski, who passed for a career-high 331 yards, celebrated by touching glasses of $46-a-bottle Dom Perignon champagne with Joe Pisarcik, his backup. It was perhaps the sweetest defeat in Eagles history.

"We gave them the magic 25," sang out tackle Stan Walters, "and then took it away from them. We got step two. Step one was to beat them outright. Step two was to beat them in the point differential."

Vermeil was thrilled about the effort rather than the final score. "It was a test of Eagle character," the coach said. Pisarcik was more blunt. "In the second half, Ron was kicking ass and taking names.... Coach Vermeil called some great plays," he said.

* * *

Sure, Jaworski threw all of those lovely passes. And those backups—Parker, Chesley, Fitzkee, and Giammona—all laughed at the pressure and played well. And Montgomery, his body aching, ran for all of those tough yards. Yet, the reason the Eagles were ready for a run to the Super Bowl was Dick Vermeil. "The Little Dictator" was the motivator who got each of the Eagles to drive himself harder and harder until the other side cracked in defeat.

"I don't know if I should use the word *hate*, but we hated the drudgery and hated how we practiced," admitted tight end John Spagnola. "But we hated it together, and that sort of hatred bonded us. We could all complain and empathize with one another. Now, I think we were all overachievers. They say the whole is greater than the sum of its parts. And I think that was true with Vermeil and this team. He brought out the best in us. He got everybody to do things that they never grasped they were capable of doing as players."

The Eagles disposed of the overrated Minnesota Vikings 31–16 in their first playoff game, atoning for a stinging one-point defeat in 1978. The Eagles defense forced and recovered three fumbles and stole five passes from poor Tommy Kramer in the second half.

Next the Eagles would face one final war with the Cowboys. Vermeil took his team to sunny Tampa, not to warm their bones but to work longer days. After all, December days in the

> *"He created an environment that was very demanding of everybody. Demanding of players. Demanding of the staff, the coaches. But I don't think he demanded more from anybody than of himself."*
>
> JOHN SPAGNOLA

east grow dark around 4:00 PM. And, as Jim Murray said, "Dick tried to invent the 28-hour day, sometimes the 36-hour day, whatever."

The winners would head for Super Bowl XV in New Orleans. The losers would pack their belongings, shake a few hands, and head home.

"Going into the game, you'd have to say that Dallas has proved it's a better football team, based on that Tom Landry is going into his 32nd playoff game," said Vermeil, who was going into his fifth. "They have beaten three straight playoff teams [Oakland, Los Angeles, Philadelphia] and we lost to three playoff teams [San Diego, Atlanta, Dallas] in the last four regular-season games. But that doesn't mean Dallas is going to win the football game."

After returning from a fast-paced week of practice in the Florida sun, the Eagles appeared ready, except for some key injuries. Bergey's shoulders were aching. Montgomery's knee was sore. Smith had fractured his jaw in the final regular-season game. Carmichael, the other receiver, was hampered by a back injury. Yet, all of the playoff teams were feeling the pain. All of them were hoping that the adrenalin, or something else, would alleviate the aches and allow them to "play in pain," as the postseason saying goes. In Vermeil's own words, the Eagles were "beat up, banged up, and shot up."

The NFC Championship Game was played on a true winter day in Philadelphia, where the temperature had plunged to 16 degrees with a wind chill factor of minus 17. Reacting to the conditions, the Eagles became a running machine. Montgomery, ignoring the cold and rock-hard playing surface, kept slipping tackles when he wasn't avoiding them altogether. At the end of the bitter day, he had rushed for 194 yards, almost as much as the Cowboys totaled both rushing and passing (206).

"We found some weaknesses in the Dallas defense which helped us," said Jerry Wampfler, the offensive line coach. "I was up in the press box and Dick kept asking me, 'Where do you want to rush?' I kept calling for the same plays over and over. We ran right at Randy White. The reason for that was that Randy was a great pass rusher and in a pass-rushing mode most of the time."

After Montgomery broke off a 42-yard scoring run in the first quarter, there was trouble for the Cowboys. The Eagles' defensive line came hard after Cowboys quarterback Danny White. On running plays, they gang-tackled Dorsett, the All-Pro running back. Carl Hairston blindsided White in the third quarter, forcing a fumble at the Dallas 11-yard line that led to Franklin's first field goal and a 10–7 edge.

Franklin made another short field goal in the final quarter for a 20–7 lead. At that point, city police, many of them mounted and some of them accompanied by attack dogs, began closing ranks along the Eagles sideline.

The Cowboys had come out running from a variety of sets, using motion and misdirection, hoping to confuse the Eagles defense. The defenders, however, won most of the individual battles, playing as if Vermeil was perched over them, exhorting them with a bullhorn.

White, who was under constant pressure from Hairston and Humphrey, struggled in the bitter cold and tricky stadium winds. He completed only 12 of 31 attempts. Jaworski (9-for-29, 91 yards) struggled, too. But he had Montgomery and, later, Leroy Harris behind him. When it ended, the Eagles had staged a clinic on ball control, piling up 263 yards on 40 rushes for a gaudy 6.6 average.

After it was over, Vermeil began hugging his players. They had been with him through another boiling summer of workouts, the longest and toughest known to perhaps any athlete. They had sweated and winced and cursed and then cursed some more. But they had stayed together for "The Cause"; actually, they had done it for Dick Vermeil, their Little Dictator. And now a teary-eyed Vermeil was hugging Leonard Tose, the owner, and Jim Murray, the general manager. All of those endless nights alongside a film projector, seeking and creating secrets, now seemed worth it.

> *"As athletes, we all want to play well, but we want to achieve things only for ourselves. But with Dick, you went beyond that. You played for 'The Cause.'"*
>
> BILL BERGEY, FORMER EAGLES LINEBACKER

Now the Eagles wouldn't be emptying their lockers, shoving their gear into large plastic bags, and driving home. They were bound for New Orleans and a chance to become champions of the NFL. Philadelphia hadn't celebrated a championship since 1960. That memorable 17–13 win over Vince Lombardi's Green Bay Packers ended with Chuck Bednarik sitting on Jimmy Taylor's stomach as the clock ran out. Only then did Bednarik rise, ending the game that was to be Lombardi's only playoff defeat.

Vermeil was overcome with joy. "I can't even visualize going to the Super Bowl," he said. "I told them it was almost unbelievable that we're going. It would be nice to go down there and win it."

Among the Eagles, there was a good feeling, an optimistic feeling. They had beaten their Super Bowl opponent, the Oakland Raiders, once before. Play the same game, they figured, and they'd be champions.

Chapter 9

Uptight in New Orleans

Let the winter winds howl and the temperature plunge to 16 degrees. Let the news spread that the Eagles were projected to lose $309,291 in 1980. And let the court battles with limited partners persist.

Leonard Tose was putting all that aside; he was going to the Super Bowl as the proud owner of the NFC champion Philadelphia Eagles.

For those lucky fans headed to Super Bowl XV in New Orleans, there would be shrimp remoulade at Brennan's, seafood gumbo at Galatoire's, and hurricanes at Pat O'Brien's. The Tose VIP traveling party would include the city's movers and shakers, stadium and office workers, some friendly police officers, some close friends from Miami Beach and Beverly Hills, Cardinal Krol, and, of course, Tose's gorgeous wife Caroline. "We liked to say we were taking 784 of his closest friends," said general manager Jim Murray, pulling a number out of the air. "It was typical Leonard. Nobody got cut. I mean, that Super Bowl, while it wasn't the tsunami it is today, there were still a billion details. It's good that we had the whole week to prepare."

Watching the game from the luxury of the owner's box would be television celebrity Phyllis George, author James Michener, and comedian Don Rickles, along with Tose and his wife. Now all that was needed to complete the fun-filled week in New Orleans was a Super Bowl win. That would create a verbal explosion in Tose's box, and maybe Cardinal Krol would bless the team for its superb play.

"It's an excellent game plan," quarterback Ron Jaworski had promised. "It's not complicated, either. You'll see some good stuff, some big-play stuff."

Vermeil said he had cut his working hours for Super Bowl week. "Why, I was in bed at 9:30 one night," the coach said. "The next night, it was only midnight. The night before that, I took the coaches to dinner." However, his valet Bow Wow said Vermeil was still going strong into the middle of the night. "He went to 2:00 the other night," Bow Wow said. "And to 3:00, too. But no fives."

> *"I just don't think you can make as good a decision at 3:00 in the morning as you can during the day. But I would never tell him those kinds of things. I'm still his kid brother."*
>
> AL VERMEIL

The Eagles had gotten four of the Raiders' game films. Leaving nothing to chance, Vermeil told Dick Coury, the receivers coach, he wanted three other reels. A few coaching friends obliged the request. "One went way back," said Coury. "Dick wanted to see it. He wanted to see films where somebody scored a lot of points on them, and one film with a team that had a defense similar to the Eagles, like Buffalo."

Super Bowl week produces a lot of feature stories and some off-beat angles, but seldom any hard news. At Super Bowl XV, Vermeil was the media darling. To the delight of countless sportswriters, Vermeil was much more candid than most head coaches. Somebody asked him to comment on a report that Oakland defensive end John Matuszak had been seen in the French Quarter at 3:00 AM, long after curfew. Matuszak, in his own lighthearted defense, said he had appointed himself the team enforcer; he would cruise the danger spots, looking for wayward Raiders, and report back to head coach Tom Flores. "I'm going to see there's no funny business," said the towering, 6'8" lineman. "He was the only guy who was caught on Wednesday, the first night we had curfew," said Flores. "When I brought him in, he told me the only reason he was out was to make sure everybody else was in. I looked at him and tried not to smile."

Vermeil could have treated Matuszak's big night out as a joke. He could have said that he was sure Matuszak hadn't seen any Eagles on Bourbon Street at that hour. However, the coach was too honest to laugh about any rule violation. Instead, Vermeil said he would have sent Matuszak home if he had been caught partying in the middle of the night.

"I think each player has a commitment to himself and his teammates," said Vermeil. "I'm not criticizing Oakland. I just don't think that's my way. Claude Humphrey has a commitment to Charlie Johnson. Ron Jaworski has a commitment to Wilbert Montgomery. And Wilbert Montgomery has a commitment to himself and to me. Something like [the Matuszak incident] is a complete display of a lack of concern for his teammates."

Vermeil said he set an 11:00 PM curfew but no bed check for the Eagles. The team was staying at the aging Airport Hilton. The hotel was located about 25 miles from the French Quarter and directly in line with one of the airport runways. Vermeil fined only two Eagles: linebacker Jerry Robinson, who was late getting to the airport in Philadelphia for the charter flight; and linebacker Bill Bergey, who was late for the Saturday practice. Robinson said his car key "broke off in the ignition."

Meanwhile, Vermeil was working his team harder than most Super Bowl teams work. Louie Giammona said the team had practices that lasted longer than three hours the week before the Eagles left for New Orleans. "Obviously, we were the best team in the league," said Giammona. "We went to Tampa on a Wednesday to practice. On Monday and Tuesday, it was cold as hell in Philadelphia. But Dick was out there coaching a guy named Dunek [tight end Ken Dunek]. He was on injured reserve and wasn't going to play, and we were standing out there, watching Dick coach him."

On one occasion during Super Bowl week, Vermeil took the Eagles

"He called Tom Landry, Chuck Noll, and Don Shula after we won the NFC championship and asked them how to get ready for the Super Bowl. Everybody said to take the first week and do your hard work at home. We did that. But when we got to the second week, we didn't back off."

CARL PETERSON

to another practice site after they had used up their allotted time at an assigned field. So, were the Eagles a tired Super Bowl team?

Stan Walters, the offensive tackle, said that all players feel tired at the end of a long season. "But it's more of an apprehensive thing than anything else," Walters said. "You're saying to yourself, 'I'm tired but I want to be at my best on Sunday, so I have to overcome it.' It gets the adrenalin going. Am I making sense? I don't think anyone in here is tired on game days. Sure, during the week I wake up groggy. But I feel better as the day goes on. I don't think it's physical fatigue. It's pressure."

> *"He was the kind of guy you'd run through a wall for. At the same time, there were times when you'd want to put him through a wall."*
>
> STAN WALTERS

Indeed, the pressure before the Super Bowl shows up in many ways. The palms can get sweaty. The voices can get tight. Worst of all, the mind can play its tricks and some players on an underdog team can start thinking about ways not to lose.

Phil Simms, a star quarterback for the New York Giants, remembers how coach Bill Parcells scripted the early plays for Super Bowl XXI. "The first four or five [were predetermined]," said Simms. "We had never done that. And we practiced those plays day after day." The Giants scored on their first drive against Denver. "Halfway through the drive," said Simms, "I looked around the huddle and every one of the players was on the edge of hyperventilating."

In Super Bowl XVII, Mark May was one of the youngest members of Washington's famous Hogs, a huge line of drive blockers. "We were mostly young guys," recalled May. "We didn't even know about pressure. It was just a fun time. The second year [Super Bowl XVIII], there was the mystique of the Hogs. It was all so different. We were almost paranoid of everything connected to the game."

A young, quick Raiders tackle named Howie Long said the pressure came from off-the-field matters. "It's not the football part," Long said. "The difficult part involves the tickets, the hotels. All kinds of distractions." Long remembered taking a taxi to Super Bowl XVIII with two teammates, Lyle Alzado and Bill Pickel. "We got stuck in traffic," Long said. "Lyle went crazy in the front seat, screaming and yelling. We finally got out and walked a half-mile to the stadium."

Dave Rowe, another Raiders tackle, recalls peeking out of the Rose Bowl tunnel before Super Bowl XI. "You start thinking about the multitude of the crowd, and it can become overwhelming," he said. "It's kind of like driving a race car. If you sat and thought about it, you'd say, 'Damn, we're going 200 miles an hour. We could get killed.'"

At Super Bowl XVI, the NFL's first cold-weather game in Pontiac, Michigan, several Cincinnati players were short of breath after an early jog on the field. A scuffle broke out in the taping line after one player cut in front of another. "The anxiety level was thick enough to cut with a knife," said linebacker Reggie Williams. "Unfortunately, there were no knives in there."

Seeking to cope with the madness at Super Bowl XV, Tose came up with a less-than-brilliant idea. The owner invited comedian Don Rickles into the Eagles locker room, hoping he could loosen up the team.

"Rickles and the jokes?" Jaworski reflected later. "I don't remember one damn joke."

There also had been a sentimental story to energize the Eagles. Vermeil had invited former coach Joe Kuharich to be his guest at the game. Kuharich coached the Eagles from 1964 to 1968, one of the worst periods in their history. When the Eagles plunged to the bottom with a 2–12 record in 1968, fans wore "Impeach Kuharich" buttons

> *"I think that when we got into the Super Bowl, we were tight as banjo strings. I think it was just the enormity of the situation, the pressure of guys wanting to perform at their best."*
>
> JERRY WAMPFLER

and plastered "Joe Must Go" stickers on their car bumpers. "Dick Vermeil really understood the tradition of the Eagles," said Jim Murray. "He wanted the Eagles to know they had a tradition."

Before he left for the Super Bowl, Murray got a call from a woman in Delaware who informed him that Kuharich was at Graduate Hospital and was losing his battle with cancer. When Murray arrived at the hospital, Kuharich was asleep. "I decided to wake him," said Murray. "Then he went into this coach's locker-room speech about how we were going to win the Super Bowl." Murray kissed his old coach on the forehead and left.

Kuharich died January 25, 1981, on the morning of the Super Bowl.

* * *

Joe Kuharich, it turned out, wasn't such a good prophet. The pressure, real or imagined, was a heavy chain that wrapped itself around the Eagles before Super Bowl XV. Neither Vermeil nor his players could shake the uptight feeling that manifested itself during the pregame introductions. As the Eagles starters appeared, they seemed stiff and uneasy, like second-graders posing for their class photo.

Oakland quarterback Jim Plunkett, who had been banged around and sacked eight times by the Eagles two months earlier, was hardly touched this time. The only Eagles sack was harmless; nose tackle Charlie Johnson dropped Plunkett for a one-yard loss midway through the third quarter. By then, Plunkett had thrown three touchdown passes and the Raiders were up 21–3 and in total command.

Jaworski, who had promised to excite Eagles fans with big plays, instead excited only Rod Martin and the Raiders. Martin, who was traded to the San Francisco 49ers during his rookie season and then re-signed by Oakland, stole Jaworski's first pass. That set up a short 30-yard drive, capped by Plunkett's two-yard pass to Cliff Branch, who scored on a little hook route less than five minutes into the game.

Then came the disallowed touchdown that seemed to weaken the Eagles' resolve. Jaworski drove the Eagles to the Raiders' 40-yard line, hitting three straight passes. On third-and-10, he threw an apparent 40-yard scoring pass to backup receiver Rodney Parker. But even as Jaworski began his drop, a flag had been thrown; head linesman Tony Veteri ruled that Carmichael, running in motion to the inside, had turned upfield too soon.

"Sid and I talked to Dick during the week about that play," said receivers coach Dick Coury. "We told Dick that we thought we could isolate Harold with the motion from the slot. Dick didn't like the idea because Charlie Smith had been our motion guy all season. We thought, 'Gosh, a high school kid could go in motion.' Dick was worried about it but he finally bought it." As it turned out, Carmichael didn't get open, and Jaworski unloaded his deep ball off a scramble. "The touchdown to Parker, that would have put us back in the game," said Coury.

Another Oakland touchdown really rocked the Eagles. From the Raiders' 20, Plunkett started to scramble on third down, then pulled up when he saw halfback Kenny King running free up the left sideline after breaking his route. Plunkett, now getting desperate, lofted the ball over defender Herm Edwards and King took it all the way for an 80-yard score, at the time the longest in Super Bowl history.

"We were in a cover-2 deep, with a five-underneath shell," said Edwards. "Cliff Branch ran up the rail and Kenny King swung into the flat." In Edwards' mind, the coverage was perfect. But when Plunkett began to move, Edwards came up to keep him from scrambling for a first down. Branch took safety Brenard Wilson deep and out of the play. "I didn't have anybody behind me," said Edwards. "The pass nicked my fingernails."

Bill Bergey insisted that Plunkett would have been sacked except for an obvious hold that wasn't called. "Carl Hairston had a bead on Plunkett," said Bergey, "and he was just tackled literally right to the ground."

Flores had little doubt that King would score once Plunkett lobbed him the ball. "Jim was looking downfield but ran out of time," the Raiders coach said. "Once Kenny King caught it, the race was over. No one was going to catch Kenny King. He can fly. Now Kenny didn't have the greatest hands in the world, so it was a big catch for him. He took off like a jet with Bobby Chandler right next to him." Chandler screened off defender Randy Logan near the 10-yard line and King coasted into the end zone.

In the space of less than two minutes, the Eagles fell out of a potential 7–7 tie into a 14–0 hole from which they never recovered. Whether it was offense, defense, or special teams, the Eagles showed none of the fire that had driven them past Minnesota and Dallas in the NFC playoffs and into the championship game.

Tony Franklin kicked a 30-yard field goal on the next series. But he had a low 28-yarder blocked just before halftime by the 6'7" Ted Hendricks, whose arms seemed to dangle past his knees.

Plunkett, a plodding pocket passer, completed three straight passes to open the third quarter. A screen to King gained 13 yards and was followed by a 32-yard pass up the left sideline to Chandler. Finally, he threw a 29-yard pass to Branch, who beat rookie Roynell Young near the goal line and spun in for a 21–3 Raiders lead. The Eagles were done.

Bergey sensed it as early as the second quarter. "I can recall in the huddle trying to get everybody fired up," said the veteran linebacker, who played with two aching shoulders and a badly swollen knee. "I'm the elder statesman and nobody looked at me. I mean, everybody's eyes were somewhere else. I just shook my head and told myself, 'Son of a gun, it's just not going to happen today.'"

Bergey's feeling was understandable. All season long, the Eagles defenders had created a union, one looking across the huddle into the eyes of the other. Vermeil had always talked about how each of them had a commitment to the other. And there were those round tables that Vermeil had ordered for training camp, simulating a huddle in the cafeteria.

"We got to the top of the mountain and we didn't get over the peak. Once again, the thing that haunts me the most in hindsight is not winning it for the town."

JIM MURRAY

Now, as the clock continued to tick down, the frustrated Eagles kept getting first downs but no points. Indeed, they gained 19 first downs, matching their total against Dallas in the NFC title game. On this awful day, the offense became a repetitive, frustrating game of gain-and-stall. "We were never able to establish offensive momentum," said Jaworski. "I sensed a lack of emotion during the game and it never seemed to get stronger.

We usually have a strong second half, a snowball emotional effect. But it just didn't swell up in the second half of this game."

Meanwhile, the Raiders kept the pressure on. On defense, they kept sending blitzers, usually safety Mike Davis and linebacker Ted Hendricks. The pressure halted second-half drives at the Raiders' 34- and 42-yard lines and the Eagles' 45. Martin halted two of the drives with interceptions, and Jaworski fumbled away a snap to end another series. On offense, Plunkett followed Flores' orders to "stay aggressive" and threw

> *"We were two evenly matched teams. We missed one play here, one play there, and that was the difference."*
>
> JOHN SPAGNOLA

13 second-half passes, leading to 13 more points and a 27–10 victory.

Jaworski passed for 291 yards, then the second-highest total for a Super Bowl quarterback. Yet, the Raiders kept forcing him out of the pocket and into his weakness—passing while on the move. And there were those three haunting interceptions by Martin, who smartly kept dropping off into the hook zones.

The scoring pass to Kenny King was obviously the biggest play for the Raiders. After that, Vermeil presumably had to junk his game plan, which was to run Montgomery on the corners and mix in Jaworski's play-action passes to Carmichael, tight ends Keith Krepfle and John Spagnola, and young Rodney Parker.

If there was one series that still haunts the Eagles, it came just before halftime. Jaworski twice found Carmichael for gains of 29 and 14 yards, the big receiver's first two substantial catches other than an early screen. A third-and-10 dump pass to Montgomery gained 16 yards and a first down at the Oakland 11.

Jaworski then fired three incompletions, forcing the Eagles to settle for a 28-yard field goal. Franklin's low kick was deflected by Hendricks, and the Eagles came away with nothing. Later, Vermeil's offense put together a 12-play, 88-yard scoring drive and Jaworski piled up some big passing stats. But there was no fire, no "flashing," as Vermeil liked to say, and defeat became a foregone conclusion.

* * *

As night fell on New Orleans, the Eagles silently filed into their dressing room. Not 90 feet away, across a Superdome corridor, the Raiders were whooping it up and tossing their chin straps into the stands high above.

With two minutes to go in the game, Tose had bolted from the owner's box and headed for the loser's locker room. His lower lip was curled, the sure sign of anger. Soon after he arrived, the room was jammed with reporters and television crews. Tose found himself alone, sitting on an uncomfortable chair, while the traffic moved around him.

"It was still a great season," somebody said, trying to be kind.

"I don't think so," said Tose, who looked very tired.

Later, Tose tried to appear optimistic. "I hope there will be another time," he said. "But knowing what you have to go through to get here, it can't be assured. God, didn't Plunkett have a helluva game?"

> *"Mr. Tose was sitting there after the game, and I'll never forget the look on his face.... Just seeing him in the midst of the press and the players, for me personally it was just like an arrow to the heart."*
>
> RANDY LOGAN, FORMER EAGLES SAFETY

Jim Murray drew a boxer's analogy that may have had some truth to it. "We were like a fighter who seems to have it all together in the dressing room and then can't get it going in the ring," the general manager said. "Two weeks ago, I'm thinking that just to beat Dallas and get in the Super Bowl is the most important thing. But then you're here, you get swept up in the hype and exposure and the enormity of the event. Suddenly, you're stunned by how much you want to win."

Vermeil didn't have to search for answers. "Jim Plunkett won some games this season and his confidence level went way up," Vermeil said. "Plus, they were physically a stronger team than us. We just turned the ball over too many times. Statistically, we beat them [in a few categories: first downs, 19–17; passing yards, 291–260; offensive plays, 64–56]. But they have a broken play for a long touchdown, and we have a broken play for a long touchdown, but it gets called back."

According to Vermeil, Carl Hairston was about to sack Plunkett before his scoring pass to Kenny King. "A guy grabs him by the face mask," Vermeil said. "They show it on television five times and no penalty is called."

"We had a great week of practice," said Flores, "and our team was relatively loose, while I thought Dick's team was tighter than hell. He went back to a training camp–type of lockdown and our guys enjoyed themselves. We had a curfew, but our guys were still able to have their own free time."

Flores said the Raiders concentrated on stopping the Eagles' blitz-and-stunt package that had gotten

"They didn't change and we didn't change. There wasn't anything magical about what happened. They just beat the hell out of us."

MARION CAMPBELL, FORMER EAGLES
DEFENSIVE COORDINATOR

to Plunkett in their regular-season matchup. "By the time we got around to the playoffs and the Super Bowl, our offensive line was really playing well," said Flores. "The whole team was. Not flawless, but we were playing like a championship team should. And we worked on that stuff. We worked on everything they did."

Why didn't the Eagles change their defensive strategy? Because the Eagles coaches made a terrible assumption. They believed the same scheme that produced eight sacks in their previous game against Plunkett and the Raiders would work again.

"This is a mistake coaches make, and I've made it before," said Chuck Clausen, the defensive line coach. "So we went into the Super Bowl planning on doing a lot of the same things. We practiced these things, but they weren't as effective as they were the first time."

Clausen said the earlier success against Plunkett left his rushers "maybe a little fat and happy. And at the same time, the Raiders are looking at these films and they're getting mad. I think they came into the ballgame with better concentration and better focus than we had which, under Dick Vermeil, was one of our strengths. As I look back on that game, you know what, we thought it was going to be easy."

If Clausen had to play the game over again, he would have taken a different approach. "I should have said, 'Hey, we had great success with those four or five things they couldn't handle. They'll handle those things now, so we need to do something different," Clausen said. "We didn't. So it was my fault."

"I know we were mentally ready," said Vermeil. "We were very, very tense at the start. But once the hitting begins, you normally relax. Instead, it seemed like their big plays drained us. We weren't even able to do anything to really get ourselves excited. Maybe they were just that much better than we are."

But Harvey Martin, the antagonistic defensive end from Dallas, had raved about the Eagles after the championship game. "It's the best they've ever played against us," Martin had said. And Bob Breunig, the Cowboys' middle linebacker, had offered a similar observation about Wilbert Montgomery. "That's as good as I've seen him run," Breunig said. "They were running draws and tosses and he was just kind of picking his daylight."

The day after the toughest loss of his coaching career, Vermeil was still puzzled. "For the life of me, I can't figure it out," he said. "I guess if I knew how the hell it happened, I'd be the wealthiest psychiatrist in America."

Vermeil said the atmosphere in the halftime locker room had concerned him. "It was an eerie, quiet feeling," he said. "There was that faraway look in a lot of players' eyes. I think that all of a sudden, there was a feeling of shock, a feeling of if we lost, like the year before in Tampa..."

Then, when he had more time to reflect on the game, Vermeil said a lot more. "We lost and I have to take a lot of the responsibility for that," he said. "I made a mistake when I set the goals for the team. Before the season, I told them our goal was to beat Dallas and win the NFC championship. I never talked about winning the Super Bowl. There was a reason for that. We weren't a world championship football team. I know what it takes to be that caliber, and we just didn't have that kind of athlete on the team. When we did beat Dallas for the NFC championship, I let the celebration go on a little too long. It was like we had accomplished our goal, not that we had one more game left. Plus, Oakland was better than us."

When asked whether he had driven his team too hard, Vermeil shot back, "All that stuff [about the Eagles being tired] is bullshit anyway. Writers who write about that kind of thing are not knowledgeable enough to know the details of the game. To me, it's an escape for writers who don't have enough depth. Nothing was written about our work habits when we beat Dallas for the NFC championship. And we worked harder then."

But Louie Giammona disagreed with his uncle and head coach. Giammona, who started four games during the Super Bowl season, said Vermeil was pushing the team too hard at the end of the long season. He remembers talking to his roommate, linebacker John Bunting, about how he felt only hours before the Super Bowl. "I remember saying to him, 'This is the biggest day of my life and I feel like [bleep]. My back is screwed up. My knees are sore.' Dick doesn't want to hear this, but he overworked the [bleep] out of us," Giammona said.

The loss to the Raiders was so heartbreaking that neither Ron Jaworski nor Bill Bergey, the team's offensive and defensive leaders, has ever been able to watch the game tape. Even now, 28 years later, Jaworski admits the loss "absolutely haunts me."

"It was extremely emotional," Jim Murray said. "Leonard had a broken heart. We were the classic overachievers. We were totally prepared for that game but I think we had an emotional letdown. You can do all the psychoanalysis of why we weren't more on top of our game. But if we had to go back and play it over, Dick would have won that game eight out of 10 times. I think his preparation plan in his training manual about beating the Dallas Cowboys was a goal in itself. The Super Bowl then became a 500-pound cherry atop the sundae. I don't know what his mind-set was. I do know, looking back,

> *"One time we practiced at the Saints' facility for about an hour and a half. Then the rain started coming down in buckets. So he pulls everybody off the field and we head for the locker room, figuring that was the end of it. But we bussed down to the Superdome and we practiced for two more hours there."*
>
> CARL PETERSON

that people said we took it too seriously. The Raiders were on Bourbon Street and we were locked up in that bad motel and practicing."

Yet, as the years slip by and other teams play in the world's greatest sporting event, one thing becomes apparent. Over the course of the 1980 season, Vermeil turned in one of the greatest coaching jobs in the history of the NFL, which has had a lot of them.

In a 1983 *Sports Illustrated* article by Gary Smith, Bill Walsh called Vermeil's work "the best coaching job in the NFL in the last seven years. Vermeil beat them with his own guts and a few people who followed him. Players of his that he'd brag to me about, I wasn't that impressed with. He convinced himself and them that they were great. He lived their lives."

> *"I don't think we played our best and that's what hurts. I don't like to lose anytime, but when you don't play well and lose, that's really bad."*
>
> MARION CAMPBELL

But in Philadelphia, the second-guessing continued for months. In the newspapers, on the radio talk shows, and at the office water coolers throughout Center City, fans replayed the highs and lows of Super Bowl XV. They wondered whether Louie Giammona had been right about the Eagles being a tired team. They shook their heads when Jaworski's name came up. And they wondered whether the Eagles would ever get back to the big one, and how long Dick Vermeil could maintain his crazy hours.

As for the Eagles' place in NFL history, Miami coach Don Shula knew all about the dark side of coming up short in the Super Bowl. "The team that loses a Super Bowl gets thrown back on the loser's heap with the other 26 teams," he once said.

There is never any assurance that a first-time entrant like the Eagles would ever make it back. Indeed, 24 years would pass before the Philadelphia Eagles reached another Super Bowl. By then, Dick Vermeil would be 1,042 miles away.

Chapter 10

Burnout

The Eagles suffered the usual hangover from the Super Bowl that always attaches itself to the losing team. Even Dick Vermeil, their unflappable head coach, couldn't seem to shake the feeling that something terrible had happened, something that would linger and fester until the Eagles returned to the Super Bowl and won it.

"We really matured as a football team last year," said Ron Jaworski, trying to find a silver lining amidst the ruins of the Super Bowl defeat. "We really hung in all of those big games we had last season and that will help us. I think it's going to be a great year. I think it's going to be an improved football team. I can sense that already."

The Eagles prepared for the 1981 season with basically the same team that flopped in Super Bowl XV. There were changes coming, of course. There always are in pro football, as one team's marginal player becomes another team's hungry overachiever. Thinking that way, Vermeil brought a cast of 128 players from 81 colleges to his sixth training camp.

Ron Baker, acquired from Baltimore in a minor trade the previous season, would become the new right guard. Free agent Steve Kenney would start at left guard, as Vermeil replaced aging veterans Wade Key and Woody Peoples. Perry Harrington, a second-round pick in the 1980 draft, became the new fullback when Leroy Harris broke his arm in the second preseason game. The retirement of Bill Bergey opened an inside linebacker spot for Al Chesley, an 11th-round pick in the 1978 draft. Vermeil didn't know it at the time, but the '81 draft would provide little help. Top pick Leonard Mitchell flopped as a defensive end and was eventually traded. Second pick Dean Miraldi, a guard, struggled with injuries. Third pick Greg LaFleur, a tight end and a great leaper, jumped only onto the waiver wire. Hubie Oliver, an undersized fullback, was the surprise star, starting 10 games and averaging 4.4 yards per rush.

What the Eagles lacked was the same dimension they lacked in all five of Vermeil's previous seasons: team speed. Montgomery was still a running back with a wiggle and a good burst, but he had been bothered by nagging knee injuries as an undersized back in Vermeil's ball-control offense. Louie Giammona was just a 180-pound spot player. The other backs were plodders. None of Vermeil's receivers were fliers. Thus, opposing pass defenses could single-up against Carmichael, Smith, Parker, and third-down specialist Billy Campfield.

Lacking a true burner, Vermeil turned to veteran coach Ed Hughes for help. Hughes had coached on offense for eight NFL teams, among them the rival Cowboys, where he introduced the shotgun offense to Roger Staubach. Now his new student would be Jaworski. This assumed, of course, that Vermeil would go along with the league trend, which was putting the ball in the air. In 1980, NFL teams averaged 489.6 passes per season. Five years earlier, they had averaged just 383.6 passes.

Early in 1981, Vermeil made a game-by-game study of all of the shotgun teams. Then he put in a call and lured Hughes to join his staff. Vermeil also sent offensive line coach Ken Iman to Buffalo for a crash course on shotgun blocking and the blind snap from center.

Sid Gillman had left Vermeil's staff after the Super Bowl; now far away in La Costa, California, he heard the news and wasn't impressed. "Miami coach Don Shula went undefeated without using it," said Gillman. "Red Hickey used it a little differently with the 49ers. What Red did was use it as a steady diet. He had three or four quarterbacks, but he ruined them. I think Red lost his job because of the shotgun, and he was a helluva coach. It destroyed his quarterbacks and it destroyed him."

Gillman feared that the use of the shotgun would destroy Jaworski, too. "I think Ron Jaworski is the best quarterback in the NFL, and I think the Eagles are the best darn organization in the league," said Gillman, who talked to the quarterback each Wednesday night during the season. "But I would never second-guess Dick Vermeil. He's a winner from top to bottom."

So the Eagles would send out Jaworski, Montgomery, and Carmichael, the familiar faces, as the foundation for Vermeil's run-driven offense, and they would play Marion Campbell's 3-4 defense as they played it the previous season. Vermeil admitted he was edgy and perhaps uncertain about this Eagles team that was almost as slow as it was in 1976 and had not yet developed a rhythmic passing game like San Francisco, Pittsburgh, or San Diego. It would be up to Vermeil to pull his team out of its funk.

"What we don't have is a championship title," said Vermeil on the eve of his sixth season. "What we have is an NFC title. My concern is that we lose the mental edge we had that got us to the NFC title. If we lose that edge, then we can't repeat."

He had bristled at the idea that the Eagles were tired of his driving style. A former player, guard Wade Key, joined the critics during the 1981 season. "They looked tired and lethargic on television," said Key, who had been cut before the Super Bowl season. "They didn't have any edge. That's a tired ball-club." (Vermeil made sure his offensive linemen read Key's remarks.)

As the Eagles prepared for the season opener with the Giants, Vermeil wore the stoic look of a clever boxer at a prefight weigh-in. He had never been a laugher: not in his first year when trainer Otho Davis gave him a harmless methylene pill, which turns a person's urine blue or pink; not when Roman Gabriel formed the "No-Name Football Players," a group of backups that wore bags over their heads with cut-out eye slits during calisthenics; and certainly not when receiver Kenny Payne, the team joker, spiked the ball in practice and called his coach "the little midget," not knowing that Vermeil was nearby.

Vermeil decided to shift into a higher gear, working even longer hours. He wanted the Eagles to renew their all-out effort and focus on one thing: playing smart, winning football. The Eagles had never lost to the Giants, their opening opponent, during the Vermeil era: 10 straight wins by a combined score of 220–100. Yet, if you didn't know it, you would have thought that the Oakland Raiders were coming in for a rematch, waving their Super Bowl rings in Vermeil's face.

Even Ed Hughes, a veteran NFL coach, was amazed by Vermeil's work ethic. "We stopped at a diner one morning, and I asked Dick Coury how long he'd been with the Eagles," Hughes recalled. "He said, 'About six years.' I said, 'God, I don't think I can do this. My body's never felt like this. I've got pains in my body that I've never felt. Working with the Cowboys, we never worked this hard. I don't know if I can take it.' Coury told me they were kind of immune to it."

> *"He wanted the practices to be tense. He wanted them to be pressure-filled. Because his view of the game was that it wouldn't be as tense as preparing for the game was."*
>
> JOHN SPAGNOLA

Vermeil felt sorry for Tose, the disappointed owner. He felt he had let down a city that had embraced him the way they embraced Eagles legends Chuck Bednarik and Steve Van Buren. The media had grown to appreciate Vermeil, who never ducked a question and offered honest answers, meaning more insightful stories. So reporters sometimes worked the "tired team" angle and let it go at that.

In the opener, Campbell's tenacious 3-4 defense held the Giants to 55 yards rushing and got to quarterback Phil Simms six times. After a tight first half, the Eagles scored twice in the second half, and the defense kept up its assault on Simms the rest of the way. The 24–10 win made Vermeil 11-for-11 against the Giants.

The Eagles kept the pressure on opposing quarterbacks, allowing just three touchdown passes in the first six games and winning them all. Montgomery, who muscled up to 198 pounds in the off-season, missed one game with a pulled hamstring. But Giammona filled in nicely, scoring once and catching a 13-yard touchdown pass from Jaworski in a 36–13 rout of the Redskins.

Minnesota quarterback Tommy Kramer, however, knew how to beat the Eagles' pressure defense. A little dump pass here to Joe Senser, his huge tight end, and a little swing pass there to halfback Ted Brown, added up to a 35–23 upset victory for the Vikings. It was shocking, not only because the Eagles had swept the same Vikings last year 42–7 and 31–16, but because Kramer kept beating the Eagles linebackers, the strength of Campbell's defense.

"It was kind of like sandlot football," said cornerback Herm Edwards. "Get in trouble, run around, and throw to somebody who is open. A lot of times he just made some big plays. That little stuff just kept their momentum going. They're the only other team [beside the Eagles] that runs the slot offense. They're patient. If there's a three-yard pass, they'll take it."

With Kramer, it was all about the quick pass, or the quick scramble, or the draw and screen plays, tactics that can frustrate a pass-rushing team like the Eagles. On offense, Jaworski couldn't handle a skidding shotgun snap. Rookie fullback Hubie Oliver fumbled away a trap play. Jaworski also threw two second-half interceptions into traffic.

The Eagles' pass rush only got to Kramer twice. Both times he slipped on the wet grass. Interestingly enough, the Vikings were never called for holding on any of Kramer's 46 passes. "I'm not going to say anything about that," said Claude Humphrey, whose hard-fought battle with tackle Ron Yary was a classic. "[Vikings coach] Bud Grant got on [the NFL office] last week about officiating. That may have had something to do with it."

Vermeil acknowledged that Kramer was the big difference. "He's good," Vermeil said. "We knew he would be a pain in the ass. We didn't get enough heat on him."

Philadelphia moved on, and Ed Hughes' shotgun scheme helped the Eagles roll to two lopsided wins in November: 52–10 over the struggling Cardinals in subfreezing weather, and 38–13 over the hapless Baltimore Colts, coached by former Eagle Mike McCormack. Jaworski threw for 529 yards and six touchdown passes in the back-to-back wins that gave the Eagles (9–2) a one-game lead over the hated Cowboys (8–3) in the highly competitive NFC East.

From there, however, the Eagles and their offense lost their way and relinquished the division crown to Dallas, meaning the Eagles would have to claw their way back to the Super Bowl as a wild-card. That's the difficult path the

Raiders had taken the previous year, with road games all the way. What worried Vermeil was his team's late-season swoon: four straight defeats (Giants, Dolphins, Redskins, Cowboys) in which the shotgun-infused offense scored only 43 points. Carmichael didn't score at all during the four-game plunge. Montgomery scored once, on a one-yard pop against Miami. Moreover, the old theme of dominating the second half that Vermeil always preached never happened. The Eagles were outscored 43–3 in the second half of the four losses. Except for Tony Franklin's 42-yard field goal against the Dolphins, the Eagles didn't score a single second-half point in the four-game slide.

"We've played very hard, very intensely," said Vermeil. "But we have no momentum. We're just not winning. The big thing for us is to get ready to play a great football game and let the chips fall where they may."

Montgomery, the thoughtful running back, felt the Eagles' confidence had been shaken. "But all that could change with one game," Montgomery said. "Those last three losses have just been uncalled for. We've beaten ourselves more than the other teams have beaten us."

* * *

The Eagles did rebound to finish the regular season with a 38–0 thrashing of the last-place Cardinals and rookie quarterback Neil Lomax, but Vermeil felt and looked weary. Truthful to himself, he knew how difficult the wild-card road to another Super Bowl would be. Oakland had just squeezed in the year before, upsetting Cleveland 14–12 on safety Mike Davis' dramatic end-zone interception in the final minute, then stunning San Diego 34–27 on Plunkett's 14-for-18, 261-yard game.

The Eagles simply didn't have enough big-game players—those quick, strong, athletic superstars who can break open a game with their innate skills. Vermeil's team could advance, but only if it played flawless football. No interceptions, no fumbles, no crucial penalties, new rhythm from Jaworski's offense, and turnovers and sacks from Campbell's defense.

The Giants, their unlikely wild-card opponent, were a rebuilding team, with a young rookie linebacker named Lawrence Taylor, but not much offensive firepower. Phil Simms was their quarterback of the future, but he was injured, forcing the Giants to start Scott Brunner, his 24-year-old backup. Brunner, who had played sparingly, was a lowly 41.6-percent passer during the season. Vermeil, looking at Brunner's game films, should have been smiling. He knew the Giants would come out running and try to win a field-position game. They had one of the league's best punters in Dave Jennings, and Joe Danelo, their veteran kicker, was sure from inside 40 yards.

Yet, despite the apparent edge, as well as the home-field advantage, Vermeil wasn't comfortable about the game. He always worried about losing, wondering if he had put in enough hours to sharpen his team. "I'm scared to death of not doing a good enough job," he used to say. "The thought just scares the hell out of me. I always feel I haven't done enough, that there's something I might have missed, that I haven't done the best that I could do."

At times, Vermeil's long nights and the many hours he was away from Carol and their three children made him feel guilty. Carol often admitted to being lonely and restless, but she endured his absence, focusing on the love they shared and the good life that football had provided.

"We're both hicks, small-town people," she said. "It would be easy to be resentful. But if you're going to be married to somebody like him, there can't be any power struggle, that's for sure. I know I sound wishy-washy, but I'm no doormat. I just don't like any unpleasantness."

A few years before, Carol and Jim Murray had suggested that Vermeil visit a psychiatrist. After the session, Vermeil returned home. The look on his face was stern.

"Well?" said Carol.

Vermeil shook his head. "It would take me a week to straighten the guy out," he said.

Carol had been calling Mike White, an old coaching friend, about her husband's mental health. White told her that Dick was a unique individual who was obsessed with coaching his team. "He gets close to his players and he regales them," White said. "He genuinely loves those players and he wins them over. His loyalty is impeccable. Most of the coaches you thought were great were intimidating and loud, and just tried to intimidate you and control you. Dick is totally from an opposite direction." White sympathized with Carol, but told her there was nothing he could do to change her husband's habits.

Vermeil had never really gotten over the Super Bowl loss to the Raiders. And now he was going to send out another Eagles team to face a crippled opponent whose starting quarterback, Phil Simms, had been injured. The Giants hadn't been in a playoff game since 1963, back in the days of Y.A. Tittle and Sam Huff.

Before the game, the talk on the street was about more than just how the Giants and Eagles matched up. According to some reports, the Eagles had thrown a drug party on the eve of the game in South Jersey, where the team stayed for home games.

> *"He creates a family atmosphere. He just has that energy, that sincerity, and it's worked every place he's ever been."*
>
> MIKE WHITE

"I had heard the rumors, I'll be honest with you," said safety John Sciarra. "You hear certain things, but when it goes down that path, you know nothing good is going to come out from continuing down that path. I did not hear them until sometime after the game. I said to myself, 'You know what, I don't even want to know about that stuff.' I never saw it happen, so it's best not to give it any legitimacy."

The game did little to erase the drug story. The Eagles staggered through a first quarter in which they dug themselves a huge hole. The Giants jumped on two disastrous fumbles by Wally Henry and rushed out to a 20–0 lead before Jaworski got to throw his first pass.

Henry, a sure-handed returner who had lost only four fumbles in three seasons, fumbled Dave Jennings' first punt with Lawrence Taylor in his face. Later in the quarter, Henry muffed a kickoff in the deep left corner, slipped trying to beat Mike Dennis to the ball, and finally lost it. "The first one, they didn't give me enough room," said Henry. "I don't know the yardage, but they're supposed to give me enough room to catch. On the kickoff, they kicked the ball into the corner, and that's a 'me-and-you' call. I called 'You…you… you.' Booker [Russell] looked like he had a lot of indecision, so I ran over and I slipped. By that time, the ball had slid on out."

The Giants turned those two gaffes into touchdowns. They also scored on a 62-yard drive that showcased Rob Carpenter's versatility. Carpenter banged for some tough yards from the Giants' one-back set, punishing the Eagles linebackers with his cutbacks. Carpenter also caught two passes as the Giants opened a 20-point first-quarter lead against the fumbling, bumbling Eagles.

"He's got big legs and he's a good, strong back," said nose tackle Charlie Johnson of Carpenter, who finished with 161 yards on 33 carries, still club postseason records for yards and rushing attempts. "You can't arm tackle him. You've got to really hit him."

The Eagles rallied in the second half, closing the gap to 27–21 as Jaworski threw 11 passes on a late 80-yard drive. Ron Smith, a former San Diego Charger, was involved in five of them; Smith caught three straight passes and drew penalties on two others.

With 2:51 left to play, the Giants deployed nine defenders within 15 yards of the ball, expecting an onside kick. Instead, Vermeil put his faith in the battered defense, ordering Tony Franklin to kick away. That was the last the Eagles saw of the ball. Carpenter gave the Giants breathing room with four straight carries, the last a demoralizing 14-yarder inside left end. The game ended seconds later with Brunner flopping on the ball as time ran out. There would be no repeat of the Miracle at the Meadowlands.

"What happened was that they got 13 points without us taking the field," cornerback Herm Edwards said. "But I'm not going to let a loss affect my life, or throw myself out the window."

Frank LeMaster, the underrated inside linebacker, was shaken by the unexpected playoff loss. This wasn't Hall of Famers Y.A. Tittle and Frank Gifford. This was Scott Brunner and Rob Carpenter, an undistinguished backup quarterback and a journeyman runner. "This loss is the most disappointing and frustrating I've ever had," LeMaster said in the loser's silent dressing room. "Mainly it's because my expectations were higher. We've got too much talent here. The higher your expectations are, the more frustration there is. I wish I had the answers."

Vermeil's game plan had been simple enough. On defense, he wanted to gang-tackle Carpenter and force Brunner to throw before his receivers made their breaks. On offense, he wanted to control the ball with a unique three-back, power I formation and just enough passing to keep the tough Giants defense (third-best in the league) honest.

It all sounded good, but on this dreary afternoon at the Vet, the Giants kicked the aging Eagles and Vermeil's game plan around for a stunning upset. "A shock they did that much in such a short time," said Carl Hairston.

But this was no regular-season game and this was not an ordinary upset, the kind that happens even to the good teams during the course of a normal season. This was a whipping by a much younger team on the rise behind a quarterback who would be out of the league in a few more years. In their run-to-daylight offense (75-25 run-pass ratio), the Giants exposed the Eagles as an older, worn-down team. "We looked like we were in the playoffs for the first time in 19 years and not them," said Jaworski.

"I believe we get out of our current players pretty much what they have to give," a depressed Vermeil said several days after the game. "If we're going to be able to win games when we fumble punts and kickoffs for touchdowns, then we have to get better people. Teams that are so-called explosive teams have explosive people. We have to find some of them. We have to have more people on the field like Wilbert Montgomery."

Normally, the head coach would give this type of assessment to his staff behind closed doors. But Vermeil was no normal coach. His workaholic father, Louie Vermeil, had told him to always tell the truth and not give any story a spin. Some assistants may have suspected what Vermeil was saying, but it was rare for any of them to offer any suggestions. As Carol Vermeil said, "He's simply not open to suggestions."

Vermeil talked about Wally Henry, his star returner/receiver at UCLA and the Eagles' return specialist, who botched those two kicks and left the field crying. "It was his intent to try to win a game for us and come up with big plays," said Vermeil. "What am I going to do, call him a stupid SOB and kick him?"

And then the reports of a pregame drug party surfaced again. The stories were vague and largely unsourced. According to word-of-mouth accounts, the party took place in Cherry Hill, New Jersey, where the Eagles spent Saturday nights before home games.

Vermeil heard the stories and tried to address them. "I related to these guys as 'my guys,'" Vermeil said. "I was naive enough to think that my guys wouldn't get involved in anything like that. It was the week after Christmas. To do so, they would have had to sneak out of their rooms at our hotel in South Jersey. If somebody sneaks out, he sneaks out. Our policy was that if they get caught sneaking out, they're fired, no matter what they did. Nobody was caught sneaking out that night."

Less than six years later, Vermeil received a call from John Spagnola, who went on to develop into a big-play tight end, catching 129 passes in 1984–85. He had given a speech at the Philadelphia Psychiatric Center in April 1987 in which he mentioned the drug party.

Vermeil recoiled at Spagnola's insinuations. "I told him you never have to apologize for telling the truth," the coach said. "If someone is involved and disturbed by it now, he shouldn't have done it in the first place. We did get rid of a few people, not a lot, but a few. These guys became professional liars. That was one of my faults at the time. I'd just say it wasn't true. It couldn't be true. These guys wouldn't do that. I know now, damn well they would."

Now, more than 20 years later, Spagnola says his remarks were taken out of context. "I think that was a mistake on my part to bring that up," Spagnola said. "There has never been anything proven about that. It was all hearsay. I kind of used it as an example of how pervasive it got to be [around the league]. Quite honestly, it's all rumor and innuendo. I didn't have any facts. And I've never tried to substantiate it. There was never anything substantial. It was unfair to the players who were involved in that game."

Nobody can doubt, however, that the Eagles played as if they had been out all night. The result was a blow to Vermeil's coaching style, his system, and his tight relationship with his overworked players.

Kicker Tony Franklin was clearly worried about his coach. "Dick can get us relaxed and motivate us," said Franklin. "The one thing he can't do is relax himself. If you could ever get him to relax over a cold beer, he can be a very funny guy. But that just doesn't happen very often. He is so obsessed with winning. That's great, but sometimes you worry about him."

There were others worrying about Vermeil. One of them was Mike White, his old friend and confidante. White worried that the recent defeats were causing Vermeil to feel depressed. "It was so tough on him," said White. "It was the total consumption that the game had for him. Sleeping in the office, there was no moderation because he couldn't do it any other way. He's not a 'poor me' kind of guy, and I could feel his emotions in our phone conversations. It was wearing on him. Carol would call, asking if I could 'pump him up.'"

White said Vermeil always felt responsible for the losses. "The losses just kill you and the wins don't last but five minutes," said White. "Pretty soon, you're almost like a merry-go-round. You can't get off. I guess we've all heard some of the distractions and the emotions. The insecurity and the low self-esteem. These are things that happen and the toughest person on you is you. And we all go through it at certain times."

"I don't think he'll ever agree that he was burned out. But he knew he was burning it at both ends."

CARL PETERSON

Time was not the only thing that made Vermeil seem older after the 1981 season. In January 1982, another driver slammed into Carol's car on the driver's side. The collision fractured her right elbow and pelvic bone. Shards of glass hit her forehead, barely missing her left eye.

"They say she could easily have been killed," said Lynn Stiles, an old family friend and Vermeil's administrative assistant. "You could see the effect on Dick. For the first time, it really hit him: how important is anything compared to life?"

Two other unexpected events happened that left Vermeil perplexed and eventually close to a mental breakdown. Three months after the car accident, the Vermeils went sailing in the Caribbean, a vacation they had planned for years but had never gotten around to taking. They were relaxed, enjoying the beauty of the rolling sea. For once, Dick had left behind his yellow legal pad and his tape recorder. But one morning they awoke feeling groggy. They shrugged off their condition and assumed it was just seasickness. Instead, it was hepatitis, a serious disease marked by inflammation of the liver.

"When his wife had that accident, I think that got Dick thinking that, hey, I'm really putting my wife through hell. I used to call her Saint Carol."

BILL MCPHERSON, FORMER EAGLES
LINEBACKER COACH

When they returned, Vermeil was told to stay off his feet for a month. But the 1982 draft was approaching, and Vermeil felt compelled to be present in the Eagles war room. His previous drafts, at least two of them bankrupted by trades made before he arrived in Philadelphia, had produced only seven starters. Four of those—Hairston, Montgomery, Johnson, and Chesley—had been picked in the lower rounds. Vermeil knew he needed more playmakers who could turn a game around with their natural athletic skills. Maybe a Lawrence Taylor. Maybe an Anthony Munoz. Maybe…

Reacting to the pressure of the moment, Vermeil slipped out of bed in his suburban Bryn Mawr home and headed for Veterans Stadium. He was greeted by his nine assistants and a small army of scouts and personnel reps, each of whom was wearing a surgical mask. Vermeil didn't think it was funny.

Several months later, Vermeil still wasn't in the mood for laughing—after another of his demanding camps, he sensed that only one of his picks, receiver Mike Quick, would help his team. Quick, a former hurdler, was a long-strider with sure hands. The Eagles had planned to draft Perry Tuttle, a smaller, quicker receiver, with the No. 20 pick. Then Buffalo coach Chuck Knox ambushed Vermeil. Holding the 21st pick, Knox flip-flopped with Denver, which owned the 19th choice, and took Tuttle. "Hey, Dick," said personnel director Carl Peterson, "see what your old friend, Chuck Knox, did to you?"

In the end, Vermeil and the Eagles won this last-minute shuffle game. Quick played nine years with the Eagles, catching 363 passes, 61 of them for touchdowns. His per-catch average was a remarkable 17.8 yards. From 1983 to 1986, he scored 42 times, or four out of every 10 touchdowns scored by the Eagles. Meanwhile, Tuttle was plagued by injuries, playing with Buffalo, Atlanta, and Tampa Bay. He caught only 25 passes in his career.

* * *

As it turned out, not even the greatest receivers caught many passes in 1982. On September 20, the executive committee of the NFL Players Association voted unanimously to shut down the season after only two weeks. Gene Upshaw, the outspoken union president who announced the strike, blamed the owners' Management Council for refusing to engage in meaningful bargaining.

"We have been left with no choice but to use our only weapon that we have left to force management to the bargaining table," said a somber-faced Upshaw. "All of the NFL training facilities will be shut down. There will be no practices, no workouts, and no training. No games will be played until we receive a fair, equitable contract."

The previous February, NFLPA executive director Ed Garvey had said the players wanted 55 percent of the owners' gross revenues to be paid into a central salary fund. They also wanted to establish a seniority-based wage scale. Jack Donlan, the owners' chief negotiator, said the clubs would never approve a revenue-sharing proposal; it would become the topic of bitter debate for several months.

As the weeks slipped by, the two sides dug in for a long fight. The league issued a gag order to its owners, yet Leonard Tose decided to speak out. He had negotiated many union contracts for his trucking company and felt he could sense the mood of negotiations. "In my opinion, now I will get fined, but screw it, I don't think there can be any compromise on the percentage they want," Tose said. "If you want to be my partner, put up some money."

Vermeil, seeking to hold his team together, said the players had a right to strike. "Since I've been here, newspaper people have gone on strike, school teachers have gone on strike, and hospital help has gone on strike," Vermeil said. "Why should a football player be any different?" Of course, journalists, teachers, and nurses don't have fast-talking agents to represent them in salary negotiations.

Pressed on the money issues, Vermeil said he thought the players deserved better pay. "I'm not sure they're getting the best leadership from Garvey, but I don't know Garvey," he said. "I'd like to see the players get more. I'm not against that."

Not unexpectedly, Vermeil started preparing game plans on a weekly basis, hoping for a fast settlement. Early each week, a copy of the plan was taken to the Hilton Hotel near the stadium by Chuck Clausen, the defensive line coach. He passed it on to one of the veterans, who had copies made for the rest of the team.

"They weren't supposed to be seen with us," said Clausen, "and we weren't supposed to be seen with them. And yet, both the players and coaches had a vested interest if we were going to come in suddenly and perform. I think we all hoped it would soon be settled."

The clandestine practice was halted when Tose closed the team's facilities. "If you don't have the players, what's the point in preparing?" said Tose. "We're closing this place down. The coaches are going out, too. I asked them to get out, go home, and visit with their wives. There's a possibility there won't even be a football season."

Vermeil argued with his owner. "We can break down film," he told Tose.

"Film of who?" Tose shot back. "How do you know which team we're going to play next?"

"Well," said Vermeil, "we can go back over our own films and make corrections."

"Dick, you've already gone over our own films 100 times," said Tose. "Why don't you just let the coaches go? If anything is settled, you can have them back here in an hour or two."

Vermeil, frustrated but unable to do anything about the silent season, returned to his Bryn Mawr home to be with Carol. Meanwhile, his players began spreading across the country. Backup quarterback—and aspiring actor— Dan Pastorini headed for New York to reshoot some scenes for a movie. Kenny Clarke, the nose tackle, said he planned to look for a job. Herm Edwards, the cornerback, said he would play some golf and rest his injured knee. Kicker Tony Franklin planned to return to San Antonio to be with his wife and newborn son. Safety John Sciarra said he might return to California, where he had an investment business.

"The owners are holding a very good hand right now," said Sciarra. "But if the players want to, they could hold a better hand. It's just a matter of going the distance."

The NFLPA's rank-and-file, more than 1,400 members strong, held together through September and October. When November came, each side started counting the weeks. The owners knew they would have to settle by late November in order to salvage a nine-game season. Anything less than that would be rejected by almost everyone, especially the television networks.

"They've got to settle it this week," said one CBS news correspondent in mid-November. "It's sweeps month in February, and my network has this blockbuster series coming up, *The Winds of War*."

John Bunting, the Eagles' hawkish player rep, also saw the urgency involved in reaching a settlement. Bunting promised that "blood will flow in the streets" if the players' demands weren't met.

Bunting was Vermeil's kind of player. An undersized, 205-pound linebacker, he wasn't taken by the Eagles until the 10th round of the 1972 draft. He arrived in camp driving a 1965 Volkswagen with 175,000 miles on the odometer. There were dents on all four of the fenders. Even Louie Vermeil would have had a difficult time restoring this $100 Bug to its original shape in his Owl Garage.

Philadelphia was a strong union city, and the striking players received enormous support from the locals. In late October, with the stadium facilities shut down and the coaches and players dispersed to various parts of the country, Leonard Tose had had enough. "Forget the season is what I say," snapped Tose, that lower lip curled in a sign of disgust. "If they are staying where they are [on issues], forget the season. I don't say it with any delight. I know the fans are upset, and I'm sorry."

At one negotiating session, the two sides looked across the table at one another for an entire hour without talking. Several weeks later, Garvey and

Vince Lombardi Jr., a Management Council assistant, began screaming at each other. Upshaw, a former All-Pro lineman, leaped to his feet, stared at Lombardi, and snapped, "Hey Vince, if you're looking for some action, here it is." Garvey laughed. "If Lombardi ever hit Upshaw," Garvey said, "and Upshaw found out about it, Vince would be in trouble."

The strike turned out to be a blessing for Mike Dougherty, the Eagles' film director. Dougherty was used to editing film until 2:00 AM, which limited his social life. "The strike came and we weren't playing all of those different weeks," said Dougherty, who was dating a special girl. "Marge and I actually started going out a lot. That's when we got engaged and eventually married in 1984. So it worked out pretty good that way."

"The Vermeil years were crazy years," said Marge Dougherty. "Dick was almost like his father. He loved Mike so much. Mike worked these crazy times. The only reason we got to know each other was the strike year, the '82 season."

Finally, just when the sniping sides appeared ready to take Tose's advice to call off the season, the owners acquiesced on several of the sticking points in the players' long list of demands. On November 17, a date nearing the unspoken deadline to salvage the season, the two sides reached a historic settlement after marathon talks in New York City. As the news spread, weary reporters scrambled to phone their sports desks. Cab drivers honked their horns. And Ed Garvey, the players' labor leader, strode past the bright lights and into the players' hotel on Lexington Avenue, feeling like a winner. The players got a minimum salary scale, increased medical insurance and retirement benefits, and a severance pay system. Each veteran would also receive a $60,000 bonus known as "money now." The four-year agreement was worth $1.6 billion. Garvey, however, abandoned his idea of a salary schedule involving 55 percent of the league's gross revenues.

* * *

While the players and owners argued, Vermeil and his wife had finally begun enjoying the idle time away from the pressures of the game. He had purchased a cabin in upstate Pennsylvania. There in the countryside, surrounded by scenic mountains, they could relax and share Vermeil's idea of a perfect evening: glasses of red Napa Valley wine, mood songs by Neil Diamond, and a good steak dinner.

Driving to the cabin, Vermeil was surprised by the beauty of the daffodils, crocuses, and roses, all in dazzling yellow, red, and pink. He and Carol were older now, but they were reaching back, trying to recapture their younger years of marriage spent in the little town of Calistoga. And then the feeling of being away from the cauldron of pro football suddenly ended. The two-month strike was over, and Vermeil headed back to his job and his players.

Vermeil knew it would be difficult to recapture the bond that had existed between him and his team. To his dismay, the strike had divided the Eagles into hawks and doves, along with some players disinterested in what Ed Garvey and Gene Upshaw had achieved.

"I don't think the strike divided us as a team," said Stan Walters, "but I think we were pretty much forced to support the union. We might have had a few players wondering about what was happening, but John Bunting did a good job as the union organizer."

Walters said he thought the strike separated Vermeil from his team. "I definitely think the strike affected him only because he lived and breathed football," he said. "Here it was taken completely out of his hands. And he probably saw his football team drifting away. Maybe not fragmented, but it divided Dick from the team and Dick from the players and Dick from Leonard Tose. He was just in the middle, wondering what the hell was happening."

Even earlier, Frank LeMaster had polled the players on how they were feeling. Their answers indicated that most of them felt mentally and physically burned out by Vermeil's long workouts and frequent "hot thud tempo" sessions, Vermeil's term for full contact. Vermeil shot back a letter in his neat, distinctive handwriting, stating that LeMaster only "thought he was tired."

The abbreviated strike season was a disaster. The Eagles allowed the Redskins to tie and then win the opener 37–34 in overtime on two field goals by Mark Moseley. The defense gave up 373 passing yards and 487 total yards in the wild shootout. After edging Cleveland 24–21 with a spectacular 21-point rally in the fourth quarter, the Eagles' offense vanished. Jaworski, who had two 300-yard games to start the season, threw six interceptions in the next two games, both losses.

In the first game after the season resumed, Cincinnati coasted to a 18–14 win after leading 18–0, as the Eagles fans began chanting, "Strike!…Strike!… Strike!" It got worse the following week. Jaworski fired four interceptions in a 13–9 loss to the Redskins. And when the Eagles lost their third game in a row, a 23–20 setback to St. Louis, the fans let Vermeil, Jaworski, and just about every other Eagle have it.

The boo-birds, it seems, weren't alone. Tose bolted to the locker room after the game and ripped into his team.

"I think the strike is still on your minds," said an angry Tose. "And if it is, then you guys should all vote to go back on strike."

Vermeil, now cast in the role of peacemaker, led Tose away from the players.

"Leonard, this isn't the time or the place for this," Vermeil said. "You shouldn't be in here saying things like that." Later, however, he defended his owner.

"Many times you guys have been emotionally upset and disturbed," Vermeil told his squad. "If you had as much invested as he has, from time to time you'd get upset, too. We certainly didn't do anything to excite anybody."

Tose said that Bunting, the player rep, had misled the players. Bunting, however, said that using the strike as an excuse was "very illogical." According to Bunting, the team had lost its confidence and the defense had made "a bad habit of getting off to poor starts."

The Eagles lost two of their last four games to finish with a 3–6 record, tied for 11th in the NFC standings. When the bizarre season was finally over, the Eagles were a demoralized team, and their fiery coach was a man headed for a mental breakdown. Tose, the demanding owner, had expected much more from the Eagles.

There was also growing tension between Tose and Vermeil, emanating from the bitter strike. Murray, the general manager, revealed that he often had to act as a peacemaker when Tose exploded after losing games, his lip curling and his voice rising. "He was respectful of Dick," Murray said. "He would vent on other people, whether it was a bartender, or Jim Murray, or my neighbors."

But now the Eagles organization faced a troubled future. The team had lost $1.4 million in 1982. Vermeil was worn down. He was so tired of the game and the weeklong pressure that on at least two occasions, he was unable to get out of his car after arriving at the stadium. It happened the second time on a Saturday, the day his daughter Nancy was graduating from Penn State. Vermeil, teary-eyed and confused, watched as his players boarded the team buses for the ride to Washington. He finally dragged himself from his car and joined them.

"I know I'm too emotional, too intense," Vermeil said. "But I've just got to be me. It isn't only this season. I've had this feeling coming over me. I'm not doing a good job of handling the deep pressure from inside. I handle losing poorly. I think it's an accumulation of being a head coach the last nine years. Two at UCLA, seven with the Eagles, and 23 years of living with Dick Vermeil."

Vermeil was burned out after only seven seasons in the NFL pressure-cooker. Don Shula had coached for 33 years, Tom Landry for 29, Chuck Noll for 23. Even Bill Parcells, the nomad of coaches, had put in 19 years. Other coaches had warned Vermeil about the need to delegate more responsibility to his assistants, but Vermeil never listened. And now he was burned out, unable to leave his car and sometimes too depressed to address his players. After only seven seasons, four of them winning seasons and one of them a Super Bowl season, Vermeil was about to walk away from his passion.

Chapter 11

"We're Getting Out"

The Eagles' loss to the Giants on a last-second field goal in their final game of the 1982 season left Dick Vermeil wrestling with his thoughts about whether he had a future in this crazy game. More importantly, Vermeil had finally become concerned about his own health and well-being.

Fellow coaches and old friends had been constantly warning him about his work schedule. Vermeil, however, had ignored their advice, plunging ahead with his 18-hour days and full-scale scrimmages during the season.

One of his closest friends was John Ralston, who had given Vermeil his first major college job in 1965 at Stanford. Ralston also spent the 1978 season helping Vermeil's offense.

"Oh, gosh, we had a couple of good players and we picked up a couple along the way," said Ralston. "And you worked like a dog. Gosh, he almost killed himself. He'd go all night long. Sometimes we'd be meeting at 1:00 or 2:00 AM and he'd say to the staff, 'I'll finish this up, you guys get some sleep.'"

As that season unfolded, Ralston felt that Vermeil came close to having a total collapse. "He almost had a nervous breakdown, just from overworking," Ralston recalled. "He would stay at it until 4:00 in the morning and then get up and try to face the team at 7:00 or 8:30 in the morning. Geez, he was going to have to cut that out or he was going to kill himself."

Now Vermeil's seventh season was over. He had suffered from neck pains and mental fatigue. "Criminy, it used to feel like the whole back of my neck was one big cramp of tension," he once said. And that Super Bowl game, the one that was followed by all those stories about the Eagles losing because Vermeil overworked them, still dwelled heavily on his mind. Just like Carol's scary car accident. Just like the sight of his players discussing the terms of their new labor agreement rather than talking football.

Ron Jaworski said the players sensed that Vermeil was burned out long before his final season. "After the players' strike in '82, when we came back we weren't the same football team and he was not the same guy," Jaworski said. "We were a team based on hard work, discipline, repetition, and preparation. When we came back after the 57-day strike, it was just a mess. Coach tried to get us going, but he couldn't get us going. That season was gone. It was gone. And I think it grated on him, wore him down."

During the last few weeks, Vermeil became even more emotional. He began losing control of his players and therefore the execution of his game plans. The final loss to the Giants left Vermeil and the Eagles with a 3–6 record. Vermeil was crushed. "We still loved him because of his emotion," said Jaworski. "But that's when we got a little bit concerned for him."

Vermeil spent the next week wondering if he should walk away from the demons and the pressure that had left him lonely and depressed. He discussed his future with Carol, who had seen how the game had overpowered her husband.

"We all know better than anybody the toll that football has taken on Dick," said Carol. "I want to see him in tune with something other than football."

Carol was fearful that her husband was headed for a total breakdown if he remained in the game. Dick finally began listening. Carol opened a book titled *Burn Out* that had been given to her husband by Monsignor George Sharkey, the team chaplain. "He needed a push, so I gave it to him," Carol would later say. "He knew what he should do, but he didn't want to do it. He was emotionally drained. The strike made him realize that life did go on, even on fall days when there was no football."

Vermeil listened intently, as if he was young again, attending one of John Ralston's morning lectures. He remembered the advice given to him long ago by his father: always tell the truth and never use an excuse. Dick still couldn't make up his mind. So Carol called an audible for him. "I've already made the decision," she said. "We're getting out." Only then did Dick finally summon the nerve to utter the words that Carol wanted to hear.

"Okay, I'm getting out," Vermeil told her. Later, Vermeil would admit that Carol "put the cap on the bottle when I was struggling to make my decision."

When the word reached Leonard Tose and Jim Murray at the end of the week, they quickly arranged to meet with Vermeil at the owner's $800,000 mansion in suburban Villanova. Tose tried to persuade Vermeil to stay, suggesting that he delegate more authority to his assistants. Vermeil, however, had made up his mind. No million-dollar bonus. No two-week vacation in Acapulco. No piece of the club. Nothing could have changed his mind.

"That was a moment that changed everybody's life," said Murray. "Dick Vermeil's life. Mine. Leonard Tose's life. But I respect Dick Vermeil, who was not afraid to resign. I think the intensity of Dick Vermeil is something that makes Carol the unsung hero in this."

On January 10, 1983, the Eagles held a joint press conference. "I am emotionally burned out," Vermeil said. "Therefore, I feel I need a break from coaching. Not a sabbatical; a break. I think it's in the best interests of my family, the Eagles organization, and the players that someone else assume my responsibility. As I said to myself 23 years ago, if I ever questioned whether I wanted to coach again, or get out, I would get out. I've made a lot of mistakes. Probably the most vivid mistake is that I probably set a tempo for 23 years that it may not be possible to keep through a 10-year pro contract. That's why I'm saying I'm just burned out."

Vermeil mentioned that he had read Monsignor Sharkey's book, but couldn't understand it. "I thought they were wrong," he said, "but no, they were right. I have too much pride to pick up a paycheck and go home. And I hope very much that my players can understand where I'm coming from."

Then Vermeil began crying, overcome by the emotions of the day. "I love these guys," he sobbed, glancing at the players who were in the room. "I love all the people in the Eagles organization."

In his opening remarks to announce the news, Tose appeared to have pulled out an old press release from the files. When he announced Vermeil's hiring in 1976, Tose had called it "a happy day for me personally and for the entire Eagles organization." To announce Vermeil's sudden departure, Tose said it was a "sad day for me personally and for the entire Eagles organization."

> *"I had mixed emotions about the position I was in. I knew one thing for sure: I was a much better coach for having been around Coach Vermeil those last few years."*
>
> MARION CAMPBELL

Tose said a lot more. "I feel happiness for Dick's welfare," the owner said. "Dick came to my house last night at 8:00 with Carol. I asked him if there was anything the Eagles organization could do, without putting any pressure on him and influencing his decision. I wanted him to stay. But I also didn't want to put the burden on him by pressing the issue. They convinced me, Carol and Dick, that this was the right thing for him. And the right thing for him is the right thing for the organization."

The owner said that Vermeil "revolutionized football in Philadelphia. No question about it. He gave us hope. Our people became character people who were proud to be associated with the organization. I think that's the difference."

Tose didn't want to endure the rigor of another search for Vermeil's replacement. Accordingly, he decided to hire from within the ranks and named defensive coordinator Marion Campbell as his fifth head coach. Campbell, who had been fired by Atlanta in 1976 after a 1–5 start, didn't really want the position. Tose, however, appealed to his loyalty as a former Eagle and rewarded Campbell with a five-year contract, an offer too good to turn down.

The players had been stunned by Vermeil's decision. They had grown accustomed to his long days and emotional roller-coaster rides. When he began snarling and scowling during the strike season, most of them passed it off. *That's just Dick*, they thought.

"I'm surprised," said tight end John Spagnola. "The intensity and emotions of Dick Vermeil are well documented as real. I know it's been a tough season for him. The strike certainly added pressure to the whole thing. We didn't play well. We had a pretty good team but didn't handle the strike well. And there was tension between him and Tose for the first time. And I can document a bunch of other things, like his daughter graduating from college [Vermeil was unable to attend because of a road game]. So it came home to roost for him."

"I never would have expected this to happen to a guy who had given so much to the program," said Wilbert Montgomery. "It feels like a big part of the team had been taken apart."

"It's a down part of my life," said linebacker Reggie Wilkes. "He's doing this for the players even though we were the ones who lost the games, and I feel bad."

"Knowing how much he puts into football," said Louie Giammona of his uncle, "to go off for a week and come up with a decision like this...I wonder if it's all that sudden."

Chuck Clausen, the defensive line coach, recalled that his father Dick burned himself out as head coach at the University of New Mexico. "I've seen this before," said Clausen. "My father burned out when he was 47 years old. He went out and got another job."

David Vermeil, Dick's youngest son, felt relieved. "He finally made a decision that was in the best interest of himself instead of everybody else," he said. David thought his father began to burn out right after the Super Bowl. "He always felt the harder you work, the better you do," said David. "So he worked more hours, and it took so much out of him."

* * *

All NFL coaches are under enormous pressure. It comes from all angles. The impatient owner. The negative press. The fans who bet $500 on the team, expecting it to cover. How did other coaches avoid becoming burned out?

"For me, it wasn't that difficult," said Marty Schottenheimer, who coached 21 years with four different teams. "My focus was always on the things I could control and not worrying about the things I couldn't."

"I think that's a term, or phrase, that [Vermeil] invented," laughed Don Shula, the modern king of longevity with 33 seasons in the league. "I don't think anybody ever thought about that type of thing. I think it might be stress over a period of time. But [it's surprising] to think that he would burn out over that short a period." Shula couldn't recall any longtime coaches who ever suffered from burnout. "All the coaches I coached against or with over the long period of time I did, that never seemed to be a factor with any of them," Shula said.

Fun-loving Jimmy Johnson never came close to burning himself out. A couple of early championships with Dallas helped. "I think once you kind of accomplish what we were able to accomplish toward winning two Super Bowls, then it's not a big deal to us," said Johnson. "You think about all the other things in life that you'd like to do. Pro coaching is seven days a week, night and day. So you don't have much time for family life, or any activities outside of football. In Dallas and even in Miami, I'd see [my wife] Rhonda not in her pajamas two nights a week. When I left in the morning, it was at 5:00 AM. I'd get home at 11:00 PM. On Thursday, I'd tape my TV show and she went with me. Thursday night and Friday were the only two nights I ever saw Rhonda that she wasn't asleep."

Sam Wyche admits he didn't handle the pressure of the game very well. "I let the pressure build, and one pressure magnified the next pressure, which was a mistake on my part as a rookie head coach in '84," said Wyche. "But then after some good counseling from Paul Brown and other friends like Bill Walsh and Hank Stram, I started handling it better. It was just relying on people that I trusted. People that I knew had been there before and trying to put into action what they said. Believe me, good advice is hard to activate."

Vermeil, of course, would agree. And if he had listened to Carol and friends like John Ralston, Mike White, and Jim Murray, as Sam Wyche had done, he might have avoided burning himself out.

Greg Kinnear, the fine actor who played Vermeil in the inspirational movie *Invincible*, remembers studying old films of the coach for his role. It was the look on Vermeil's face during that final season in 1982 that disturbed the actor most.

> *"He's got great tenacity. He just has that energy about him, you know, a little larger than life."*
>
> GREG KINNEAR,
> STAR OF THE MOVIE *INVINCIBLE*

"Honestly, I didn't know much about Dick, to tell you the truth," said Kinnear. "I was watching him that last season in Philadelphia, when he seemed to have what the media was calling a breakdown. I don't know what it was, but there was a look in his eyes, just a demeanor and an intensity about him that I've never seen before. And I've seen a lot of movies. There was just an unequivocal intensity about the guy that I think was kind of inspiring for all of us who worked on the movie."

Indeed, Jaworski couldn't help but think of what might have been if Vermeil had been able to pace himself. The Super Bowl team in 1980 was strictly a collection of hard workers who overachieved with a 14–5 record. "We were built on the work ethic, we really were," Jaworski said. "On Monday, Wednesday, and Friday, you'd throw ball after ball after ball. Mike Dougherty would tape every shot. And this was in the off-season. But that's how we got better. And we accepted that. We accepted the team concept. It was an incredible group of guys. We covered each other's asses."

"If Dick could have gotten himself under control, we'd have won a lot of Super Bowls, no question," said Jaworski. "We finally got a speed guy in [free-agent receiver] Ron Smith. We threw for all of those yards and I'm going, 'Ho, ho, baby.' Then the goddamn players struck. It blew everything."

Chapter 12

Staying Close
to the Game

Each year, it seems some retired coach or quarterback turns up on the set as a new celebrity for one of the sports television networks. It seemed like a natural move for Dick Vermeil and his agent, Bob Goldy. Vermeil was full of energy and statistics and knew the league, top to bottom. Goldy called CBS producer Terry O'Neil and there was immediate interest. Vermeil was given an audition and hired as a color analyst. His play-by-play partner was former Eagle Tom Brookshier.

"He would analyze things, break it down," joked Brookshier. "How many times somebody went to the john the night before the game. With him, he had everything out here."

Brookshier recalled when he and Vermeil were returning from a game that first season. "Kansas City or somewhere," said Brookshier. "I'm relaxed. I'm having a cocktail. All of a sudden Dick says, 'Well, I'll be darned. I would have had 14 of the 16 games and beat the point spread.'"

Vermeil, however, paid no attention to point spreads in his early years with the Eagles. Ron Jaworski says most of the negative mail he received was from gamblers. "The games we won and didn't cover, or we didn't go over," he said. "I'd be called an MFer and everything else. There were games where we backed off in the fourth quarter when we were way ahead. Rather than score, we'd just run out the clock. Was Dick naïve about the spread? No question. The coach didn't care about that. He cared about winning and ultimately respecting his opponent, too."

There was one memorable game in which the Eagles were within field-goal range with only seconds to play. Vermeil elected to have Jaworski take a knee, running out the clock instead of waving in his kicker. The winning Eagles were greeted by boos as they left the field.

> "He's probably the most intense worker I've ever been around in football."
>
> Tom Brookshier, television announcer and former Eagles cornerback

Vermeil, stunned by the reception, asked a security guard why the fans were unhappy.

"You didn't cover, Coach," said the guard.

As a football analyst, Vermeil became more aware of the game's off-the-field aspects. He also was treated as a star in almost every city except Dallas. When he and Brookshier entered a locker room, players would greet Vermeil and start asking questions. "Some coaches didn't like him in the locker room," said Brookshier. "They'd come over and say, 'You're coaching my team.'"

Vermeil and Brookshier quickly became the best pro football combo in television. They were an odd pair. Vermeil was all business and focus. He arrived for a game with a load of charts and worksheets. He could tell you, for example, that from 1983 to 1992, the average rating for a Pro Bowl quarterback was 89.1, the average rating for a Super Bowl quarterback was 89.9, and the average rating for a Super Bowl–winning quarterback was 91.3.

A more detailed offensive sheet included 34 categories that Vermeil called "per-game values." For example, NFL teams averaged 20.52 points per game in 1986. They averaged 65.12 plays per game, and 18.96 first downs. Defensively, teams allowed 324.23 yards per game and achieved 2.26 take-aways per game. Vermeil also made a study of the red zone; it included 40 categories for each of the 28 teams. In 1992, the Eagles, then coached by Buddy Ryan, ranked as the top offensive team for points scored from outside the red zone (137). The Steve Young–led San Francisco 49ers ranked first in points scored on offense (407).

The sheets were compiled in Vermeil's distinctive all-caps writing style. He would jot his name on the right side of the sheet ("Vermeil, '93"), like some Renaissance painter. Brookshier remembers Vermeil holding a flip card against the steering wheel, memorizing the players' names as they drove to a game.

Yet, unknown to Vermeil, the CBS brass had begun to question his on-air personality. The most common objection was that Vermeil was a poker-faced analyst who used too many statistics and never cracked any silly jokes. It was too late in his life to become an on-camera comedian, of course. So CBS gave him some of the worst games on the 1987 schedule, where his nuts-and-bolts style wouldn't matter anyway.

"They said he overprepared," Brookshier had said. "How the hell can you overprepare? He's not an actor. Big John [Madden], he's somewhere between Happy the Clown and a coach. He's not really a football person anymore. He's a personality. Dick, he's a very, very articulate guy."

Vermeil loved his job. There were rap sessions with other NFL coaches. He was invited to sit in on quarterback meetings. And sometimes, coaches who used to be rivals would ask Vermeil about certain plays or players. "I'd watch a team practice on Friday morning," he said. "I'd be in their locker room. I'd visit with coaches, players, and management. I'd sit in and have film sessions with the quarterbacks. I was really into football."

One morning, Vermeil arrived at the Minnesota Vikings complex when they unlocked the doors at 7:45 AM. "We were putting stuff in the deer feeder before Bud Grant was in his office," said Brookshier. "They could not get enough of Dick's observations on their teams."

They would ask Vermeil about burnout, too, and he would retell the story. "I kept pushing myself harder and harder and harder," Vermeil would say. "And what usually happened by the end of each football season, I had nothing left to push with. I remember people used to say that the team ran out of gas at the end of the year. The guy who ran out of gas was me."

Vermeil said there were a number of coaches who were on the brink of being burned out. "Believe me, you'd be surprised," he said. "There were winning coaches, not just losers. Guys winning big. They just didn't know how much longer they could do it."

CBS, however, didn't care about Vermeil's little chats with other coaches. The network wanted more punch lines and fewer stats. When Vermeil's contract came up for renewal, CBS president Neal Pilson hastily suggested a token contract for six events. Vermeil, who had rejected what he called "an unbelievable offer" from NBC two years earlier to remain with CBS, brushed aside Pilson's offer.

"I don't think Neal meant to hurt Dick at all," said Brookshier. "I think it took place around and under him, and all of a sudden, he was left with the bag."

Vermeil admitted that his pride had been hurt by the treatment he received from CBS. "I don't think the situation was handled as well as it might have been," said Vermeil. "But I've lost before. I can handle this."

"He came to visit me once in the hospital. He was drawing plays on the IV bottles."

TOM BROOKSHIER

Ted Shaker, the executive producer for CBS Sports, said he felt Vermeil "might have been too intense." Vermeil said Shaker's only criticism was that "it might help if he was a little more spontaneous." Vermeil agreed. "I sometimes do overprepare," he said. "So I can see where that might be a negative. But I'm not an entertainer."

It wasn't long before Vermeil was back in the stadium booth. ABC came calling with a three-year offer to do major college games. It included an escape clause that allowed Vermeil to return to coaching. Vermeil accepted and soon joined partner Brent Musburger in the ABC booth. He was back in the broadcast business, memorizing the names of 19-year-old kids from Casa Grande, Arizona, and Fountain Valley, California, and their matching jersey numbers.

* * *

During Vermeil's television career, the Los Angeles Rams had tried to lure Vermeil back to the sideline. Vermeil had become a close friend of Rams owner Georgia Frontiere when he worked under George Allen in the late '60s. But each approach was rebuffed; Vermeil still wasn't sure he was ready to coach again. Moreover, he wasn't sure that Carol would be there applauding his return to the NFL's sweat box.

Then Vermeil received a call from Taylor Smith, Atlanta's executive vice president and son of owner Rankin Smith. The Falcons had fired Dan Henning in 1986 after a 7–8–1 season in which they lost seven of their last nine games. The team had major problems on defense. It had been nine years since their last defensive Pro Bowl player, defensive end Claude Humphrey.

Smith ultimately offered Vermeil $1 million per season, with the possibility of owning a small percentage of the club. Vermeil, however, didn't want to make a snap decision on whether he wanted to get back into coaching. "I just don't want to get across a meeting table from them," Vermeil said. "If I get across from the table, they'll probably make it so good they'd make me take it."

And how did Carol Vermeil feel? "If you've got to do it, you do it," she said, according to her husband. But there was another family matter for Vermeil to consider. Louie, his father, was very sick back home in Calistoga. Vermeil flew back to be with him and the family over the Christmas holiday. "I went for a hike in the mountains that I roamed as a kid," he said. "I walked for six or seven hours." During that long, thoughtful walk, Vermeil made up his mind to reject Smith's blockbuster offer.

"To the people who have as much money invested in pro football as these owners do, they deserve the kind of effort I made in Philadelphia," Vermeil said. "I just don't know if I can redo that again. My boys were against it. Carol was against it, although she thought we were going."

Louie Vermeil died of cancer on March 21, 1987. Dick had been with his father on Christmas, the saddest holiday any of the Vermeil family would spend together. After his father's death, Vermeil returned to the highly competitive world of sports television, wondering if he would ever get back onto the field.

Early in 1994, Vermeil was tempted to coach again. This time it was his former team that expressed interest in bringing the city's beloved coach back for another crack at the Super Bowl. There was a new owner in Philadelphia; Jeffrey Lurie had purchased the Eagles in May 1994 from auto magnate Norman Braman for $185 million. (Braman and his brother-in-law had bought the team from a cash-strapped Leonard Tose in 1985.)

Lurie came from a suburban Boston family that owned a movie theater chain. Eventually, the family got into publishing and formed a $3.5 billion conglomerate. Lurie himself became a Hollywood movie producer whose films reflected his interest in social issues and values. He was always interested in sports and remembers watching the historic New York Giants–Baltimore Colts championship game in 1958 on television with his father, Morris John Lurie. He was seven years old. Two years later, his father died of cancer.

"I think the game turned me on to NFL football for life," Lurie said. "I was never so impressed with the tension and excitement of a championship game coming down to sudden-death overtime...wow!"

It was too late to hire a new coach in Lurie's first year. But after the Eagles lost their last seven games under Rich Kotite, a coaching change was inevitable. Lurie wanted a dynamic leader, a coach who could excite the fans like he had been excited watching the Colts-Giants game.

There were numerous talks between Lurie and Vermeil. Lurie actually stirred the competitive fire within Vermeil during their discussions. There were plans for a new training facility and a $512 million, 66,000-seat stadium. Talks had progressed to the point where the Eagles offered Vermeil $8 million over five years. Now Vermeil's competitive fire was raging. He began assembling a staff that would include Jerry Rhome as his offensive coordinator.

And then, just as quickly, the deal fell apart. Two lawyers could stop Jim Brown in his tracks, and it probably was the lawyers who got in Vermeil's way. The sticking point was control; Vermeil wanted it all, but Lurie wouldn't budge. He had already hired Joe Banner as vice president, another little guy who knew all about the tricky two-year-old salary cap. So Vermeil backed away and Lurie hired Ray Rhodes, the defensive coordinator for the Super Bowl champion San Francisco 49ers.

"It's clear that it would have been a terrible, terrible mistake [to accept the Eagles job]," said Vermeil, who believed that Lurie misled him. "I knew there was a potential problem down the road when it came time to put things into writing. Suddenly, Jeffrey's tune changed. He didn't want wording about who would have the final say. But Jeffrey Lurie made me aware that there was still a fire within me that hadn't gone out. I'll always appreciate that."

Carol Vermeil grew wistful after the decision was made. "It would have been very nice if the Eagles thing had worked out," she later said. "But we both believe there is a reason for things happening the way they do."

Two years later, there would be another sliding team and another owner who would contact Vermeil. This time, there would be no debate over control. The owner would not only extend her hand; she'd give Vermeil a big, welcoming hug.

Chapter 13

Return to the Promised Land

On December 18, 1994, the Eagles added Dick Vermeil to their prestigious Honor Roll. Vermeil was the 23rd inductee. Seven of the players he coached had already been inducted. At least publicly, the belated honor was attributable to Vermeil's work schedule in the ABC television booth.

Under Rich Kotite, their lame-duck coach, the Eagles had lost five games in a row, falling to 7–7 after a 7–2 start. And with the New York Giants on a four-game winning streak that showcased their defense and a young pass rusher named Michael Strahan, the Eagles were in danger of making it six losses in a row.

Vermeil sensed danger, too, but in a different sense. The word on the street was that Vermeil was the hot candidate to succeed Kotite, who had struggled with quarterback injuries, morale problems, and the loss of two All-Pro free agents, defensive end Reggie White and linebacker Seth Joyner. Rather than embarrass Kotite, Vermeil suggested to Eagles public relations director Ron Howard that the ceremony be postponed until the following season.

"I left it up to them," Vermeil said. "I thought it would be unfair to Rich for me to appear right after the newspaper article that mentioned me as a candidate to be the next head coach."

The Eagles gave away the game. The Giants turned an interception and a fumbled kickoff into 10 fourth-quarter points to win 16–13. The winning field goal came with 54 seconds left. As Kotite and the Eagles struggled to find any kind of offensive rhythm, chants of "We want Dick! We want Dick! We want Dick!" cascaded from the stands.

Vermeil winced at the outpouring of affection. "I was told that the plans [for the ceremony] had already been made, and they wanted to go through with it," he said. "But I felt badly."

Jeffrey Lurie, the owner, gave Vermeil a grand introduction at halftime, while Kotite and the Eagles were plotting game strategy for the second half. "Dick Vermeil personifies leadership and intensity and competitiveness," Lurie told the sellout crowd. "He's a true winner. He represents everything we all strive to be."

Though Vermeil passed on the Eagles job, his rekindled interest in coaching didn't surprise 83-year-old retired passing guru Sid Gillman. "Hell, yes, I expect him to get back into coaching," said Gillman. "Dick Vermeil is too good a coach to be out of it. Being out of it has been great for him. I think his perspective has changed a little bit. He knows you don't have to start at 6:00 in the morning and go until 4:00 in the morning. Oh, I'm sure he'd do it differently. I'm sure he would."

The Eagles eventually hired Ray Rhodes, a fire-and-brimstone defensive coordinator from the San Francisco 49ers. Rhodes' problem: he couldn't prevent the Eagles' slide to 3–13 in his fourth year and couldn't win in the NFC East (a 3–9 divisional record in 1997–98). Lurie sent Rhodes packing after the Eagles finished with a drab 20–10 loss to the Giants in 1998, a club-record 13th defeat.

Meanwhile, the St. Louis Rams had also been faltering. Quarterback Jim Everett, who had some big years in 1988 and 1989 when he threw 60 touchdown passes, was getting old. The running game, an old Rams staple in the '80s and early '90s, was slipping. Interestingly enough, the Rams had traded both Everett (1994) and running back Jerome Bettis (1995) during their plunge to the bottom of the NFC West. Even the move to St. Louis for a sweetheart deal in rent, facilities, and guarantees, plus a new 66,000-seat dome stadium, didn't help. And in her moment of desperate need, Rams owner Georgia Frontiere turned to Vermeil, an old friend, to provide a new direction.

* * *

The Rams had considered Vermeil several times in the past, but this time was different. The once-proud Rams had won only 36 games in seven seasons. They had kept changing quarterbacks, running backs, and defensive schemes under John Robinson, Chuck Knox, and Rich Brooks. And when the seasons were analyzed, the Rams simply couldn't win the close ones. They lost 25 games by a touchdown or less in that forgettable seven-year stretch. Moreover, the Rams defense finished in the top half of the league only once (1996), barely making the cut in 12th place. Some critics joked that the Fearsome Foursome had been replaced by the Fearful Foursome.

Vermeil had rejected the Rams at least three times in the past: 1991, 1994, and in December 1996. John Shaw, the club president, wasn't discouraged. New Yorkers are persistent, and the Brooklyn-born Shaw went to the phone again. The Rams had been talking to Jim Mora, Vermeil's old friend. George Seifert, the Super Bowl–winning coach in 1989 and 1994, said he wasn't interested in coaching the lowly Rams. Shaw then made an early-morning call in mid-January 1997 to Vermeil, who eagerly accepted over the phone. The only downside of the hire was that Vermeil knocked Mora, his old coaching pal, out of a job. Vermeil's hefty cost to the Rams: $8 million over five years.

"I left the game because I had to," a misty-eyed Vermeil said at his first press conference in St. Louis. "I'm not embarrassed to say that. Fourteen years later, I'm coming back because I have to. It's just something that's missing. And I'm excited to say that."

Television analyst John Madden noted that the NFL had changed since Vermeil left in 1982. "Dick Vermeil is not coming back to the game that he left," said Madden. "I'm not saying he can't do it. I'm saying I don't think I could, and it's going to be difficult for him. It's a different game."

> *"Everyone thought that when he was out of football for those 14 years that things would pass him by. Or that he would be out of touch. But that wasn't true."*
>
> MIKE WHITE

Vermeil, however, felt that his years in television had given him an opportunity to visit with coaches, players, and club management, including the so-called capologists. They were the deal-making money wizards who knew the tricks of keeping their teams under the salary cap.

"I don't believe there are divisions of a pro football team," Vermeil told Peter Downs of the *St. Louis Times*. "I don't believe there's a football side and a business side and a personnel side. I think it is a football organization and there is only one side; that's the Rams side."

Vermeil's hires provoked some humorous digs from the media. The graying seniors on his coaching staff included 64-year-old offensive line coach Jim Hanifan, 61-year-old quarterbacks coach Mike White, and 67-year-old receivers coach Dick Coury. At the other end of the age spectrum were the young hustlers: defensive line coach Carl Hairston (45), defensive coordinator John Bunting (46), and running backs coach Wilbert Montgomery (42). As much as anything, the new hires were a show of loyalty by Vermeil, who had worked with or coached each of them.

"That was his way of repaying me for what I've done for him," said Montgomery, who was a great back and now a rookie coach. Montgomery related this phone conversation with his old head coach.

"How does 'Coach Montgomery' sound?" Vermeil said.

"It sounds great, Coach," said Montgomery, who had been working in a paper company and hosting cable television and radio shows. Soon, Montgomery would coach an assortment of running backs, including vagabond Lawrence Phillips. Two years later, however, he would be tutoring a very special player named Marshall Faulk.

Before Vermeil's arrival, the Rams had been a soft team. In the second half of tight, tough games, they would crumble, showing little heart. From 1990 to 1996, a seven-year period, the Rams defense gave up 30 or more points in 35 games. They were at their worst at the end of the 1995 season; the Rams allowed 45 points to Buffalo, 35 points to Washington, and 41 points to Miami. The Redskins ranked 18th in total offense that year, and the Bills were 20th. Miami ranked a more-respectable eighth

(21st in rushing), but only because it still had Dan Marino firing fastballs at age 34.

So Vermeil's major problem, aside from getting tougher players on defense and stabilizing the quarterback position, was changing the Rams' casual attitude. It was similar to his challenge in Philadelphia, where the organization once resembled "a country club," as Roman Gabriel had said.

"What we're trying to do is bring in the kind of person whose personal character traits were developed long before he ever became a pro football player," said Vermeil. "Those guys have opportunities to be a positive influence on other people. You don't worry so much about motivating them. They motivate you. Sometimes you'll end up with less talent doing that. But you'll end up with 16 more consistent games."

Undersized linebacker Mike Jones (6'1", 240 pounds) was one of Vermeil's character players. A plodding running back at Missouri, Jones went undrafted in 1991. The scouts described him as a "slashing runner who will not go down without putting up a fight." Jones was signed by Vermeil as a free agent after the Raiders had switched him to defense, based on his excellent work habits. Two seasons after the signing, Jones would figure in one of the most memorable plays in Rams history.

"After I met Coach Vermeil, you can't do anything but love the man," Jones told Bernie Miklasz, a columnist for the *St. Louis Post-Dispatch*. "He comes at you with the truth. If he wants something, he lets you know it. He's going to push you. But you're going to love him for what he does."

Vermeil's first season began with a rousing 38–24 rout of the New Orleans Saints, who had also hired a former Super Bowl coach, Mike Ditka. Before a vociferous home crowd, an excited Vermeil joined the pregame introductions, running past a line of high-kicking cheerleaders and jumping into the arms of offensive tackle Fred Miller. The Rams rallied from a 17–14 halftime deficit to dominate Ditka's flat Saints as Lawrence Phillips scored three touchdowns. Vermeil, who had rescued Phillips from a troubled life of domestic assault and drunk driving, hugged his new back and flipped him the game ball.

"If you'd write a scenario for a first game back with a new program after all these years, you would want to write it that way," said Vermeil, referring to the 24-point second-half rally. "Fourteen years is a long time to wait, but it makes this win so much sweeter."

The sweetness was short-lived, as the Rams would win only once more over the next 11 games, falling to the bottom of the NFC West. Tony Banks, their journeyman quarterback, continued to play erratically, and Vermeil's running game collapsed behind poor blocking. On defense, the Rams lacked the fire that characterized Vermeil's Philadelphia teams.

Jeff Wilkins kicked a 25-yard field goal to edge the Washington Redskins 23–20, and the Rams would win two more games against losing teams, New Orleans and Carolina, to finish at the bottom of the division with a 5–11 record.

By then, it was clear that the Rams needed a more consistent quarterback, a quicker running back, improved pass blocking, and new leadership in the huddle. Despite the challenges, Vermeil refused to second-guess his decision to return to the game after his 14-year career in television.

"It's way too late for that," he said. Then he admitted that the Rams lacked an inspirational leader. The big man in Philadelphia was Bill Bergey, a rowdy linebacker. "Do I have a Bergey here?" said Vermeil. "Hell no. Bergey would take a locker room and get them ready to play. Do we have that type of person here? I don't recognize who he is. We have some silent leaders."

The next year, the Rams sank even deeper into the depths of the NFC West. Over the last 11 weeks, they won only twice and finished with a 4–12 record. They were beaten eight times by superior quarterbacks: Steve Young (49ers); Dan Marino (Dolphins); Randall Cunningham (Vikings); Chris Chandler (Falcons); and Steve Beuerlein (Panthers). Banks, still Vermeil's best option at quarterback, regressed, throwing only seven touchdown passes and getting sacked 41 times.

"I'm embarrassed," Vermeil said after getting pounded by the Saints 24–3. "A junior high coach could have done better than I did."

Banks was sacked seven times in the rout. "You guys see it," Banks grumbled when asked about his offensive line. "But I'm not going to point fingers."

"I don't know what's wrong with us," said veteran free safety Keith Lyle. "We're going up against New Orleans and we feel we match up very well with that team. And then we're flat. I don't get it."

A drained Vermeil, however, promised results in his third season after losing to the 49ers in the final game, San Francisco's 17th straight win in the series. "I'm giving it everything I've got," Vermeil said. "The Rams will succeed. We've got good ownership, good management. Nobody interferes. There is no reason not to succeed. It just takes time."

In an extremely busy off-season, the Rams hired Mike Martz as their new offensive coordinator, drafted speed receiver Torry Holt in the first round, signed guard Adam Timmerman as a free agent, and executed a blockbuster trade with the Indianapolis Colts for unhappy Marshall Faulk, a gamebreaking running back with 4.48 speed. With Martz, it was actually a two-for-one deal; he brought with him free agent Trent Green, a tall, big-play quarterback. On defense, the Rams made two changes at linebacker, elevating London Fletcher, a 6'0" dynamo, and adding free agent Todd Collins, a 248-pound run-stuffer.

Martz represented a daring change for the Rams. Vermeil had always been a one-back, play-action, ball-control coach. Martz, who would now run the offense, was a thrill-a-minute play caller, willing to take risks with skilled players. "I told him, 'Dick, if I get this job, we're going to attack the defense every game for four quarters,'" said Martz.

> *"He takes on a fatherly persona that you don't even realize is happening when you're there. I was just blown away when I first met him."*
>
> MIKE MARTZ, FORMER RAMS
> OFFENSIVE COORDINATOR

Martz, another member of the California-bred family of coaches that included Vermeil, Ralston, Walsh, Prothro, and White, said Vermeil gave him total freedom to make the offensive calls. The Rams also added Al Saunders from the Kansas City staff to coach the Rams' stable of speed receivers. John Matsko came over from the New York Giants to assist and eventually replace Jim Hanifan as the offensive line coach.

"I think [Vermeil] felt comfortable that we knew what we were doing, and it was a relief to him," said Martz. "The fact is, that's the way he wanted it done. It was kind of understood that there would be the intensity and the attention to detail. He just wanted to make sure everything was covered. That's how he coached. I just wanted to make sure we were pleasing him."

Martz said Vermeil never caused any disruption during offensive meetings or practice sessions. "He was just so awesome," said Martz. "Letting you be yourself. He was more of a father figure for me. He was like a velvet hand. He would punch, but you didn't know you were getting punched. He'd say, 'I think you ought to think about this.' Or, very quietly, he'd say, 'Incidentally, John, you screwed up.' I think it was somewhat of a relief to him that way. You know, he wanted to be the head coach, but he didn't want to do all these other things. He loved the fact that we took advantage of our personnel. He was not necessarily a conservative coach."

The personnel changes reflected the philosophy of former Dallas coach Tom Landry in regard to losing teams. "The basic problem you face is developing a losing pattern," said Landry. "The most difficult thing in coaching is to overcome that feeling you're going to lose. You can only do it by bringing in new blood."

> "He's the hardest-working, most motivated guy I've ever been around. But this is not his best quality. His best quality is that he's a helluva guy."
>
> LYNN STILES

Lynn Stiles ran the football operations and coached the tight ends. Stiles said Vermeil still believed in hard work and attention to detail.

"All the quirks are still there," said Stiles. "But he's not digging trenches like he used to. He can stand and look at the horizon. He's developed a great chemistry, and it's not just the athletes. It transcends the whole organization. And he's letting the lieutenants make decisions."

Vermeil had an ethical slogan for the Rams' new approach: "Gotta Go to Work." It might have been an old line uttered by family members who worked in Louie Vermeil's Owl Garage. Or maybe the motivational cry from some forgotten high school coach. Or maybe it came from remembering his inner voice when he pushed himself away from the pillow after a three-hour snooze in Philadelphia.

Whatever its origin, the Rams bought into it. And Vermeil bought into a request from the team's got-a-gripe executive committee to lighten up the workload. Hanifan, Vermeil's offensive line coach, had been moving in NFL coaching circles for 27 years and had never seen a coach allow his players to be at home on Saturday nights. "We have a Saturday walk-through at home, and the next time we see the fellas is Sunday morning for breakfast," said Hanifan.

"When he came back to the Rams after that layoff, I think he found the game had changed a lot. Dick went to a different phase that played to his strengths as a head coach, and he did a magnificent job."

AL SAUNDERS, FORMER RAMS AND CHIEFS ASSISTANT COACH

The day before Christmas in his third season, Vermeil agreed to change the time of an 11:00 AM holiday workout, but refused to cancel it. Yet, when the Rams executed a near-flawless practice, Vermeil shouted, "The hell with it," and gave them Christmas Day off.

Stiles, the coach's key assistant, presented an interesting view of Vermeil. "What we're talking about is the most unique coach in my lifetime who has ever coached the game of football," said Stiles, who began coaching under Vermeil at UCLA in the mid-1970s. "He's the most unique because of his tremendous desire to have a relationship with his players and his coaching assistants. It's the 'it' principle, as I call it. People say, how do you get 'it' done? Well, the 'it' principle is coach-to-player, player-to-coach, and player-to-player. That's what gets it done. And it's not always about the team with the best personnel. It's the same thing when a player retires, he's finished the game. What does he miss the most? The camaraderie in the locker room. That's what 'it' is, that's what it's all about."

Saunders, the new receivers coach, said Vermeil adhered to four principles. "He says that first, you've got to have a plan," said Saunders. "Then you've got to hire good people who have character and values, your staff and the players. Then you've got to work hard. Finally, you've got to show them that you care."

*　*　*

Vermeil seemed to have "it" all together. He had his plan, a fine staff, and a vastly improved roster. And, of course, they all knew that he cared. So the Rams went to training camp in 1999 with a new quarterback, an explosive back, an upgraded receiving corps, and a vastly improved defense with heart and without the bickerers of another time.

"He was under a lot of pressure that third year," said Jim Thomas, a beat writer for the *St. Louis Post-Dispatch*. "There was a feeling that he better do something. What helped Dick Vermeil was that John Shaw felt that firing Rich Brooks after two years [before Vermeil was hired] was done too quickly and was cold-hearted."

Then, even before the summer ended, the optimism flowing from a great training camp turned to doubt. The third preseason contest against New England was played with the intensity of a playoff game. Rodney Harrison, the Patriots' highly competitive strong safety, came on a surprise blitz and slammed into quarterback Trent Green, tearing the ligaments in his left knee. The season-ending injury suddenly left Kurt Warner, an obscure star from the indoor Arena League, as the starting quarterback.

Green had been sensational in preseason play, completing 28 of 32 attempts (two of his four incompletions were drops). But now the quarterback directing the Rams offense was Warner, a man who had stocked shelves in a grocery store after being cut by the Packers back in 1994. Vermeil tried not to sound devastated. "It hurts," he said. "But we will rally around Kurt Warner and we will play good football."

The resurrection of Warner's career made a heartwarming story for the local media. In three seasons with the Iowa Barnstormers, he had thrown for 10,486 yards and 183 touchdowns. Those gaudy Arena League numbers were nice enough, but what concerned the Rams were his NFL stats: Warner had appeared in only one game, mopping up for Steve Bono in the final game of the 1998 season, and had thrown only 11 passes. Fearing the worst, the desperate Rams added journeyman Paul Justin as a backup in a trade with the Oakland Raiders.

Nobody was quite sure how Warner would perform. Not Vermeil. Not Martz. Not any of his offensive teammates, now huddling up with their new quarterback. Warner, however, was a believer. A man of deep faith, he hosted a weekly Bible study for a dozen or so players, including Isaac Bruce, the Rams' premier playmaker.

The opening game was against Baltimore, a team in transition without much of a pass defense. In his debut, Warner passed for 309 yards and three touchdowns in a rousing 27–10 win. Vermeil was thrilled as well as relieved. Then he got carried away and predicted a win in their next game against Atlanta, the Super Bowl runner-up from a year ago. "Dick Vermeil told us then that we were going to beat Atlanta," said Kevin Carter, the defensive end. "And I think that added confidence and started us going."

The Rams made a prophet out of their coach, whipping the Falcons 35–7. Warner was getting more and more comfortable with what Martz was feeding him. Faulk kept twisting and weaving through the tiniest of holes. The Rams' receivers kept making those hard, clean cuts to get open in Martz's high-powered offense. Meanwhile, Tony Horne and Az-Zahir Hakim kept breaking off long, dazzling kick returns. In their first six games, the Rams scored 217 points, only 68 fewer points than they scored the entire year before. They won all six games by an amazing average of 25.7 points.

One of the wins was a 42–20 laugher over the San Francisco 49ers, a team that had beaten the Rams 17 straight times. "We hadn't beaten them since 1990," said Kevin Carter. "I mean, 17 straight losses. And I've been here, I guess, for 10 of them." Warner gave the game another perspective. Warner said the Rams couldn't be regarded as a threat to win the NFC West until they beat the 49ers. "Until we beat the mystique," he said.

"6–0," sang out Vermeil, almost giddy in his mood. "6–0, not too bad."

Then came two close losses to Tennessee (24–21) and Detroit (31–27) on the road. "Losing those two games was a character-builder for us," suggested Todd Lyght, the left corner.

In other years, the Rams would have taken the defeats in stride. They would have thought about another ugly workweek coming up, about taking it easy on their tired, old bones. But things were different with these Rams. As Carter said, "We were sick over those two losses. Just sick."

The Rams regrouped. Warner and a relentless pass defense carried the Rams to a 35–10 rout of Carolina. And then came the 49ers in a rematch, the team that had tied, handcuffed, and blindfolded the Rams during that remarkable streak of 17 straight wins.

The Rams went out and dominated the game by a 23–7 score, sweeping the 49ers for the first time since 1980, the year of the Jack Youngblood–Nolan Cromwell–Jackie Slater–Vince Ferragamo team.

Martz's offense kept running up and down the field like a track team, scoring from all over on both spectacular catches and breathtaking runs. Faulk was particularly brilliant behind the offensive line of Orlando Pace, Tom Nutten, Mike Gruttadauria, Adam Timmerman, and Fred Miller.

"What I think he did was to back off the Xs and Os a little bit and devote a majority of his time to personnel and focusing on the emotional climate of the team, and he was spectacular at it."

AL SAUNDERS

It figured that eventually there would be some nickname to describe the Rams' explosive offense. Somebody came up with a jazzy slogan—"The Greatest Show on Turf"—and it caught on. The fans loved the speed, the big plays, and the sideline swagger of these Rams after so many years of suffering. Opposing defensive coordinators were forced to study "The Show" until long past the midnight hour, just as Dick Vermeil used to do in Philadelphia.

After sweeping the 49ers, the Rams would win five more games in a row before losing a meaningless finale to the Eagles 38–31. Vermeil cleaned the bench at halftime, using backups while resting his starters for the upcoming playoffs.

Warner was on fire during December. In four straight wins, he threw for 351 yards against Carolina, 346 yards against New Orleans, 319 yards against the New York Giants, and 334 yards against Chicago. His final passing stats were Arena League–like: 4,353 yards, 41 touchdowns, and a league-high quarterback rating of 109.2.

In the opening playoff round against Minnesota, an NFC wild-card team, the Rams won the way they usually did. Warner, behind near-perfect protection, passed for 391 yards and threw five touchdowns to five different receivers. The final score was 49–37, but it wasn't that close. The Rams led 49–17 with 8:13 to go. After that, the Vikings scored three garbage-time touchdowns with Jeff George firing many of his 50 passes all over the field.

The following week, the Rams proved they could win a tense, defensive struggle. Tampa Bay, the NFC Central winner, held Faulk to 44 yards rushing and three dinky catches for five yards. Warner threw 43 passes but only one of them went for a score. That was a daring third-and-4 throw to Ricky Proehl; Proehl beat cornerback Brian Kelly for a 30-yard touchdown with just 4:44 left to play. That was enough to edge the Bucs 11–6 and send the Rams to the Super Bowl for the first time in 20 years.

Warner had been given an option on Proehl's touchdown. Faulk was the primary receiver, dipping into the line and finding the nearest open spot for a short first-down flip from Warner. But if Bucs safety Damien Robinson came on a blitz, Warner was to go deep to Proehl racing down the left sideline. Bruce, meanwhile, ran a deep route along the right sideline as a decoy.

Martz, noting that both Holt (bruised ribs) and Hakim (dehydration) were out of the lineup, said he played it too conservatively until the big play to Proehl. "We were jittery," he said. "That's not us. We had a lot in the game plan for Holt and Hakim. When they came out, I could have handled the play-calling a little better."

"If we screw it up, you won't be thinking about how great this offense was," said Jim Hanifan, the veteran offensive line coach. "I don't think we'll be remembered as one of the great offenses unless we go all the way."

* * *

Unlike Super Bowl XV, when he was consumed by the game during the warm-ups, Vermeil was loose and engaging before his Super Bowl XXXIV contest against the AFC champion Tennessee Titans. "At Super Bowl XV, the president of the United States could have been sitting behind our bench in the front row and Dick wouldn't have known it," said Ron Jaworski. "In the Super Bowl with the Rams, I was down on the field in the pregame warm-ups and he gives me this big hug. He said, 'Where's Carol?' He wanted to know where she was sitting. I said, 'Wow, he's really calm and relaxed.'"

Martz was loose, too. "I've never been so relaxed in my whole life," he told Vermeil as they hugged before the game. The Rams offense gave an indication of Martz's mood on their first two series: Martz fed Warner 11 pass plays and only five runs. By the end of the first half, Warner had thrown for 277 yards, a Super Bowl record. Martz had called 36 passes and only eight runs, a lopsided 82-18 pass-run ratio. Yet, while Warner was completing 19 passes to eight different receivers, including a tipped blooper to tackle Fred Miller, he was being knocked around by the Titans' rush, which included a heavy dose of blitzes.

Greg Williams, the Titans' scheming defensive coordinator, knew his rushers had to put their hands and pads and helmets on Warner to prevent another 328-yard, three-touchdown game as he had against the Titans earlier in the regular season. So Williams threw everything he had at the Rams, including loops and stunts by his down linemen and blitzes by Blaine Bishop and Denard Walker. Warner survived the early pounding with only one sack, but he went down numerous times, bruising his ribs and causing Vermeil to pace and frown along the sideline.

> *"I can't describe it, but everybody he meets feels like they're real important, and that's a quality not many men have."*
>
> MIKE MARTZ

"How did he get hit?" he snapped at Hanifan. "Get their asses knocked off."

Warner and the Rams offense, playing like alley fighters, drove inside the Titans' 20-yard line on each of their first five possessions. Yet, they came away with just a 9–0 halftime lead.

"Everybody's singled up," growled Vermeil. "Every single guy. It's like steal-ing." But not in the red zone, where Warner completed only one of 11 attempts, a little six-yarder to Torry Holt on first-and-20 near the end of the fifth drive.

"They can't stop us," Vermeil told the Rams in the dressing room during a Super Bowl halftime break that seemed to last forever. "We're stopping our-selves. All we've got to do is keep protecting [Warner]."

Warner finally drilled a nine-yard scoring pass to Holt midway through the third quarter to open a 16–0 lead. There was dancing along the Rams sideline, a weaving two-step that didn't go unnoticed by Jeff Fisher, the Titans' coach. "They're celebrating right now!" screamed Fisher. "Look at them over there. They're already celebrating!"

The Titans refused to feel the pressure, which sometimes dooms teams who trail in the second half of the Super Bowl. Quarterback Steve McNair, who had a shaky first half (66 yards passing, 12 yards scrambling) suddenly found his rhythm. Eddie George, their heavyweight running back, began picking the right holes and making others when the Rams clogged his way. Together, McNair and George pulled the inspired Titans into a 16–16 tie on touchdown drives of 66 and 79 yards and Al Del Greco's 43-yard field goal with 2:12 left to play.

Now the pressure was building on the Rams. Coaching from the press box, Mike Martz reminded himself of his philosophy. "I've always been a passing guy within the framework of the people we had," Martz had said. "Both tight ends were hurt during the early part of the year, so Ricky Proehl took the part of a tight end and we became a four-wide receiver team."

In the biggest game of his coaching career, Martz decided to take a shot. He sent in a pass play called 999 H-Balloon. "The '9s' are 'go' routes," said Martz. "It was four vertical routes, and Bruce was on the right outside." Holt was the only receiver lined up on the left side. Hakim ran the same deep route to Bruce's inside. Holt did likewise on the left side, and Proehl ran a post route. Warner, behind a wall of arm-jamming protectors, had to wait until Bruce cleared his defender, Denard Walker. That gave pass-rushing end Jevon Kearse time to break into the pocket and hurry Warner's throw.

The ball was underthrown. All Warner could do was hope that Bruce's athletic skills would take over. Indeed, Bruce wheeled back and caught the ball inside Walker near the Titans' 38-yard line. Instinctively, he slipped away from Walker, veered back inside, and outraced two Titans into the end zone, completing a 73-yard scoring pass. Jeff Wilkins added the PAT and the jubilant Rams were in front 23–16 with only 1:54 left to play. Vermeil began counting down the time. "A minute and 54 seconds away, guys, and we're the world champs," he said at one point. "Get after them."

McNair, however, wasn't finished. Running or passing on nine straight plays from a shotgun set, McNair took the defiant Titans from their own 12 to a first down at the Rams' 10-yard line with five seconds left. The Georgia Dome was rocking with the kind of ear-shattering noise that accompanies once-in-a-lifetime drama.

What was Martz thinking, high above all the drama? "All of us in the box were thinking overtime," admitted Martz.

Down below, Hanifan and White inched closer to each other along the tense Rams sideline. "Right before the snap, Mike White and I were holding hands," said the 66-year-old Hanifan. "I kept saying, 'Please God, please don't let them get in.' I was hoping there weren't any television cameras on us."

McNair had already pulled off one miracle, retreating and scrambling away from Kevin Carter and Jay Williams, then firing a 16-yard strike to Kevin Dyson at the Rams' 10-yard line. The Titans had called their final timeout. Vermeil was pacing the sideline, hoping for one more big play from his weary defense that had been fighting McNair for 10 straight plays.

McNair was ready, and took one final shotgun snap, the defining moment in the most dramatic finish in Super Bowl history. There was Dyson, slanting inside near the 5-yard line. McNair threw another strike and for a moment, Dyson seemed to have a lane to the end zone. But linebacker Mike Jones, closing fast, grabbed Dyson and wrestled him to the Georgia Dome turf as Dyson's arm stretched futilely toward the goal line as time expired. The dramatic tackle preserved the Rams' 23–16 win. Another few inches by the lunging Dyson would have produced the first overtime in Super Bowl history.

"I thought I was going to get in there," said Dyson. "I didn't think he had a good grip on me and I stretched out. I was just short. To come this far and be a half-yard short is just a sick feeling."

Coach Jeff Fisher said the Titans vowed at halftime to come out battling. "We told ourselves that we were going to come out and win this game," said Fisher. "We had time. We had a minute and 54 seconds. We came six inches short."

In the midst of a confetti storm, Vermeil cradled the gleaming Super Bowl trophy. Soon owner Georgia Frontiere embraced it, too. Earlier, Vermeil had crossed the field to shake Fisher's hand and congratulate the losing coach on a tenacious

"I don't think there's ever been anybody quite like him, and probably never will be. He's everybody's dad. I'm like one of his kids. He calls to check with you. He's got a whole country full of kids."

MIKE MARTZ

effort. "I wish I could share this with Jeff Fisher and his staff," said Vermeil. "I've been in both locker rooms now, the winning and the losing locker rooms. I know the feeling."

Warner, who passed for a Super Bowl–record 414 yards, was named the game's MVP, completing perhaps the most unlikely season in football history. Martz's bold play-calling had something to do with that; the Rams dismissed the notion of running the football, passing on 78 percent of their 59 plays. Marshall Faulk had only 10 carries for 17 yards. But numbers were insignificant in this Super Bowl, which was a test of Vermeil's four principles of coaching: have a plan, have good people on the field and on your staff, work hard, and show that you care.

There was, of course, a wild celebration on the streets of St. Louis, which had never celebrated an NFL championship. There were good feelings, too, in the homes of every Eagles player who had played for Vermeil in Super Bowl XV. Three of them—Bunting, Hairston, and Montgomery—had finally earned their Super Bowl rings 19 years later as Rams coaches.

* * *

Less than 72 hours after the game, Vermeil made another teary-eyed announcement. He was retiring as coach of a championship team, just as his old friend Bill Walsh had after winning Super Bowl XXXIII with the Joe Montana–led San Francisco 49ers. Walsh cited burnout, the same condition that had forced Vermeil to leave the Philadelphia Eagles in 1983 after seven seasons. But now Vermeil had a different reason. "You can always make another one of those," Vermeil said, glancing at the glittering Lombardi Trophy. "The high of coaching for me is the relationship with the players."

It was the free-agency system that Vermeil worried about. Every Super Bowl team has its share of egos and contract problems, and Vermeil simply didn't want to face the possibility that he would have to cut any of his players.

"The Rams' Super Bowl was bittersweet for me. I was just glad that Coach Vermeil had an opportunity to win the one that he missed."

WILBERT MONTGOMERY

"I don't want to participate in that," he said, tears welling in his eyes. "I don't want to cut the squad. These are my guys, okay?"

Vermeil also wanted to go out with a championship, and on a more personal point, he wanted to spend more time with Carol, his wife of 44 years, and with his three children and 11 grandchildren. He owned a sprawling 110-acre ranch outside of Philadelphia that former Eagles personnel director Carl Peterson had dubbed "Yosemite Lodge." It was there that Vermeil wanted to retire and rejoin his family.

"I don't want to be the head coach here in training camp or in the middle of next season and tell myself, 'I should have retired when I was on top,'" Vermeil said. "To see the expression on people's faces Sunday after that ballgame at our party was worth all the three years of work. Just to see how much joy it brought to them. So I've made the right decision. But I'll tell you this. There will be times, just like making the right decision to come here, that I'm going to say to myself, 'What the hell did I do that for?' But that's life."

For her part, Carol Vermeil raised a simple question: "What else do you have to prove to yourself?"

Some of the Rams players were left in tears, if not total shock. "A lot of guys are going to realize those moments with him, how special they were," said linebacker London Fletcher. "Him getting in front of the team in meetings and crying and getting emotional. You take a team that was 4–12 and lead us to a Super Bowl championship, that was unbelievable."

"He's unusual in the aspect that he cares about you," said offensive tackle Fred Miller. "That's hard to find in today's line of work, where money is more important, that's the big issue."

Said Mike Jones, the defensive hero of Super Bowl XXXIV, "We're going to be Vermeil guys for the rest of our lives." Jones remembered his first meeting with Vermeil. "He gets up and walks around his desk," said Jones. "I'm like, what are you doing? Then he sticks his arms out, like for a hug. I'm like, I never had a coach hug me like that."

These Rams were a family. Vermeil brought them together in a very special season that ended with confetti falling in their joyous faces and their coach crying without shame. There would never be another season quite like the 1999 season. Not with Dick Vermeil gone.

Chapter 14

One Last Time

When Dick Vermeil returned to Philadelphia after the Super Bowl season, a lot had changed since he left in 1997. Jeffrey Lurie, the Hollywood movie producer who had purchased the Eagles in 1994 from Norman Braman for $185 million, had already hired his second head coach. The newest man in charge was Andy Reid, a figure as formidable as a courthouse who lived by the forward pass. Reid came from Green Bay, a team that had been using Bill Walsh's so-called West Coast offense since the early 1990s. The quarterback was Donovan McNabb, the second overall pick in the 1999 draft. Picking four spots lower, Vermeil had chosen receiver Torry Holt, who caught seven passes in the Rams' dramatic Super Bowl win.

The Eagles' playboy owner, Leonard Tose, had long ago been forced out of the game by gambling debts. By his own admission, Tose lost more than $25 million at the blackjack tables in Atlantic City. After 16 years as an NFL owner and countless good times in Miami Beach, Acapulco, and Las Vegas, Tose found himself a pauper. "It's hell to be 80 and broke," he would say. Eventually, he would be forced to move into a junior suite at a downtown hotel. In the sad, lonely years that followed, he was supported by a small circle of loyal friends. One of the benefactors who helped pay the bills was Dick Vermeil.

The Eagles had fired Tose's general manager, Jim Murray, in 1983. "Abolishing the position," as Tose put it. He then turned the team over to his daughter, Susan Fletcher, naming her vice president. "Instead of an adopted son," explained Tose, "I have a real daughter." The scene grew so chaotic that Tose and his daughter had planned to move the franchise to Arizona. Tose, however, pulled out of an enormously attractive deal with Canadian real-estate developer James Monaghan. The reason given was a political plum: dozens of new luxury boxes to grow the financial pie for Tose at aging Veterans Stadium.

Soon there would be a new 108,000-square-foot training complex with fields trimmed like the greens at Augusta, and a new 67,594-seat stadium with the same impeccably groomed surface. Vermeil's Eagles had trained at the ancient JFK Stadium—where the field was choppy and had a distinct odor after city police horses performed at a charity event each year—and had played their home games at Veterans Stadium, with its rock-hard synthetic surface that players despised.

Meanwhile, the NFL had evolved into a pass-crazy league, and the ever-changing rosters and soaring eight-figure salaries brought on by free agency left many coaches shaking their heads in amazement. Some of the good ones, such as Jimmy Johnson, Joe Gibbs, and Jim Mora, were forced out the door because of glaring cap mistakes. On the field, there was more strutting and gyrating, mostly by free-spirited receivers and running backs, who called their childish acts "part of my package."

Dick Vermeil stayed busy with speaking engagements and his involvement with many Philadelphia-area charities, even as he approached his 64th birthday. One of his favorites was called Eagles Fly for Leukemia. It was started in 1969 in support of tight end Fred Hill, whose three-year-old daughter Kim had developed acute lymphatic leukemia. Eagles owner Leonard Tose, general manager Jim Murray, and Stan Lane, one of Hill's neighbors, spearheaded the original drive. Despite his crowded schedule, Vermeil eagerly joined in.

Yet, with all of his personal appearances, his involvement in charity work, and his frequent visits back to his beloved Calistoga, Vermeil still missed coaching. It brought to mind Tom Flores' old line after he moved from the sideline to the general manager's office with the Raiders. "It's interesting," Flores had said. "You go all the way to the weekend and, all of a sudden, you're outside looking in."

Al Davis, Flores' boss, had suggested that NFL coaches could last only 10 years because of the stress. Davis proposed that all coaches take a one-year sabbatical. "Not a bad idea," said Flores. "But it doesn't work that way."

It happened that Vermeil had coached for exactly 10 years and taken his own kind of sabbatical away from the sideline. In his much calmer world, there was Napa Valley wine and Carol, his loving wife, at his side. Vermeil wasn't drawing bootleg plays on paper napkins anymore, but his mind was never very far from the game that still fascinated him. The average age of the 31 NFL head coaches in 2000 was 50.6 years; 14 were in their forties. Vermeil, trim and full of energy, could still beat most of them in a sprint. And there was an unshakable feeling that he could beat them on the field as well.

If Vermeil had checked the league standings on the day of his 64th birthday, he would have found that only two of the six division winners from 1999 (Indianapolis and his former Rams team) were leading their divisions. Jacksonville (3–6) had slipped to fourth place after winning 14 games in 1999. Seattle (2–7) had dropped to fourth, Washington (6–2) to second, and Tampa Bay (4–4) to third. None of the six would repeat as division winners. Only three (St. Louis, Indianapolis, and Tampa Bay) would make the playoffs.

Even the most loyal fans were left wondering exactly which players would return to their favorite team each year. Vermeil must have wondered, too; the ever-changing nature of the game was one reason, maybe the biggest reason, that he had retired from the Rams with the Super Bowl confetti still in his hair. Vermeil said he couldn't stand to see loyal players, the ones he hugged in those joyful moments, leave "The Cause" for the cold cash of another team. It was the same empty feeling he had at UCLA, when he felt bad about leaving because he couldn't take all of his assistants with him to Philadelphia. In the new millennium, coaches also had to deal with ego-driven agents, increasingly impatient owners, and players being arrested seemingly every other weekend.

Vermeil knew that if he returned to coaching, he needed more support than he sought when he coached the Eagles in the mid-1970s. Not just from his assistant coaches, but from his scouts, his capologists, and his trainers. If he had remained with the Rams, he would have had to replace center Mike Gruttadauria, offensive tackle Fred Miller, defensive end Jay Williams, and linebackers Mike Morton and Charlie Clemons. (All five jumped to other teams as free agents in 2000.)

All Vermeil knew was that he desperately wanted to reenter this adventurous and insecure world, even if it was for mad and crazy coaches. How adventurous and insecure? With the game now a contest of passing and catching, an injury to your starting quarterback could send a team plummeting to the bottom of the division; after all, the Kurt Warners of the world were in short supply. The cap system almost always left some teams with marginal backups. The truly great scouts—Bobby Beathard, Bucko Kilroy, George Young, Ron Wolf, and Tony Razzano among them—had left the game, leaving behind what Bill Walsh once called "big guys in trench coats with stopwatches who don't know anything about evaluating talent."

* * *

In Kansas City, meanwhile, Carl Peterson was spending his frustrating days wondering if the Chiefs were ever going to return to the Super Bowl. The Chiefs had won Super Bowl IV after the 1969 season behind cool quarterback Len Dawson and a great defense, led by Buck Buchanan and Willie Lanier. In the 1990s, the Chiefs played like a Super Bowl team in December but then always flopped in the playoffs. The Chiefs won 102 games in the '90s mostly under Marty Schottenheimer, one more than those excellent Dallas teams over the same period. The Cowboys, however, had claimed two Super Bowl trophies. The Chiefs never even got close.

Since Super Bowl IV, the Chiefs' playoff record was 3–9. It was 3–7 under Schottenheimer, who could never squeeze enough offense out of five different quarterbacks, including a near-retirement Joe Montana. The Chiefs were bounced out of the playoffs in the first round five times. Their best chance at the Super Bowl was in 1997 when the Chiefs finished 13–3, winning six games by less than a touchdown. Pete Stoyanovich made 26 of 27 field goals and won four games with his leg.

Yet, in the divisional playoff game at Arrowhead Stadium, the Chiefs offense fizzled and the defense couldn't stop two scoring drives by John Elway and the Denver Broncos. The 14–10 defeat was one of the most painful for Schottenheimer, who had endured a lot of them with the Chiefs. "It's the reality of life," said Schottenheimer. "I'll always be thinking about the season until the Super Bowl champion is crowned. Then I'm able to forget it because everybody is 0–0 for next year."

Peterson, the Chiefs' president and general manager, was thinking about the next season, too. He had been hired by owner Lamar Hunt, who liked his bold move to the United States Football League in 1983. Peterson left his personnel job with the Eagles to become president of the USFL's Philadelphia Stars a year before Vermeil resigned. Hunt said Peterson's risky move reminded him of his own nerve in 1960, when he put an American Football League team in Dallas and challenged the Cowboys.

Peterson and Vermeil had been virtually inseparable since they first met in Los Angeles in 1974. Vermeil, hired by UCLA to succeed Pepper Rodgers as head coach, had retained Peterson as his receivers coach and confidante. They headed east to join the Eagles, but Peterson left his best friend in 1988 to run Hunt's football team.

> *"Coach Vermeil was more than a coach. I mean, Coach was a family builder. He loved guys who grew up in a family. He helped guys who didn't know how to develop a balance in their lives."*
>
> BILLY LONG, FORMER CHIEFS ASSISTANT
> STRENGTH AND CONDITIONING COACH

And now, after 13 years and what seemed like a lifetime of playoff misery, Carl Peterson was headed back to Philadelphia to talk with his old friend. Not about ideas or personnel or visiting training camp, but about a shocking offer: Peterson wanted Vermeil to come out of retirement at age 64 to coach the struggling Chiefs. Before leaving Kansas City, Peterson had conferred with Stiles, the Chiefs' vice president of football operations and one of Vermeil's lifelong friends.

"If we make a change," Peterson said, "what direction do you think we should go?"

"Well," said Stiles, "there's a guy you and I have known for a long time. His first name is Dick."

"Dick Vermeil?"

"Yeah, Dick Vermeil."

Peterson initially dismissed the idea. "He just retired," he told Stiles.

"No one keeps pace with Dick Vermeil. You just hope to stay in the same ballpark. He's the first guy in here in the morning and the last guy to leave at night."

LYNN STILES

"He's not retired," said Stiles. "I sat with him in a booth at one of our games this season and his whole demeanor was about coaching."

Peterson thought back to the recent phone conversations he had with Vermeil, and suddenly the idea of seeking Vermeil didn't seem so implausible. "I could tell every time I talked to him that there was still a void," recalled Peterson. "He missed the coaching. I think he second-guessed himself when he stepped away too quickly in St. Louis. He just wasn't finished with it."

On January 2, 2001, Peterson and Stiles boarded an early-morning US Airways flight bound for Philadelphia. They would eventually end up at the doorstep of Vermeil's log cabin lodge in the distant countryside, about a 45-minute drive from the airport.

Peterson had learned that Dan Snyder, who owned the Washington Redskins, and assistant Pepper Rodgers had visited Vermeil just one day earlier. Snyder had fired Norv Turner 13 games into the 2000 season. Presumably, his visit was to ask Vermeil to recommend a replacement. Yet, Peterson knew Snyder was a persistent man with a load of money to offer. And, of course, he knew about Vermeil's desire to coach again.

"I'm not going to spin my wheels, Dick," said Peterson. "You can have Dan Snyder and Pepper Rodgers in your house, but you won't let me in? Listen, I'm just going to come and sit down with you and Carol and tell you why I think you should be the head coach of the Kansas City Chiefs."

Vermeil knew all about the Chiefs' history of late-season flops. The offense needed a big-play back. The offensive line was solid, a tradition with the Chiefs. Tight end Tony Gonzalez had caught 93 passes the season before, and receiver Derrick Alexander had led the AFC in yards per catch (17.8). Elvis Grbac, the quarterback, was a hot-and-cold guy but had a promising season in 2000.

The Chiefs defense was another matter. The big problem: poor tackling, especially in the secondary. While the Steelers and Raiders liked big hitters in their secondary, the Chiefs always seemed to favor speed over toughness and tackling skills. The linebackers weren't bad, but the Chiefs' front four seemed to get tangled in too many hand fights, allowing big running plays.

As Peterson and Stiles got settled, Vermeil started a fire in what Stiles later described as "a fireplace big enough to walk into."

"We had a game plan and we spent the late afternoon and early evening at his place, covering everything," said Peterson. "Lynn and I probably did as fine a recruiting job on Dick and Carol as we ever did recruiting players at UCLA."

Vermeil broke open a bottle of wine during a lull in the talks. Meanwhile, Peterson pulled out his yellow pad, the one with all the issues involved in the hiring process. It was a cozy winter scene among old friends. Lori Peterson, Carl's wife, had flown in from Pittsburgh where she was working for HOK, the design company, on the Steelers' new stadium project. Flames flickered in the huge fireplace and there was talk of other times like this and other faraway places.

At one point, Vermeil left the room. Carol looked at Peterson and Stiles, two old family friends, and shook her head.

"You guys are good," she said. "You're very good."

When Vermeil returned, Peterson laid it all on the line. "Dick, we've known each other for so many years," Peterson said. "Your very essence, your very being, is to be a football coach. And I don't think you've got that out of your system yet. Therefore, I think you need to come to work for the Kansas City Chiefs."

Peterson felt he had a natural edge. Vermeil had been a color analyst for some Chiefs preseason games and had met owner Lamar Hunt and his wife

Norma. When Vermeil was coaching the Rams, they always played a charity game against the Chiefs known as the Governor's Cup Series.

The recruiting session then moved to a quaint Italian restaurant. As they headed for dinner, Peterson and Stiles felt they were close to a deal. Vermeil was never good at hiding his feelings. His response to their questions clearly showed his interest. And when Peterson went for the final answer just after the end of the meal, he was sure that Vermeil would be his next coach.

> *"I heard from Lamar and Norma on more than one occasion that Dick and Carol were their favorites. They loved him."*
>
> CARL PETERSON

Peterson stood up, turned to Vermeil, and said, "C'mon, let's go to my office." Vermeil, with a look of curiosity on his face, followed Peterson into the nearby men's room, which Peterson promptly locked for privacy.

"Okay, now let's discuss the hard part," Peterson said. "I mean, what I think you should be compensated. I need you for three years."

Then Peterson threw his knockout punch. His offer: $10 million for three seasons. Vermeil was taken aback. Just as he was pondering the figures he had just heard, a knock came on the door. Peterson pulled the lock and the two men returned to the table.

Meanwhile, Lori Peterson had presented Carol with a piece of jewelry designed with a Chiefs theme, a nice touch near the end of the evening.

"I think I stunned him," Peterson said later. The blockbuster offer was more than Dick Vermeil had earned with the Rams and Eagles combined.

Peterson told him they were staying at the Philadelphia Airport Marriott and had an early-morning flight back to Kansas City.

"I think I need to go home and think about it," said Vermeil, trying to hide his true feelings of gratitude and growing interest.

"Just give me a call in the morning," said Peterson, who already sensed that the Chiefs had gotten their man.

At 6:00 the next morning, the phone rang in Peterson's hotel room. It was Vermeil. "I'll take the job," Vermeil told him. A broad smile broke out across Peterson's face. He had lured Dick Vermeil back into coaching, and everything was right again with the Chiefs and his view of NFL football. As Peterson and Stiles later walked along an airport concourse, in that triumphant moment, Peterson felt like throwing a clenched fist into the air in celebration. Bring on the Raiders. Bring on the Broncos. Bring on anybody.

Before Vermeil began work in his office at Arrowhead, there was a not-so-small matter to clear up. NFL commissioner Paul Tagliabue had ruled that signing Vermeil would cost the Chiefs their second- and third-round draft picks, plus $500,000, because of Vermeil's prior employment as a consultant with St. Louis. The Rams, who gave Vermeil a $2 million bonus for winning the Super Bowl, felt he would remain retired through 2001. Peterson said Vermeil would pay the $500,000 assessment.

"It was just the total package," Vermeil said, explaining his sudden interest in coaching the Chiefs. "First, there was an expression of need. There was a personal relationship. And they represented a fine organization. Going to Kansas City isn't like starting over. I put in three tough years with the Rams. They told me I could coach there as long as I wanted to. I know there was all of that radio talk that they forced me out. But we had a great relationship with ownership and management. If I had known my feelings then, I wouldn't have gone."

Vermeil said that Carol never wanted him to retire anyway. "She is for me doing what I love to do. I'm a relationship leader. I'm used to a leadership role, and I missed that," he said.

In fact, Carol seemed overjoyed that her husband was going to coach again. "Once you've become king," she said, "it's nice to be the king."

* * *

Vermeil's Chiefs didn't play like kings, though, at least not at the outset. Vermeil had acquired two new offensive talents, former Rams quarterback Trent Green—the man who had been replaced by Kurt Warner prior to their Super Bowl run—and Priest Holmes, a 5'9" free-agent running back who had gone undrafted in 1997 because of a poor workout at the NFL's scouting combine.

Holmes proved to be the best free-agent signing of the Vermeil era, and quite possibly of any era. In 2000, the year before Vermeil arrived, the Chiefs' best back was Tony Richardson, a 233-pound fullback not known for any wiggle or burst. Accordingly, the Chiefs finished 25th in rushing (91.6 yards per game).

Then Holmes arrived, swiping Richardson's job and rushing for 1,555 yards. Holmes won the league's rushing title on the last day of the season, gaining 117 yards in a 21–18 loss to Seattle that ended the Chiefs' year at 6–10.

General manager Carl Peterson tried to find some humor in the losing season that also prevented tight end Tony Gonzalez from playing in his third Pro Bowl because of a torn knee ligament. "We still have an appointment in Hawaii," quipped Peterson. "For mai tais."

Gonzalez had another brilliant season. He caught 73 passes, often against double coverage. Gonzalez, Holmes, and kick returner Dante Hall gave the Chiefs some memorable afternoons. Over the years, it always seemed to be that way for the Chiefs. The offense and special teams would produce some remarkable stats, but the Chiefs would flop in the drive for the playoffs.

"It's a little disappointing," said Vermeil of his first season in Kansas City. "I anticipated being better." The defense, which had its moments (holding seven teams under 21 points), too often gave up big plays on decisive drives. Trent Green didn't help the cause either, throwing a team-record 24 interceptions.

Also not helping matters were Vermeil's first two drafts; each failed to produce one legitimate long-term starter for his troubled defense. Tackle Ryan Sims, the sixth pick in the 2002 draft, was eventually traded. Taken in the third round in 2001, tackle Eric Downing never panned out. Linebacker Scott Fujita and safety Shaunard Harts, two low picks, were plugged in for a year.

So it wasn't surprising that Vermeil and the Chiefs struggled through another disappointing season in Vermeil's second year. Only their high-powered offense and three squeaker wins (40–39 over Cleveland, 17–16 over Buffalo, and 24–22 over San Diego) allowed the Chiefs to finish at 8–8. In the game against the Browns, it was Dwayne Rudd's premature helmet-tossing penalty that allowed 42-year-old Morten Andersen to boot the winning field goal as time ran out.

According to defensive end Eric Hicks, what the Chiefs remembered most of all was the 24–0 "whupping" they got in a season-ending loss to Oakland. Whupping? The Chiefs possessed the ball for only 19 minutes, 45 seconds and gained only 176 yards in a driving rainstorm. The Raiders rushed 60 times for 280 yards before the Chiefs limped off the field, shut out for the first time in 139 games.

As *Kansas City Star* columnist Joe Posnanski noted, "No team in NFL history has frittered away a season quite the way this Chiefs team did. This team will lead the league in scoring. Do you know how hard it is to score more points than any other NFL team and not even finish with a winning record? Only one other team has pulled off that neat, little trick, the 1985 San Diego Chargers. And they turned the ball over 49 times. (The Chiefs turned it over only 15 times, losing only two fumbles)."

"I'm not going to talk about what needs to be fixed," said Vermeil, always mindful of individual criticism after the battle. "I just got my ass handed to me. I don't feel like talking about next year right now."

One Chief, who preferred to remain anonymous, said the defense "hated [Greg Robinson's] system all year. That's no secret." Under Robinson, the Chiefs played a 4-3 base with a read-and-react, protect-your-gap philosophy. Some of the younger Chiefs preferred an aggressive blitzing style to fit their showboating personalities.

Eric Warfield, a veteran corner, was baffled by how the Chiefs struggled all season. "It's to the point where it's unexplainable," Warfield said. Obviously, he hadn't watched too many defensive game tapes.

They say nothing is ever certain in pro football. But from 2001 to 2005, the certainty was that the Chiefs defense would rank lower than Trent Green's offense. The unit that Vermeil sent out with crossed fingers and a little prayer probably missed more tackles than any defense in the league. During the Vermeil years, the Chiefs defense was ranked 23rd, 32nd, 29th, 31st, and 25th. In those five seasons, the Chiefs surrendered 1,835 points and 213 touchdowns.

"I knew I had to go offense," said Peterson, referring to the composition of the roster. "That was his forte. And when you have a head coach, you want to give him all the things that he needs to win. Assistant coaches, players, facilities. As I always say, 'an environment to win in.' As good as an offense we had—and we had some top offenses—we were equally poor on the defensive side."

Under Vermeil, the Chiefs twice led the league in offensive production, scoring 483 points in 2004 and 403 points in 2005. The most crushing season, however, was 2003, the year the Chiefs opened with a nine-game winning streak, scored a club-record 484 points, sent nine players to the Pro Bowl, and finished with a 13–3 record.

Vermeil even liked his reshaped defense that year. "Now we've got three first-rounders playing," he had said. "We've got [free safety] Jerome Woods and [defensive tackle] Ryan Sims back from injuries. And we signed [defensive end] Vonnie Holliday and [linebacker] Shawn Barber." Vermeil couldn't stop talking about Barber. "I don't think the Chiefs have ever had a better weak-side line-backer," he said. "He's a leader, with a lot of charisma and a great work ethic."

Actually, Vermeil felt the Chiefs upgraded their defense in 2002 despite some dreadful numbers (allowing 399 points and 27 touchdown passes). He noted that the Chiefs jumped into the top 15 among defenses based on the second half of the season. The defense didn't have Woods or Sims, but it held their last eight opponents to an average of 19.9 points. The Chiefs shut out Arizona and held St. Louis, Vermeil's old team, to one touchdown.

In the off-season, there was concern about Holmes when he underwent hip surgery. Yet, he bounced back with a 1,420-yard season in 2003. Holmes also caught 74 passes, proving to be a more versatile back than the Chiefs had expected.

Leaving nothing to chance, the Chiefs drafted Penn State's Larry Johnson, a 228-pound power back with 4.46 speed and great body lean. "He will compete for a backup slot," grumped Vermeil, who had wanted the Chiefs to draft Tyler Brayton, a 6'6" defensive end snapped up by Oakland five spots below Johnson. Brayton was a useful, but not exceptional, starter with the Raiders, sometimes sliding over to linebacker.

The Chiefs got off to a great start, beating defending AFC North Division champ Pittsburgh 41–20 after a season-opening 27–14 win over San Diego. Against the Steelers, Holmes scored three touchdowns and Hall streaked 100 yards on a kickoff for another score.

The streak continued for nine weeks. The Chiefs defeated two division winners (Baltimore 17–10 and Green Bay 40–34 in overtime on Green's 51-yard pass to Eddie Kennison). Green threw for 400 yards against the Packers, easily outdueling Brett Favre, who threw an interception that free safety Jerome Woods returned 79 yards for a touchdown.

The eighth and ninth victims were Buffalo (38–5) and Cleveland (41–20). Now there was excitement and belief. Then the Chiefs stumbled, losing to Cincinnati 24–19 because they couldn't stop Rudi Johnson (165 yards), then three weeks later to Denver 45–27 because they couldn't put a hand on Clinton Portis (218 yards, club-record five touchdowns).

Yet, there was a good feeling all around after a season-ending 31–3 rout of the Bears in which Holmes scored his 26th and 27th touchdowns, a league record. The Chiefs owned home-field advantage against their first playoff foe, an Indianapolis team that had a lightweight defense based on quickness. Surely Vermeil's line would shove them around for Holmes and keep them away from Green.

* * *

With their 13–3 record, the Chiefs held the home-field advantage throughout the AFC playoffs. Surely this would be the breakthrough year, the year in which Dick Vermeil would take his third different team to the Super Bowl. Yet, this was a season in which the AFC was loaded with ambitious teams besides the Chiefs: New England (14–2), Indianapolis (12–4), Tennessee (12–4), and Baltimore (10–6), led by 2,000-yard rusher Jamal Lewis and a tenacious defense.

In their first divisional playoff game, the Chiefs lived up to their reputation as a defense that played tentatively, as if they were afraid to lose. Quarterback Peyton Manning shredded the Chiefs secondary with a spray-it-around attack, passing for 304 yards and three touchdowns. The Colts also ran for 142 yards behind their mammoth line to win a 38–31 shootout.

The Chiefs got a punishing 176-yard rushing game from Holmes. Green, the Chiefs' other weapon, had a decent game, too. But he couldn't match Manning's quick start that gave the Colts leads of 14–3 and 24–10 and forced the Chiefs into a desperate game of catch-up.

"Neither team punted," said Peterson. "There was no defense. They scored first, we scored. They scored, we scored. They finally held serve and beat us. We had no defense. That was our Achilles' heel. We just couldn't stop anybody and it killed us."

Holmes got his running lanes and Green went untouched. Yet, the poor Chiefs couldn't cope with Peyton Manning's offense that generated 434 yards to win the wild ping-pong match. The Colts scored on six of their first seven possessions. According to Lynn Stiles, the vice president of football operations, defensive coordinator Greg Robinson changed his game plan 48 hours before kickoff.

"He changed it on Friday," said Stiles. "We played a soft defense, read-and-react, each guy responsible for a gap. If you get blocked and you're in the gap, that's okay. It sounds good, but then it spills over and you have a $10 million [running back] being pursued by a $30 safety trying to make a play downfield. We had no pressure. Our defensive linemen were down in their stances for 30 seconds or more, into their isometric contractions, before the ball was snapped with three to five seconds left [on the play clock]. [Robinson] gave them a Rembrandt, a still picture. We didn't reroute the receivers. If I didn't know better, I'd think it must have been a fix."

Stiles said Vermeil never asked for Robinson's resignation. "You know Dick," Stiles said. "He's a loyal, loyal, loyal guy. So Dick wouldn't fire him. He fired himself."

Robinson walked into Vermeil's office after the bitter playoff loss to the Colts and said he was leaving. Vermeil, who wept at a press conference to announce that Robinson had resigned, said he was "stunned" by the decision.

"Tough to say good-bye to Greg," said a teary-eyed Vermeil. "I've watched him coach since he was a kid. It seems like just the other day he was called a genius. I'm going to miss him."

Robinson agreed with Vermeil that his resignation was a necessity. "I wanted it in the worst way for it not to be," said Robinson, whose name had been attached by fans to a website called firegregrobinson.com.

Most of the Chiefs' defensive players supported the decision. "To lose the way we lost to Denver, to Minnesota, and then in the playoffs to Indianapolis, certainly it would have been hard for any guy to come back after that," said defensive end Vonnie Holliday. "He tried everything he could to get this team going."

"I feel very hollow," said Robinson. "I didn't experience what we were really trying to get done. I'm like the coach who says, 'We didn't lose; we just ran out of time.' Unfortunately, my time has run out."

Vermeil and Peterson quickly agreed to bring Gunther Cunningham back as defensive coordinator. Cunningham's defensive units had led the league in scoring defense in 1995 and 1997. But those units featured Derrick Thomas, the league's best blitzing linebacker and a natural leader. There was nobody close to Thomas in the years that followed Vermeil's arrival. And there were no defenders quite like Dale Carter, James Hasty, or Mark McMillian, the 5'7" nickel back who had eight interceptions in that memorable 13–3 season in 1997.

Off that thrilling but ultimately heartbreaking season, the Chiefs signed Vermeil for two more years. Peterson remembered how the Rams had won a Super Bowl in Vermeil's third year and how the Eagles had reached the Super Bowl in Vermeil's fifth year. "They had wanted to run him out of town after his second

> *"I went up to visit him in training camp when he was coaching Kansas City. Somebody walked me down to pretty much the worst, darkest room in the entire facility. There was a cot sitting there and a couple of television monitors, where he could watch playbacks."*
>
> GREG KINNEAR

year with the Rams," said Peterson. "I had some conversations with [Rams president] John Shaw, and frankly, he was ready to say good-bye to Dick. I told him, 'John, just trust me, you've got to let him get his program going.'"

In his last two seasons, however, Vermeil didn't finish his usual drive to the top. His 2004 team, beset by injuries and poor pass defense, fell to 7–9. The defense, with two new starters up front (defensive end Jared Allen, a pass-rushing rookie, and defensive tackle Lionel Dalton, a 315-pound free agent cut by the Redskins), ranked 31st in the league based on yards allowed.

The signs that 2004 was hardly another magical drive to the Super Bowl, as Vermeil had achieved in Philadelphia and St Louis, came as early as the third game. Kris Brown, a kicker without much range, boomed a 49-yard field goal with two seconds left, giving the struggling Houston Texans a 24–21 upset. A year before, the Chiefs had manhandled the Texans 42–14, scoring 28 points in less than 12 minutes.

The Chiefs split their next two games, then enjoyed a 56–10 rout of Atlanta in which Holmes and Derrick Blaylock each scored four touchdowns. "We felt our big people could control the game," said a jubilant Vermeil. "We sort of set the tone all week that we would put the game in the hands of our big people on the offensive line." A week later, there was a 45–35 revenge win over the Colts in yet another shootout; Vermeil's high-powered offense gained 590 yards. Yet, the Chiefs couldn't shake their old habits. Bad tackling. Weak run defense. Costly turnovers.

In one midseason stretch, the Chiefs lost four straight. They led in each game, only to lose by three points to Tampa Bay, seven points to New Orleans, eight points to New England, and three points to San Diego. Larry Johnson, their second-year back, carried them to four late-season wins, but the Chiefs lost again to Doug Flutie and the playoff-bound Chargers 24–17 in their final game as Trent Green threw four interceptions. The Chargers rested many of their regulars, but it didn't seem to matter. The only shining moments for the Chiefs came as Gonzalez was running rings around the Chargers secondary. He finished with 14 catches, giving him 102 receptions for the season, a new league record for tight ends.

"It's incredible because he continues to do it year after year," said Green. "They double-team him a lot of times and he finds a way to get open. That's about the only positive out of today."

Vermeil had done everything possible to bring the Chiefs a championship. During the off-season, he invited units of his team to his home for cookouts. He lightened the workout load. He drove his points home in meetings, but let his veteran staff—Al Saunders, Mike White, Gunther Cunningham, and Peter Giunta—do most of the coaching. So now there was just one more season to play out.

"Anyone 69 years old is a lame duck," Vermeil conceded just before his final season. "I'm on the last year of my contract. And I just feel that if this football team is playing very well, then I think maybe my approach still works. My process still works and I can keep coaching. If it is not doing well, and Lamar Hunt isn't experiencing a successful season, or a good football team, then I think I will leave."

"He is so genuine. He does it the right way with values. He does it with honor. And he does it with dignity."

AL SAUNDERS

After starting out as a win-one lose-one squad on its way to a .500 record, Vermeil's final team closed with a determined drive to reach the playoffs. The Chiefs won five of their last seven games to finish 10–6, but they fell one game short. Their two losses were on the road against NFC East teams, the Cowboys and Giants.

Both games were lost in the final minutes. The Cowboys drove 68 yards and scored with 22 seconds left for the lead. Then Lawrence Tynes missed a 41-yard field goal at the final gun, leaving Dallas with a 31–28 win. Against the Giants, the Chiefs couldn't locate Tiki Barber, who rushed for a club-record 220 yards in the 27–17 win. Barber scored the decisive touchdown at the end of a 10-play drive, and the Giants pulled loose a fumble and intercepted Green, all in the final 2:48.

Vermeil's final season proved a few things, both positive and negative. Larry Johnson, who ran for 1,750 yards and scored 21 touchdowns, emerged as a great back. Trent Green, who threw for 20,117 yards and 111 touchdowns in five seasons, became a Pro Bowl quarterback. (Peyton Manning, arguably the league's best pure passer, threw for 20,902 yards over the same period.) The Chiefs' offensive line, anchored by Willie Roaf and Will Shields, was among the best in the league. Tight end Tony Gonzalez developed into a certain future Hall of Famer. The Chiefs defense, on the other hand, was still too easy to push around. It lacked fighters. Indeed, maybe the defense should have followed the advice of former coach George Allen, who felt a flat team sometimes needed a good bench-clearing fight to wake up.

"Every team that's worth a darn has to get internal leadership," Lynn Stiles said recently. "That's one of the things we lacked at Kansas City."

At the very end, after the Chiefs had drubbed the Cincinnati Bengals 37–3, Vermeil began hugging his players and his assistant coaches. His coaching career that had started 46 years earlier as an assistant at Del Mar High in San Jose was over. The Kansas City players, now as emotional as the Super Bowl team that they never became, stood and cheered. "My heart is pounding," said Carol Vermeil, who was cheering with them. "I have been very philosophical because I'm not thinking about the loss, because it's a huge loss. I think of it as another awesome chapter in our lives." Then she headed for the Chiefs dressing room to meet her husband. "That's the first time ever in my football career," she said afterward, referring to her venture into the steamy locker room. "It was a big lovefest."

"We didn't win a Super Bowl for you," Vermeil told owner Lamar Hunt. "Sooner or later, Carl [Peterson] is going to take you to a Super Bowl and I'll go with you." This was a wish that Vermeil would never fulfill. Hunt, a classy, soft-spoken man, died of prostate cancer on December 13, 2006. Peterson was fired after the 2008 season, his 20th with the Chiefs.

On January 4, 2006, Vermeil stood before the local media and formally announced his retirement, this time for good. There were tears in his eyes as he spoke. "It's tough," he said. "But it's the right thing to do."

As a final gesture to his coaching staff, Vermeil purchased custom-made suits as Christmas presents for his 20 assistants. "I wanted them to look sharp," he cracked.

As his eyes glistened, Vermeil recalled that several times during the pregame warm-ups on the road, some fans would scream out, "Hey Vermeil, why don't you cry for us?"

"Sooner or later, I got tired of all that," he said. "But, hey, that's me."

Vermeil briefly reflected on the inability of the Chiefs to reach the Super Bowl. "Did we get done what we wanted to get done?" he said. "Not quite. Did we fail? No way. No way."

He couldn't end the press conference without mentioning his veteran staff. "My coaches, I see these guys and they know how I feel," said Vermeil. "You know why? Because I tell them I love them. Why feel something about somebody and not express it? What good does it do?"

> *"The NFL misses him, and we are all better people for having been around him. He was a very special man and a unique human being in a unique business."*
>
> AL SAUNDERS

Finally, the coaching career of Dick Vermeil was over. They will not soon forget him in Kansas City, or St. Louis, or Philadelphia, or in those hidden California towns in the Napa Valley where his career began.

"He probably has the largest legacy of any man I know," said Lynn Stiles. "I mean, Vince Lombardi was a great coach, but what about the people who were close to him? I don't know. Dick Vermeil's legacy will be marked on the basis of his relationships with the people he coached, and the people he surrounded himself with. Not the wins and losses or the Super Bowls. That's not what Dick Vermeil was about."

Epilogue

When the mood strikes, Dick and Carol Vermeil return to Calistoga, the little town in Northern California's wine country where they both grew up. They live in a sprawling 110-acre lodge outside of Philadelphia, but Vermeil has never been able to break his ties with the Napa Valley.

The trips back home, however, are more than just a pilgrimage to remind themselves of their youth and the Owl Garage, where Vermeil worked for his father Louie and where Carol used to hang out. Returning to Calistoga just seemed like the natural thing to do. Vermeil has always felt the same way about the people in his life. The players he coached and the coaches with whom he worked, sometimes until they dozed off at 4:00 AM. There were ties to them, too, and Vermeil never forgot.

He hired John Ralston as the Eagles' offensive coordinator in 1978, 13 years after Ralston had given Vermeil his first major coaching job at Stanford. He brought Wilbert Montgomery, his former star running back, into the coaching world in 1997 with the St. Louis Rams. In 1983, several months after he had left the Eagles, Vermeil paid an unannounced visit to publicist Jim Gallagher, who had recently had his right lung removed. "Hey Jim, just want to come up and say hello," said Vermeil, who stayed for an hour of warm conversation.

Vermeil also liked to mend ties that had been broken. Soon after joining the Eagles, he made Chuck Bednarik an honorary coach. Bednarik, the greatest player in Eagles history, had divorced himself from the club. "He was a helluva coach," said Bednarik. "When Dick Vermeil left the Eagles, I left, and I've never been back."

Joe Kuharich, the most scorned coach in the history of the Eagles, was diagnosed with cancer in 1980. Vermeil appointed him as a low-key aide. Kuharich, who had left the team in 1968, was thrilled. He was back in football, thankful to be participating on the fringe of the game.

From Calistoga to Kansas City, there are hundreds of players and dozens of assistant coaches who remember Vermeil's driving style as well as his genuine affection. Long, hard workouts. Attention to detail. Endless statistics, printed in his distinctive all-caps handwriting. Sometimes the kind of nasty language heard on the New Jersey waterfront after the Eagles bungled a play. And at the end of a tough, close victory, the teary eyes and the big hug.

Vermeil knew hardly anything about drugs and nothing about point spreads. Presumably, they don't snort cocaine or gamble in Calistoga. The Calistogans sip their choice wines and enjoy company at dinner. They are honest, genuine, caring people, and Dick Vermeil was among the most famous of them all. Yet, there is no Vermeil Avenue or Vermeil Stadium in Calistoga. He would never have approved the honor.

* * *

I first started talking to Dick Vermeil about collaborating on an autobiography while he was coaching the St. Louis Rams. He rejected the idea, even after the Rams won a Super Bowl and he retired with the championship that had eluded him in Philadelphia.

After yet another unsuccessful attempt at coaxing a book out of Vermeil when he was coaching in Kansas City, he explained his reluctance in a letter.

"Thanks for your letter wondering about a Vermeil book of some type," he wrote. "As I think I mentioned once before to you, I'm really not interested in any type of autobiography as I personally don't think there is that much there."

The decision to proceed with this biography proved that Vermeil was totally wrong. He was a remarkable coach, unique in his ability to drive his players to exhaustion but not lose their affection. Vermeil loved the game and his players so much that he was often moved to tears. His weepy press conferences were sometimes ridiculed as maudlin. But as Hall of Fame defensive end Bruce Smith said after learning of his selection, "I cry because I am not less than a man, but because I am a man."

Without interviewing Vermeil, I had to rely on three sources: previous interviews with the coach when I covered the Eagles for the *Philadelphia Inquirer*; recollections from former players and assistant coaches; and clippings from the team's excellent archive. I found Vermeil to be an honest, sentimental man whose fanatical work habits would have threatened the stability of most families. As it turned out, his tenacity almost caused him to suffer a mental breakdown after coaching the Eagles for seven years.

Although Vermeil returned to win a Super Bowl and coach for eight more years, we are left to wonder what might have been if he had throttled his excessive work habits. Ron Jaworski, Vermeil's quarterback in Philadelphia, says the Eagles "could have won a lot of Super Bowls" if Vermeil had delegated more authority as he learned to do in St. Louis and Kansas City. That may be overstating it, but surely Vermeil could have enjoyed a longer coaching career, perhaps as long as 25 years.

As a former selector, I would vote Vermeil into the Pro Football Hall of Fame without stopping to think about it. Of course, most selectors are bound and tied by statistics, so Vermeil's candidacy remains a question mark. But Vermeil always wanted his career to be judged by what he meant to his players and coaches, not by wins and losses. The words *genuine, honest, caring, dedicated,* and yes, *loving,* are almost always part of any conversation about Dick

"When you look at what he did with those players, where their loyalty still lies, where the passion is, that's one of the things that's missing in the world today."

Jim Murray

Vermeil. Sure, Vermeil drove his players like no coach has since Vince Lombardi cracked the whip, and occasionally a fist, in Green Bay. Yet, Vermeil made them better players and, more importantly, better people.

Vermeil would have been a better coach in an earlier era, before so much uncertainty crept into the game. Catering to thrill-seeking television networks in the 1970s, the NFL owners reshaped the rules to showcase a pitch-and-catch game between the quarterback and receivers. It was a return to the wild and wide-open years of the old American Football League, which put the ball in the air to sell tickets. While Vermeil was working as a television analyst, the owners and players agreed to a free-agency/salary cap system, another variable to clutter the minds of head coaches.

The Lombardi years (1959–69) would have been kinder to Vermeil. It was a simpler game with a shorter schedule. His focus on work ethic would have been in step with society. His affection for his players would have been accepted as a love-in. Instead, we can only ponder Vermeil's career as a coach who lived by Louie Vermeil's book and his own remarkable source of energy.

After the 2005 season, he finally retired from this crazy, unpredictable game we call professional football. I shall always remember his honesty and availability, as well as his marathon-length workouts that often extended my own dinner hour past 8:00 PM. And in that Eagles season of 1980, the unexpected Super Bowl season of grit and belief, Vermeil was at his best. It was one of the greatest coaching jobs in NFL history.

Vermeil's passion now is Napa Valley wine. He and partner Paul Smith formed a winery called OnThEdge, which features a cabernet named Jean Louis Vermeil, named after the former coach's great-grandfather. The grapes come from vineyards once owned by Vermeil's other great-grandfather, Garibaldi Iaccheri.

"It's something I always wanted to do," said Vermeil. "It's a way to pay respect to my heritage."

So Dick Vermeil has returned to his roots, working the vineyards and enjoying the simple life as he did as a Calistoga teenager. For old time's sake and maybe more, Vermeil rebuilt one of Louie Vermeil's race cars and shipped it to the old Calistoga dirt track, where so many family memories were made.

"All the old guys came out of the woodwork to watch Dick take that car around the track, spinning his wheels and everything else like Louie used to do," said Tom Brookshier, Vermeil's old television partner. "The local newspaper ran a picture of Louie from the '40s. He had this hat on and he looked just like Dick. Just like the guy on the sideline."

Acknowledgments

It was fourth down. Three previous attempts to get Dick Vermeil interested in doing a book on his coaching career had failed. I would like to sincerely thank Tom Bast, editorial director for Triumph Books, for proceeding with this project rather than punting it away. I am also thankful for the assistance of Adam Motin, who guided me through the manuscript and gave it direction.

As with all unauthorized biographies, there were many contributors who knew Dick Vermeil and were eager to talk about his boyhood and his coaching years that followed. Carl Peterson and Lynn Stiles, who were almost always in step with the coach, were generous with their time. Mike White, who knew the Vermeil family and coached with him in St. Louis and Kansas City, was especially helpful in discussing Vermeil's coaching style. Al Saunders, another Vermeil assistant, reflected on his unique career and how he was able to change after burning out in Philadelphia.

Former Eagles general manager Jim Murray, a wonderful storyteller, was able to re-create the coast-to-coast coaching search and shared countless other stories with me. I am grateful to Greg Kinnear, the actor who played Vermeil in the movie *Invincible*, for taking time to discuss his impressions of the coach before jetting off to Europe to start another film project. Marion Campbell, Vermeil's fine defensive coordinator, interrupted his vacation and spoke with me from somewhere in the Bering Sea. The other coaches who proved invaluable to me included Bill McPherson, Dick Coury, Jerry Wampfler, Pepper Rodgers, Bill Walsh, John Ralston, Chuck Knox, Jim Hanifan, Sam Wyche, Don Shula, Jimmy Johnson, and Mike McCormack, Vermeil's predecessor. Wyche, Shula, and Johnson were particularly helpful in discussing burnout. Dr. John Trotta, a noted clinical psychologist, left me with a better understanding of burnout, its cause, and its symptoms. Another coach, Tom Flores, took me back to Super Bowl XV, the game in which his relaxed Oakland Raiders dominated the uptight Eagles.

Among the players I interviewed, John Sciarra was a wizard with memories of his UCLA years and the aborted Rose Bowl rebellion against Vermeil's lengthy workouts. We talked over a two-hour lunch on Balboa Island, California. Other players who were gracious with their time included Bill Bergey, Ron Jaworski, Randy Logan, Stan Walters, John Spagnola, Wilbert Montgomery, and Carl Hairston. Mike Dougherty, the Eagles' video director, gave me his impressions of Vermeil from a different side. Former Eagles publicist Jim Gallagher was an excellent source of stories from the Vermeil era, as well as a walking directory for phone numbers.

I am indebted to Derek Boyko, the Eagles' director of football media services, and staffers Brett Strohsacker and Matt Haley for their help in researching the Vermeil years in the team's archive rooms. In addition, Donald Deeley, a Temple University student researcher, responded to many requests as if he were the quarterback in a two-minute drill. Two public relations directors, Rick Smith (St. Louis) and Bob Moore (Kansas City), were diligent in supplying me background on Vermeil's time with their teams. Ryan Anderson of the Rams, Brad Kuhbander of the Chiefs, and the Pennsylvania Horticultural Society helped me with their research.

Finally, I would like to thank my partner, Marie Schebesta, for accepting the long nights that were necessary to complete this book. Like Carol Vermeil, she did it with good spirit and belief in the cause.

Appendix

Dick Vermeil's Off-Season Conditioning Manual

When Dick Vermeil took over as head coach of the Philadelphia Eagles in 1976, he implemented his own conditioning and training program, one designed to maximize the potential of each and every one of his players. Vermeil's belief in preparation and a strong work ethic led him to create an off-season conditioning manual that was distributed to all players. The following are selected pages from the coach's 1977 manual; they illustrate the level of commitment and effort Vermeil demanded from everyone in the Eagles organization.

1977 OFF-SEASON CONDITIONING MANUAL

PHILADELPHIA EAGLES

THE PHILADELPHIA EAGLES
Veterans Stadium, Philadelphia, Pennsylvania

Gentlemen:

The enclosed booklet is your off-season conditioning program,
specifically designed to prepare you for training camp in July and
the N.F.L. season. These booklets are to be turned in when you
report this summer, so take good care of it. Many hours of work have
gone into the preparation of this booklet and believe me it will be
well worth your efforts to follow the prescribed routines. As you
know, nothing comes easy in professional football. Everyone is
looking for a winning edge. Our edge has to come from outworking
our opponents in every phase of the game and this certainly includes
off season conditioning. It is my feeling that those that dedicate
themselves to the way of life they have chosen succeed, and if we
are to succeed in PHILADELPHIA each and every man must get himself
ready to play through proper training mechanics. It is all a matter
of dedication.

You all know how hard we work in training camp. All this program
will do is make hard work a little easier on you and allow you to
recover more rapidly in between those double sessions. The increase
in strength will show up in a positive improvement in your performance.
This is especially true of the linemen. There is no substitute for
strength and no excuse for the lack of it! Strength is one attribute
of professional athletes that an individual can improve through hard
work.

I don't have to tell you that professional football is physically
more demanding on your body than any other professional sport because
you are the people that put their bodies through the grind of pro
football. The bumps, bruises and injuries are many, therefore anything
you can do to prevent injuries is a very intelligent way of approaching
your job. Good off season condition definitely helps prevent injury
and prolongs professional athletic careers. Very few athletes make
the kind of money after retirement that they make while playing, and
it has to be very obvious to all those involved that proper off season
work can and will help you make a good salary over a longer period of
time. The program is in your hands. What you do with it is
specifically up to you. If you are SELF MOTIVATED and DEDICATED you
will go to work immediately. We are going to win in PHILADELPHIA! It
is just a matter of being PERSISTENT. Go to work. The job you save
may be your own.

Sincerely,

Dick Vermeil

INTRODUCTION

Tom Tellez, the Head Track Coach at the University of Houston and very well respected exercise physiologist, when he spoke to the Eagles during training camp last summer pointed out the fact that YOUR performance as an athlete is affected by seven basic factors.

1. Skill and Technique

2. Strength

3. Flexibility

4. Endurance

5. Speed

6. Mental Concentration

7. Rest

The exclusion of any one of these factors will detract from optimum performance. During the next five months (15 of February to the 18th of July) you can by training increase your strength, flexibility, endurance and as a by-product of the first three, speed.

The program that we are going to outline for you in this training book is a five day a week program. And each day's workout should begin and end with the flexibility routine that we have out-lined for you in Section 2. So at least 10 times a week you will be going through this routine. You will notice that there are 23 different exercises and it is important that you take the time to learn each exercise and do it right. After using the book for a week or two you'll have the routine down pretty well and you will be able to move fairly quickly and easily through the routine without having to refer back to the book.

On Mondays, Wednesdays, and Fridays from February 15th until June 13th you will be involved with the recommended weight program that we have outlined for you in Section 3. We have designed three different programs, so that each athlete will be involved in that type of program best suited for his individual needs. It would be impossible for us to overemphasize to you the importance this aspect of your training can have for you, your professional career, and for the 1977 Philadelphia Eagles football team. We will be a stronger football team in 1977 because of what you do during the next five months. One month before we start training camp we are going to have you switch your weight program from three days a week to two days a week as you step up your running program in preparation for camp.

During the first couple weeks of your weight program, work yourself gradually toward the weight (or number of plates) that you really want to use as you build greater strength and power. If you are on Nautilus, concentrate on good form and experiment with the number of plates you can work out with for each exercise. The interior linemen should work with a little lighter weight and do three sets of 10 on each exercise during February. By March first you should be in the kind of shape you need to be in to extend yourself on each exercise and really build up your strength.

Although the regular running program doesn't start until April 4, you should get out and jog for 10 to 12 minutes two days a week and play as much racquetball, handball or basketball as you can fit into your schedule. Starting April 4 you will find in Section 4 a workout schedule which will take you right up to the time you start camp. This schedule has been devised on the advice of both track coaches, exercise physiologists, and football trainers.

To review, flexibility before and after each workout; lift on Monday's, Wednesday's and Friday's; jog two days a week, play as much

racquetball, handball and basketball as you have time for, and
starting April 4 start the countdown to camp with the organized
running program outlined in Section 4.

In Section 5, Otho Davis has prepared for you a section on
diet and rest. These are important aspects of training and
conditioning and we felt you should have this information.

The last section of the book is a place for you to keep a record
on what you have done in your conditioning program. This section
should be a record of your improved strength and conditioning.
Your heart rate will go down the more you run and your strength will
go up remarkably as you lift.

Ron O'Neal will supervise the in-town conditioning program. Otho
Davis and Chuck Clausen will be available to discuss any specific
questions you might have in terms of off-season conditioning.

From time to time we will be asking you to report on the progress
you have made.

STRENGTH AND POWER DEVELOPMENT

The following three strength development programs were designed specifically for the National Football League athlete. For the purpose of strength development, we have divided the squad into three broad categories.

1. Interior Offensive and Defensive Linemen

In this group, the player must generate a tremendous amount of explosive force on every down and his performance would be benefited by increased muscle size and body bulk as long as he maintains his flexibility, movement and agility. Program A was designed for the athletes in this category and you will notice that explosive movement of relatively heavy weights exercising the basic muscles groups that the interior linemen use is basic to this program.

2. Skilled Athletes

Running backs, receivers and defensive backs.

This group of athletes will all benefit from increased strength and muscular endurance, but not necessarily from an increased muscle bulk. Where it is available, we will recommend to this group of athletes, the Nautilus Weight Machines. Nautilus Weight Machines not only increase strength and endurance, they also increase flexibility, and the athlete achieves maximum muscle development through the full range of motions. (Program B Nautilus or Program C free weights).

3. Linebackers and Tight Ends

Since the nature of your job involves many elements of both the interior linemen and the skilled athlete, you should pick the program which best serves your own particular needs. If you have good size, muscle bulk and power for your position, you should exercise as a skilled athlete.

(Program B or C). If you have marginal size, muscle bulk and power for your position, you should exercise as an interior linemen. (Program A).

Each of the following three programs is made up of exercises which strengthen football muscles and football muscle groups, and each exercise included in your weight program was selected because it will develop muscles which will make you a more effective professional or will strengthen muscles which will give you more protection from injury. You will find that these programs will not only increase your ability to generate more force and power because of your increased strength, but you will gain a great deal of muscular endurance which will make you a more effective football player longer on each down and a stronger player during the latter stages of each game.

Warm Up - It is extremely important that you precede each weight work out with the recommended flexibility routine. If you are lifting weights (not using Nautilus) you should start each exercise with one warm up set using a relatively light weight and doing 10 to 15 repetitions.

Note - You are going to get sore and stiff and temporarily lose some flexibility during the first two weeks of this program. It can't be helped, you are going to put a tremendous stress on your body that your body is not used to. Your body will adjust, however, to this increased stress. The stiffness and soreness will leave and as your flexibility will return and then eventually increase.

PROGRAM A

This is a heavy weight, low repetition program designed to make you a more powerful and dominating athlete. This program will concentrate on developing your legs and hips so that you are more explosive on the snap of the ball, your arms, chest and shoulders so that you can gain greater control of your opponent after the ball is snapped and the muscles around your knee, neck and shoulders so that you will be less susceptible to injury.

In this program, after a warm up set of 10 to 15 repetitions with a light weight, on your first set use a weight where you can do six repetitions. Then add some weight and try for five repetitions, keep adding weight after each set so that on your fifth and final set you are only attempting to get two repetitions. In addition, to your basic power exercises, we are recommending some additional exercises for the development of your neck, the muscles that support the knee and your stomach muscles.

<u>Note</u> - Make sure you have a spotter to help you on these exercises, if you are working out at Vet's Stadium, the trainers will be supervising your work out.

PROGRAM A

1. Bench Press	5 sets of 6-5-4-3-2 repetitions
2. Parallel Squats (use a Squat Rack or Bench)	5 sets of 6 repetitions each set
3. Military Press (can use a weight rack)	5 sets of 6-5-4-3-2 repetitions
4. Dead Lifts	5 sets of 6-5-4-3-2 repetitions
5. Cheat Curls (use heavier weights, don't have to use strict forms)	5 sets of 6-5-4-3-2 repetitions
6. Power Cleans	5 sets 6 repetitions each set
7. Nautilus Neck Exercise	1 set in each position, 8 to 12 repetitions

<u>Note</u> - If the Nautilus neck machine is not available, do ISO neck
exercises with a buddy holding your head for resistance. Exercise
your neck in all four directions for six to eight seconds in each
direction.

8. Cybex Knee Exercises

<u>Note</u> - If you are not in Philadelphia and can't use the Cybex, do
leg extensions on the Nautilus or Universal weight machine. Plus
leg curls on the Nautilus or Universal weight machine. If you are
using the Nautilus, do one set of 8 to 12 repetitions of leg
extensions and one set of 8 to 12 repetitions of leg curls. If you are
using the Universal weight machine, do 3 sets of 8 to 12 repetitions of
the leg extension and 3 sets of 8 to 12 repetitions of leg curls.

9. Nautilus Torso Machine Pull Over Exercise

$\qquad\qquad\qquad\qquad\qquad$ 1 set of 8 to 12 repetitions

10. Nautilus Hip and Back Machine   1 set of 12 to 15 repetitions
using a light weight for
flexibility

<u>Note</u> - During the first two weeks on Program A (the month of February)
rather than doing 5 sets on a 6-5-4-3-2 repetitions basis, do only
3 sets but work for 10 repetitions per set. This will allow you to
use a lighter weight and your body can adjust more gradually to the
tremendous stress put on it by weight training.

Note - You should use a weight belt to support your lower back when
doing squats, dead lifts and power cleans.

Note - On the Dead Lift make sure you keep your head and eyes up as
you lift and you should start with a lower weight and work up a little
more gradually than you do on other exercises to prevent lower back
strain.

9

DAY	DATE	WORK-OUT DAYS	PROGRAM
Monday	May 16	31	5 Minute Run (Easy Pace) - Weights
Tuesday	May 17	32	8 X 110 at 18 sec. each; 8 X 110 at 18 sec. each
Wednesday	May 18	33	5 Minute Run (Easy Pace) - Weights
Thursday	May 19	34	3 X 330 at 60-75 sec. each; 8 X 110 at 18 sec. each; 8 X 110 at 18 sec. each
Friday	May 20	35	5 Minute Run (Easy Pace) - Weights
Monday	May 23	36	5 Minute Run (Easy Pace) - Weights
Tuesday	May 24	37	3 X 330 at 60-75 sec. each; 8 X 110 at 18 sec. each; 8 X 110 at 18 sec. each
Wednesday	May 25	38	5 Minute Run (Easy Pace) - Weights
Thursday	May 26	39	3 X 330 at 60-75 sec. each; 8 X 110 at 18 sec. each; 8 X 110 at 18 sec. each
Friday	May 27	40	5 Minute Run (Easy Pace) - Weights
Monday	May 30	41	5 Minute Run (Easy Pace) - Weights
Tuesday	May 31	42	4 X 220 at 40 sec. each; 8 X 110 at 16 sec. each; 8 X 110 at 16 sec. each
Wednesday	June 1	43	5 Minute Run (Easy Pace) - Weights
Thursday	June 2	44	3 X 330 at 50-65 sec. each; 3 X 330 at 50-65 sec. each; 8 X 110 at 16 sec. each
Friday	June 3	45	5 Minute Run (Easy Pace) - Weights

THE BEST PLAYING WEIGHT

Being in condition includes achieving one's best playing weight. The athlete in many situations can decide for himself at which weight he participates best by using the scale, tape measure, performance, fatigue and his age as guidelines. This athlete carries no excess weight to consume needlessly the energy needed for participation.

The objective of losing excess fat is to reduce the energy cost of moving about additional poundage, which results in an associated reduction of body reserves. Thus, weight loss helps achieve a body weight conducive to maximal physical efficiency and optimal health. The safest way to lose weight is through oxidation of fat depots. This is best accomplished by restricting total calorie intake. It may also be accomplished by removing bodily fluids--this is a dangerous method that carries the risk of losing enough electrolytes to cause a disturbance of the finely balanced concentration of electrolytes in the body fluids.

PLANNING THE DIET

Since athletic activities require more energy than is needed for the daily routine of living, a greater amount of energy-producing food must be consumed. Each athlete has his own requirements depending upon his particular nutritional assessment. As soon as an athlete gets into condition and has reached his best playing weight, the caloric intake must balance the output.

In planning a suitable diet, allowances for individual differences must be taken into consideration. For example: age, since younger athletes require more protein than older players; season or climate, since less is needed when the termperature is relatively high, more when it is low; and physique of the individual, since a 180 pound quarterback will not eat as much as a 260 pound lineman.

Foodstuff Groupings   1. Milk Group - four or more glasses (NOT BEFORE
                           A GAME)
                       2. Meat Group
                       3. Vegetable/Fruit Group
                       4. Bread and Cereal Group

From these basic four groups of food, an athlete can select and consume a variety of appetizing and nourishing foods of sufficient calories to balance the daily expenditure of his athletic energies. The diet must be adequate and flexible enough for maintenance and repair, provide sources and reserves of available energy and aid the athlete to reach his best playing weight.

Meal Patterns. Juggling calories should not mean missing meals; meal regularity aids nutrition, morale and discipline as well as the efficient utilization of nutrients. For protracted and exhausting sports, some athletes may require five light meals. Breakfast can and should be a welcome meal since the digestive and nutritional states of the body are at their lowest upon awakening in the morning and need replenishing for the day's activities. Carbohydrates are supplied by the fruit juices, fruits, jellies, jams, breads and cereals. Lunch and dinner meals are generally selected from the same basic food groups

4

and slight differences between these meals depend upon personal preferences. Both meals are built around a serving of meat, poultry or fish that may be preceded by an appetizer of fruit, vegetable juice or soup.

Before the afternoon practice session, the main serving at lunch should be an easily digestible food. Noon meals prepare the athlete for the afternoon practice session, which should take place three to five hours afterwards. This allows sufficient time for digestion, absorption and conversion of the foods so that the blood needed for the process is shunted from the gastrointestinal tract to the musculature of the trunk and extremities.

After practice sessions, the athlete should not eat until his body has reverted to its normal pre-practice physiologic condition, which may take as much as one hour. The size of the servings varies with the athlete. He must discipline himself to satisfy wisely his appetite and hunger. Much versatility must be shown by those who prepare and serve these meals to provide top quality nutrition while preventing the meals from becoming boring and monotonous.

REST-SLEEP

The span of life of the species is determined by evolution and for a given generation by heredity. It is affected by numerous factors of the social and natural environment. Man as a rational being has the chance to evade unfavorable and consciously to use beneficial environmental factors so as to retard the rate of physiological (function of living organisms) aging, to prevent premature pathological (disease) aging, and to prevent physical fatigue factors.

Physical activity and rest are two impartible linked factors. Intensive processes of nutrition, food absorption, and recovery of structural proteins and high-energy compounds take place in the organism during rest following sufficiently intensive physical work. The greater the loading has been, within physiological limits, the more intensive are the processes of self-recovery brought into play. At optimal intensity of physical work, it is precisely during rest following fatigue that intensive recovery takes place, accumulation of new structural proteins, vital minerals, and other body building components, enhance activity. If the exercise is regularly repeated, body changes become firmly established and lead to growth of the working organs, to structural and functional perfection.

The biological meaning of rest is that it makes it possible for the neuro-muscular processes set in motion by work to run in a more proficient and integrated fashion.

When we work or train, we make definite pauses in the course of the day. A part of the recovery process takes place during these pauses. To a certain extent it is expedient to fill these intervals with a different kind of activity. It is known that recovery after muscular activity is faster if the work continues involving other muscles. On a broader base the principle of active rest implies alternation of physical with mental work, of certain interests with others.

The fundamental part of the recovery process, however, takes place during night sleep. In the course of evolution sleep has arisen with the development of the neuromuscular system and serves it primarily. In experimental sleep deprivation, it is principally the refined body characteristics such as perception, attention, memory, abstract thinking, and many other neuromuscular activities that are affected.

When rest and sleep are insufficient with respect to the work done, functional overloading takes place before recovery has an opportunity to be completed, even before the hard or optimal work capacity has reached its initial level. Thus, the exaltation phase of the "feeling good phase" of a workout are missing. This results in exhaustion and wearing out of the body.

So the ideal ratio is achieved when optimal physical activity is combined with optimal rest (most recent studies show that optimal rest for the athlete is around 9 hours per day). Thus for an athlete to meet the ideal ratio requirements means that the biosynthesis of the body predominates: hypertrophy or enlargement of the working tissues and increased capacity for mental and physical work occur.

Sources

Most of the background material and quotes from Dick Vermeil came from the major newspapers in the cities where he coached, including the *Philadelphia Inquirer* and *Daily News*, the *St. Louis Post-Dispatch*, and the *Kansas City Star*.

There were many other sources. Two of the best were "A New Life," the insightful *Sports Illustrated* story by Gary Smith of how Vermeil learned to slow his pace and enjoy life in a new world without football, and "Calistoga Roots," a nostalgic four-part series by *Daily News* columnist Stan Hochman that shed light on Vermeil's youth.

Other sources I referred to include the *Washington Post*; *USA Today*; *New York Daily News*; *Los Angeles Times*; *Indianapolis Star*; *Philadelphia Inquirer Magazine*; *Philadelphia Journal*; *The Sporting News*; *Philadelphia Bulletin*; *Dallas Morning News*; *Atlanta Journal-Constitution*; *College and Pro Football Weekly*; *Atlantic City Sun*; *UCLA Media Guide*; *Stanford University Media Guide*; *Look Magazine (1967)*; *Athlon Sports Pro Football Annual*; *NFL Record and Fact Book*; *Napa Sonoma Magazine*; *Calistoga Visitors Guide*; and *Calistoga Press-Democrat*.